David Burton was born in New Zealand in 1952, the son of a prominent caterer. After graduating with an MA in sociology from Canterbury University in 1974, he worked for four years as a chef in London and New Zealand. He discovered Asian food while returning home overland through the East, and continues to visit Asia regularly. He is the food and wine editor of the *Evening Post* in Wellington, contributes to a variety of newspapers and magazines, and has written eight books, including the highly successful *The Raj at Table* and *Savouring the East*. He has won seven New Zealand Food Writer's Awards, most recently Food Feature Writer of the Year for the third time in a row.

French Colonial Cookery

*A Cook's Tour of the
French-speaking World*

DAVID BURTON

faber and faber

First published in 2000
by Faber and Faber Limited
3 Queen Square London WC1N 3AU

Phototypeset by Intype London Ltd
Printed in England by Clays Ltd, St Ives plc

A CIP record for this book
is available from the British Library

ISBN 0-571-19024-3

10 9 8 7 6 5 4 3 2 1

To Andrea and Rea

Contents

Acknowledgements

On my travels throughout the French-speaking world to research this book, I frequently encountered curious reactions. Why would a *Neo-Zélandais*, they all wanted to know, be writing about *la cuisine coloniale*? Perhaps, I answered, it is because I am a colonial myself, albeit *hors de la francophonie*.

While some might claim this book glorifies and sentimentalizes European colonial oppression, this is to ignore the resilience of the indigenous cultures throughout France's former colonies which, taken together, create the delicious multi-cultural savour of *la cuisine de la francophonie*.

During all the hospitality and genuine kindness shown me in France and elsewhere, I never once felt the need to discuss the warrior ethos in New Zealand society, the early entry of *utu* into the vernacular, nor, indeed, the sabotage of the Rainbow Warrior in Auckland harbour or a proposal to restore New Zealand's trampled *mana* by having France return the remains of all New Zealand war dead from French soil. And I'm probably in the minority of my compatriots who can see the amusing side of the French rugby team forcing the All Blacks to play a qualifying match for the 2003 World Cup, which New Zealand is co-hosting with Australia. As a New Zealander, this book is my olive branch to France, my tribute to her beautiful food and wine, which happens to be her greatest cultural tie with my country, especially nowadays when we, along with everywhere else in the Anglo-Celtic world, are in the midst of a Great Culinary Renaissance.

Our chefs owe their skills to the French tradition, and the meteoric rise in the quality of New Zealand wines has also been fuelled by considerable French expertise and goodwill. In years to come, when all the many young olive groves and vineyards now in the ground bear fruit, life in the Antipodean wine regions will be more like the Midi than ever. We will never be *mediterranéens-et-demi* in the style of the *pieds-noirs*, but there is also nothing stopping us becoming quarter Anglo, quarter Pacific and *demi-mediterranéen*, with olive trees and lemons growing in our backyards.

I first thank my late father, Frederick – caterer, chef and gourmet – for leaving me his library of French cookery and wine books, especially, for the purposes of this work, his copy of Countess Morphy's 1935 classic, *Recipes of All Nations* (inscribed 'To the birthday of the best combination of a linguist and an earl from the friends who consider him their best friend.'). I also thank him for inculcating in me an early taste for Périgord truffles, frogs' legs, chianti, olives, fillets of anchovy, salami, muttonbirds and toheroa soup.

In particular, I would like to thank the Bibliothèque Nationale in Paris for granting me access to the wealth of historical material which informs this book. I also thank the staff at the Papeete Public Library, the Scholcher Library in Fort-de-France, Martinique, and the Lafcadio Hearn Collection at Tulane University, New Orleans.

I would like to thank the following for their time, and invariably their hospitality: *Wellington*: the Embassy of France; Steve Logan of Logan Brown Restaurant. *Akaroa*: Ursula Brocherie; Marie Le Lièvre, the Akaroa Museum; James Ullrich, general manager, French Farm Vineyards. *Christchurch*: Antoine Le Lièvre. *Paris*: Bruno Croissant and Deborah Roseveare. *Marseilles*: Réné Laporte. *New Orleans*: chef Dominique Maquet, Dominique's at the Maison Dupuy; chef Gregory Picolo, the Bistro at the Hôtel Maison de Ville; Gary B. Froeba, general manager, Omni Royal Orleans Hotel; Raymond A. Toups, executive chef, Omni Royal Orleans Hotel; Gene Bourg; chef Etienne Devlin, Hotel Provincial; Gunter and Evelyn Preuss, Broussard's Restaurant; chef Harvey Loumiet, Broussard's Restaurant. *Quebec:* Institut de Tourisme et d'Hôtellerie du Québec; Institut Québécois de l'Erable. *Pointe-à-Pitre*: Le Cuistot Mutuel. *Fort-de-France*: Charles Bourdin, directeur d'exploitation, Hôtel La Batelière; chef Jean Pierre St Aude, Hôtel La Batelière. *Le Diamant*: Marie-Yvonne and Hubert Andrieu, Hôtel Diamant les Bains; sous-chef Roger Silvestre, Hôtel Diamant les Bains. *Tangier*: Eduard Le Blanc. *Fez*: André Benoît; Jean-Claude and Yvette Delrieu. *Pondicherry*: Madame Lourdes Louis. *Papeete*: Tahiti Tourism; the Hyatt Regency. *Noumea*: New Caledonia Tourism. *Ho Chi Minh City*: Hoang van Cuong; Helen Lowy, New World Hotel Saigon; the owners of Globo and Camargue; Bibi of BiBi's; chef Laurent Billy at Billabong.

I thank Les Editions Maritimes for their kind permission to reproduce passages from *Cuisine Coloniale: Les Bonnes Recettes de Chlöe Mondésir* and to the owners of the copyright to Herbert Joseph Limited for their kind permission to reproduce Countess Morphy's recipe for Crabes Farcies. The author and publisher would be interested in hearing from any owners of copyright, particularly that to *La Bonne Cuisine aux Colonies*, by R. de Noter, published about 1927, probably in Paris. Please note that the metric cup – 250ml – has been used throughout.

List of Illustrations

Introduction

The cooking of the French-speaking world – *la cuisine de la franco-phonie* – is a fascinating subject, yet woefully neglected ever since Quérillac's delightful *Cuisine Coloniale* was published in Paris in 1931. How timely that I should have chosen the summer of 1996, of all years, in which to temporarily settle in Paris myself and begin trawling the Bibliothèque Nationale for this, the updated version. For that summer saw the outbreak of a furious debate between France's leading chefs, a debate which elucidates the central issue of this work. I refer to the War of the Herbs and the Spices – between the conservative upholders of traditional French cuisine on the one hand, as exemplifed by Joël Robuchon, and on the other hand, the innovators led by Alain Senderens.

As chef de cuisine of Lucas Carlton in Paris, Senderens is famed for introducing spices and aromatics in ways which often seem inspired by the cooking of France's former colonies, such as the North African idea of adding cinnamon to pigeon and cumin to lamb, the scenting of fish with star anis, as in Vietnam, or of lobster with vanilla, as in Tahiti and New Caledonia.

It all began innocently enough in May 1996, with a press release from a public relations firm which, on the face of it, was nothing more than a promotion of French regional foodstuffs, signed by Joël Robuchon and a dozen or so leading chefs, notably Alain Ducasse, Bernard Loiseau and Georges Blanc, then president of the prestigious Chambre Syndicale de la Haute Cuisine Française.

However, the statement went much further than a mere defence of French regional cuisine, condemning the globalization of cooking which threatened its very existence, and attacking certain chefs who 'wish to mix everything with anything on the plate to give the impression of innovation at all costs'. Reading more like a manifesto than a press release, it accused the experimenters of smothering flavours, of using spices to camouflage second-rate ingredients, sneeringly characterizing their style as *cuisine cache-misère* – a reference to an old-fashioned coat which buttoned up to the chin, its purpose being to conceal the wearer's lack of linen.

As an unofficial spokesman for this reactionary faction, Robuchon repeated the argument for tradition and back-to-basics on a number of occasions, openly criticizing the experimenters for suffocating the national cuisine with a battery of alien flavours. 'Nobody knows what they are eating any more,' he complained.

Using expressions which seem alarmingly nationalistic, Robuchon advocated 'purity', while Ducasse spoke of 'polluting elements'. The French culinary identity, others claimed, was threatened by 'bastardization', 'cross-breeding', even by *cosmopolitisme* – a word much used by the Vichy regime in the 1940s with respect to a supposedly corrupting Jewish influence on French cultural life.

That summer I frequently spluttered over my morning *café au lait* as I read the latest instalment in the French press, but felt cheered by the reaction of Senderens and colleagues such as Michel Guérard and Marc Veyrat. Criticism of a three-star chef by another, let alone by a group, was unprecedented. Understandably, Senderens felt dismay. 'It is not right for chefs to turn against one another,' he protested. 'We are artists and we should respect rather than attack each other's differences.'

Behind the scenes, in the kitchens, events took an even nastier turn, with this chef being rumoured to be going bankrupt, and that chef to be a member of Le Pen's National Front. In September 1996 the acrimony reached its peak with the resignation of some twenty top chefs from the Chambre Syndicale.

That such passions were aroused may seem, on the face of it, to be merely another example of the French ability to turn almost anything, food included, into an intellectual debate. Yet the issues run much deeper than that. In a sense, the Herbs are justified in their fears, for the Spices do indeed rattle the very foundations of classic French cuisine.

Since its appearance in the mid-seventeenth century, modern French cuisine has based its worldwide pre-eminence on the championing of herbs, salt, pepper and acidic flavours at the expense of spices, saffron and sugar. The style, as manifested in La Varenne's landmark cookery book, *Le Cuisinier français*, published in Paris in 1651, represented a complete break with the medieval past.

The aristocratic cuisine of medieval France, and indeed of most of Europe, had been characterized by a heavy use of spices, introduced by traders and returning armies, and also reflecting the strong influence of the Arabs, who by the end of the ninth century had conquered Sicily, the Iberian peninsula and parts of the eastern Mediterranean. Through their aroma, colour and lustre, saffron and spices had been thought to have mystical connections and hence divine healing powers.

In *Viander de Guillaume Tirel*, a fourteenth-century French cookery book, we read: 'Spices that belong to the present cook are first ginger, cinnamon, clove, grains of paradise, long pepper, mace, spice powder . . . saffron, galingale [and] nutmeg.' Grains of paradise have been identified variously as cardamom, or melegueta pepper, while long pepper, along with cubeb (another medieval spice now fallen out of favour) are related to black pepper and similar to it in flavour.

Sugar, too, had entered savoury French cooking in a big way by the end of the fourteenth century, and by 1560 the physician to the recently deceased Henry II of France was writing: 'There is hardly anything today prepared for the stomach without sugar. Sugar is added to baked goods, sugar is mixed with wines, water with sugar is tastier and healthier, meat is sprinkled with sugar, as are fish and eggs. We use salt in no more places than sugar.'

To create a new cuisine, La Varenne and his seventeenth-century contemporaries banished sugar from all but the dessert course, and elevated salt and pepper to an importance unprecedented since Roman times. They stressed butter on the authority of Galen and Dioscorides, reinstated Apicius's herb bouquet and, most significantly in the light of *la cuisine de la francophonie*, declared native herbs to be superior to imported spices.

'Fine herbs are wholesomer, and have something in them more exquisite than spices,' claimed Charles, seigneur de Saint-Evremond in one of his letters. Parsley in particular was now prized. In 1654 Nicolas de Bonnefons asserted in *Les Délices de la campagne* that parsley was 'our French spice, which seasons countless preparations and is used almost everywhere in food'. Nevertheless, like La Varenne, Bonnefons used a lot of pepper in his recipes, speaking of 'pepper and spice' as if they were two different categories. Pepper, in effect, was declared an honorary French citizen, while with the exceptions of nutmeg, mace and cloves (which were retained, though in a much reduced role), spices became alien outcasts.

The French now used disdain for spices as an expression of their own culinary superiority. Escorting Princess Marie de Ganzague, new wife of King Ladislas IV, on a journey from France to Poland in 1648, John the Husbandman complained that the banquets served en route had been so full of saffron and spices that no Frenchman would be able to eat them. The Countess d'Aulnoy recounts in 1691 being tantalized on several occasions in Spain by sumptuous meals which spices and saffron had rendered inedible. By the beginning of the eighteenth century a German was warning his compatriots that lovers of spicy food would be disappointed in France.

And so things continued for the next three centuries. As French cuisine steadily became more refined, respect for it grew throughout the Western world. Escoffier claimed French cooking was a branch of diplomacy and that he had personally placed two thousand French chefs around the world.

From the nineteenth century and right up until the 1980s, virtually every restaurant in the English-speaking world with any aspirations to quality aspired to be French. This is not to say they always succeeded and, indeed, in the decades following World War II, when restaurant culture really began to take off, the menus they actually produced were more of an amalgam of French with Italian and central European – what used to be called 'Continental cooking'. Nevertheless, French cuisine was held up as the undisputed model.

By 1996, however, things had changed. French cuisine, which during the twentieth century had successfully managed to reinvent itself twice – first with a revival of regionalism inspired by the efforts of Curnonsky and others in the 1920s, and later by the reforms wrought by nouvelle cuisine in the 1970s – was now facing a crisis.

In Paris, three-star Michelin restaurants were beginning to go broke. Robuchon sold his illustrious restaurant on avenue Raymond-Poincaré in favour of teaching, while at France's oldest and formerly most prestigious restaurant, La Tour d'Argent, recently stripped of one of its Michelin stars, I could not help but notice the shabby uniforms and soiled white gloves of the waiters. Moreover, the celebrated Parisian café was vanishing: in the course of the 1990s, the city lost 30,000, leaving only 10,000.

Meanwhile, the action in both the restaurant and fashion worlds, inexplicably, was turning from Paris to London. Terence Conran's succession of gastro-domes competed for media attention with the latest venture by Marco Pierre White, and in a turn of events which the French would have considered laughably unlikely only a decade earlier, London replaced Paris as the restaurant capital of Europe. In the United States, Australia and New Zealand, restaurants began to stray further and further from the French model.

What happened? Throughout the New World there grew the feeling that French cuisine might be caught around the neck by the noose of

The Great Tradition. For all its refinement, people began to feel it lacked excitement, healthiness and, above all, originality – all important culinary parameters in Australasia and the United States.

Spurred by health and dietary concerns, there had been a sharp reaction against the lard, the cream and the butter which form the cornerstone of the cuisine of northern France. True, as part of a love affair with all things Mediterranean, Provençal cooking found fresh popularity, but not nearly to the extent of that of neighbouring Italy.

Meanwhile, in New World cities such as Los Angeles, Sydney and Wellington, chefs had begun stirring the global melting pot, tossing in spices and aromatics from their Asian neighbours and using the French rule books for firewood. This grafting of Asian ingredients on to the cooking of France, Italy and the Mediterranean, is the style which has variously been called East meets West, fusion or, given the geographical ties of its main proponents, Pacific Rim.

Only time will tell if the incorporation of Asian flavours is here to stay. Perhaps, as the Australian author Barbara Santich suggests in *Looking for Flavour*, the worldwide movement towards regional autonomy is already having its corollary in cuisine. Perhaps fusion food seems more natural to an urban context, while regionalism may develop in provincial areas where cooks enjoy a closer relationship with land and sea. One thing is certain, however: even though the Pacific Rim food fashion is now showing signs of receding, it is leaving an indelible tidemark, if only because a taste once acquired is rarely relinquished. Nouvelle cuisine may be long gone but the lighter approach to sauce-making remains, green vegetables are still steamed and served green, and restaurant food is still plated up out in the kitchen; nobody has yet gone back to the old way of serving from platters at the table.

There are a great many antecedents to fusion food in the colonial cooking of the European powers, antecedents which give a whole new respectability to the idea. Note that I'm using the word 'antecedent' rather than 'origin' here, since I'm not claiming any unbroken lineage between European colonial cooking and fusion food we see today. One major difference is that today fusion food is a matter of choice, of a conscious search for the new, perhaps even innovation for its own sake. The various European colonial cuisines, on the other hand, emerged from expedience, of having to substitute new ingredients found in the colony for unavailable ingredients used to make the traditional dish back home in the old country.

Any traditional cuisine you care to mention is a fusion to a greater or lesser extent. Looking at the tomatoes in Italian cooking today, or potatoes in German cooking, or chillies in Indian cooking, we can say these are all culinary fusions, in the sense that none of these absolutely fundamental ingredients were known to the culture concerned before Christopher Columbus's voyage to America, and seedlings for those plants were brought from the opposite end of the earth.

Prototypes for such fusion food exist in Anglo-Indian cooking, in the *rijstafel* of Dutch Indonesia, and the cuisines of former Portuguese enclaves such as Malacca, Macau and Goa. Nowhere, however, have such colonial fusions reached the level of evolution as the Creole cuisine of France's former colonies – Louisiana, the French West Indies, French Guiana, Réunion, Mauritius and other small islands of the Indian Ocean.

I believe *la cuisine de la francophonie* offers a solution to French cuisine's contemporary crisis, in the sense that its repertoire offers a spicy variation on the old regional dishes of France itself.

The French are right to be extremely conservative about their own cuisine, since respect for tradition is necessary for its preservation. Yet rules and traditions also impede progress. If French cuisine needs to be shown a French way to loosen up and get spicier, as I believe it does, then the solution, the model, *la cuisine de la francophonie*, has been sitting under their very noses all this time. As Elizabeth David wrote of the French in *French Provincial Cooking*: 'When they settle abroad they soon realize that if they are going to be well fed they must also be flexible in the manner of adapting local ingredients new to them.' This book seeks to codify those adaptations, and to find the common global threads which interconnect them.

As fusion food goes, French colonial cookery is restrained, employing a relatively narrow range of flavours, and never too much of any strong condiments.

La cuisine de la francophonie, indeed, is France's untapped treasure, its fusion food which evolved centuries before Californians and Antipodeans even dreamed up the word. In its own uniquely hot and spicy way, French colonial cookery might even be regarded as a form of *cuisine du terroir*.

Wellington, New Zealand, May 2000

I The Caribbean

The French West Indies remain France's most coveted colonial possession, still showing little desire to be anything otherwise. Some might say this is simply due to fear of the consequences of independence on the part of a client culture – and of a client economy, dependent upon French government spending for about 70 per cent of the gross national product. Among the populace, however, Francophile sentiments undeniably run deep, if only because a little Gallic blood flows in so many mulatto veins. Significantly, *les mulâtres* – the descendants of French settlers and African slaves – form the largest group in the population.

For in *les Antilles* – in Martinique, Guadeloupe and assorted small satellite islands such as St Martin and St Barthélémy – France succeeded, as she did perhaps nowhere else, in her *mission civilisatrice*. Martiniquans and Guadeloupians may be people of colour, but whether of mulatto or purely African ancestry, by their mannerisms, speech, gestures and especially their cuisine, they are French.

Since French culture is largely led by its food and wine, it is not for nothing that the Antilles have the reputation of offering the best food anywhere in the Caribbean. This is evident enough from the advanced restaurant culture on the islands. The importance that the entire populace at large places on eating well is also obvious from the freshness and huge variety of produce on sale at fruit and vegetable markets, and the avidity with which they pursue supplies of fresh fish.

In an everyday scene on Guadeloupe, crowds of eager buyers rush up and down the wharf at Pointe-à-Pitre clamouring with money-filled hands every time a catch of fish is brought in by small aluminium fishing boats (see plate 3).

Serious haggling goes on at the early morning fish market in Fort-de France (see plate 2), the capital of Martinique. Opulent arrays of fresh fish shimmer in the morning sun, of all shapes and sizes, from tiny silver garfish to the gorgeous crimson red scales and canary yellow eyes of the vivaneau, or silk snapper (*Lutjanus vivanus*). Such fish would have been familiar to the original inhabitants of the islands – Arawak Indians who came from the South America some three thousand years ago. Indeed, archaeological analysis of ancient kitchen scrap heaps indicates the Arawak were used to catching over 40 species, by trapping, by damming rivers, with poisoned arrows, even by drugging the fish by pouring juices from narcotic plants into streams.

A ghastly holocaust befell the Arawak in about the tenth century when both Martinique and Guadeloupe were conquered by the less culturally advanced, but considerably more war-like Caribs, also Indians originally from South America. All Arawak men were executed and the women enslaved. Since they now became the cooks, this aspect of Arawak culture was saved, but unfortunately it does not appear to have been their strongest point. Essentially, it was very primitive. One Arawak culinary legacy which still survives, however, is the concept of a cake made from cassava, a tuber native to the Caribbean. This was originally made by pounding the cassava root and squeezing out the poisonous juices between two heavy flat rocks to make a thick pancake.

Eating cassava raw was a common method of suicide for Arawak slaves, since there is easily enough prussic acid in the bitter cassava root to kill you. Cooking the juice turned its poison into a harmless starch they called *moustache*, today better known to the makers of English nanny's puddings as tapioca. The ground meal is also mixed with finely desiccated coconut for *farine coco* – coconut flour – which also has its fans. On the whole, however, cassava use is in decline nowadays, not surprisingly, for – Peter Gordon's cassava chips possibly notwithstanding – it is hardly a taste everybody must experience at least once in a lifetime.

A major Arawak gift to the modern world was the pineapple, the cultivation of which they had practised in South America. But their biggest contribution was also the simplest – the barbecue. It was their one and only way of cooking, either grilling at the end of sticks over hot embers, or on a frame of green sticks, bones and animal hides placed over the embers. It was as much a means of smoking as it was of cooking, used for preserving strips of game meat after a hunt. Known as a *brabacot*, this frame of green twigs was adopted by the first Spanish colonists, who called it *barbacoa* – hence barbecue.

The first French to arrive in the Caribbean in the seventeenth century were pirates. Only a few struck it rich with plundered treasure from the Spanish Main, the remainder living almost as wild an island life as the Caribs. They, too, readily adopted the *brabacot*, only their word for it was *boucan*. Some say *boucan* derives from a Carib word *boucacoui*, meaning 'fire of herbs', but it is more likely derived from *mukem*, in the Tupi language of two Amerindian tribes from the interior of French Guiana (the Emérillons and the Oyampis) in reference to the wooden frame upon which meat was either cooked, dried or smoked. By adopting this method of cooking and drying meat from the Amerindians in French Guiana, these *boucaniers* invited the English nickname that has stuck ever since – buccaneers.

Barbecuing still runs red hot in the French islands today. In Guadeloupe professional barbecuers set up beside the road on the fringes of the jungle. Firewood is apparently not an issue, so these barbecuers deploy massive horseshoe-shaped batteries of metal drums whose beds of glowing coals are hot and deep enough to chargrill rows of whole spatchcocked chickens, sending tempting smoke signals far and wide to prospective customers slowly approaching along the winding jungle roads in their cars and rickety buses. The chicken is either eaten on the spot, perhaps with rice, or bought as a takeaway. This is *poulet grillé*. True *poulet boucané* involves smoking the chicken over embers placed in a drum which has been cut through the middle, the top half attached with hinges and acting as a tightly fitting lid. From time to time, the lid is lifted and water is sprinkled over the coals to produce more smoke.

In the case of fish, a lighter hand is used, and the smoking effect is even better. In French Guiana, pirates devised a special fuel mixture to burn for smoking fish – sugar cane, rice and bread – which was supposed to perfume the fish and give it the colour of toast. If the smoked fish technique had not preceded the buccaneers, they would have made culinary history!

Salade d'Avocat et Poisson Boucané
(avocado and smoked fish salad)

¼ teaspoon salt

juice of 2 lemons

4 tablespoons extra virgin olive oil

¼ teaspoon ground black pepper

pinch of sugar

2 shallots, finely chopped

1 large clove garlic, crushed

3 courgettes, sliced into rounds

300 g (10 oz) smoked fish

1 avocado

2 large tomatoes, blanched,
  peeled and quartered

½ bunch fresh coriander, leaves
  only,
  chopped

400 g (14 oz) dried pasta (macaroni
  or pasta spirals)

Whisk the salt into the lemon juice to dissolve, then add the olive oil, black pepper and sugar. Whisk together. Add chopped shallots and garlic and leave to marinate for 15 minutes.

Pour a little oil in a pan and sauté the courgettes. Set aside.

If the fish has been hot-smoked, it will not require cooking. Cold-smoked fish will need 2 minutes in the microwave, or about 6 minutes in a pre-heated 200°C (400°F/Gas 6) oven, wrapped in foil. Flake or chop the fish, and pour any cooking juices into the marinade.

Cut the avocado into large dice and add to the marinade, gently mixing to coat the avocado. Add the courgettes, tomato and chopped coriander.

Cook the pasta and divide between four plates. Pour over the remaining ingredients and serve warm.

SERVES 4.

Inflaming buccaneer appetites still further were casks of madeira plundered from the Spanish, which they made even sweeter by adding sugar along with a dash of lime, and then, just to completely blot out the madeira, a sturdy taste-proofing layer of spices – cinnamon, cloves and nutmeg.

Sang-gris, a recipe learned from their Spanish rivals, was likewise favoured by the first French settlers on Martinique – a few hundred men who landed in 1635, built a fort and repelled the Caribs. Their leader was Belain d'Esnambuc. Some call this gentleman a buccaneer, while the French prefer the term *filibustre* – 'filibuster' – perhaps believing it to be a more genteel term for a pirate; d'Esnambuc is still honoured, after all, with a statue in the corner of Fort-de-France's town square.

For the next twenty years these men, and others who subsequently joined them, donned straw hats and flannel waistcoats or perhaps a costume of solid grey cloth imported from Holland, and set about the weary task of clearing the jungle and planting crops. Sugar cane plantations were established in Guadeloupe in the early seventeenth century (the date is uncertain, but the Compagnie des Iles decided to build the first sugar factory there in 1642) and in Martinique after the importation of plant stock in 1654, by a Brazilian Jew called Benjamin da Costa. Sugar cane, in the form of slavery and rum, was to radically alter the course of the Caribbean's social and culinary history.

Rum was invented by the English on Barbados in the early 1600s, its name a shortening of the seventeenth-century English words rumbullion and rumbustion, meaning tumult, rumpus. And a tumultuous early career it had, as the habitual tot not only of pirates but also of seventeenth- and eighteenth-century New England slave traders, who would buy molasses, distil it into rum, exchange the rum for slaves in West Africa, then sell the slaves to cane planters in the West Indies for more molasses.

By the end of the seventeenth century, with the massive sugar plantations and the allied rum industry well established, a new class of planters took time out in their comfortable mansions to evolve a simplified formula for the Anglo-Indian punch[*] that had earlier made its way to the British islands.

The new recipe was dubbed *petit punch* (little punch) now commonly shortened to *ti-punch*. Rather than make their punch English-style, in advance with enough to fill a huge bowl, the French planters would have their slave servants assemble *ti-punch* in glasses on the spot. This became a sort of ritual, a performance, during which conversation might stop. The servant would squeeze a few drops of lime into a glass, add a dash of cane syrup, a two-finger measure of rum and plenty of water. 'One of sour, one of sweet, three of strong and four of weak' went the same formula in the British islands.

On less formal occasions, the makings were left out for guests to concoct according to taste. In the nineteenth and early twentieth centuries, *ti-punch* became the mainstay of bars throughout the French West Indies. Since rum was then so very cheap, only the sugar syrup

---

[*] See my *The Raj at Table*, Faber and Faber, 1993.

was paid for – the rum being free, left on the table as indifferently as if it were water.

The popular image of the cane planter relaxing on his verandah with a cocktail must have had a fair basis in truth, for there still exists in the Antilles a wide class of mixed rum and fruit juice punches known as *planteurs*. So popular have these *planteurs* proven with tourists, especially when gilded with the baroque accoutrements of sliced fruit, striped straws and naff miniature umbrellas, that there is nowadays a snobbish reaction against them by native Martiniquans, who either continue the tradition of *ti-punch*, or increasingly, drink the rum dry.

But regardless of whether this punch is *blanc* (white) *paille* (light straw yellow) or *vieux* (dark – aged at least three years in old oak), if it is to be drunk neat, the label on the bottle must carry the magic words *rhum agricole*, indicating it has been distilled directly from crushed sugar cane. Only industrial rum is made from molasses, say the connoisseurs, much of it poor quality and coloured with caramel, barely fit to soak a rum baba. Because *rhum agricole* requires the juice of fresh sugar cane, it can only be made during the harvest season, usually by smaller artisan distilleries on Guadeloupe, Marie-Galante and especially Martinique.

Visiting these smaller distilleries, often housed in ramshackle corrugated iron-roofed buildings with whitewashed walls and equally antiquated machinery, or the nearby sugar refineries which fill the air with a ripe, sickly-sweet smell for miles around, is to be transported back to an earlier age.

At the Clément distillery, the impression deepens with a visit to the Clément family mansion, built between 1820 and 1840 and now officially listed as one of Martinique's historical monuments. It is indeed a treasure, for elsewhere in the Caribbean, most great houses have succumbed to hurricanes, termites, revolutions and hard times, their splendid paintings and furniture long gone.

With the ferns and flowers of a luxuriant garden screening out the nearby plantations of sugar cane, the red-bricked verandah speaks of pre-dinner punches made with the Clément family's own fine rum. Inside, the library, the games tables, the four-poster beds, the silver, porcelain and expanses of French polished mahogany all recall a life of house parties from plantation to plantation, of races, picnics, cock-fights, love affairs and duels.

As in many of the old planters homes, the Clément dining room is dominated with an enormous dining table seating fourteen, upon which are set the finest silver candelabra. In a corner of the room a Chippendale-style case displays treasured bibelots, while a Martiniquan sideboard stores the crockery.

The dishes presented in such dining rooms attempted to reproduce as exactly as possible those served back in France. But of course this was impossible. France lay on the other side of the Atlantic, and the only imported comestibles were those which could survive an arduous sea journey, such as wine, cognac and hard cheeses.

So from the very first days, locally grown tubers (yams, sweet potatoes, green bananas, taro) graced the colonists' tables. Desperately missing French bread, they quickly turned cassava meal into mock versions of the flat buckwheat cakes known as *galettes de sarrasin*. The Bretons, of which there were many among the settler population, diluted the batter and made lacy pancakes, rolled Breton-style like table napkins.

As elsewhere in the French empire, palm trees were sacrificed for their tender hearts which were eaten in salads. It became known as *chou palmiste* (cabbage palm), *chou coco* (coconut) and *chou glouglou*, according to the type of palm it came from. They also tore into the native avocado with gusto.

A host of unfamiliar but exquisite native fruits awaited French degustation: the soursop, its prickly skin ripped open to reveal a tart, fragrant flesh, snow white and semi-liquid; the guava, also unprepossessing on the outside, but with a deep coral-coloured flesh; the papaya, its smooth patchy gold skin mottled with green and rusty brown, its pink flesh miraculously hanging in the balance between solidity and liquescence. Along with coconut, mango and banana, these tropical fruits faced the formidable French dessert battery and in no time a new class of bavarois, flan, mousse, soufflé, coulis, blancmange and fritter was added to the *grand repertoire de la cuisine*.

The rivers teemed with enormous freshwater shrimps known in Martinique as z'habitants (in Guadeloupe as ouassous), the coastline with rock lobster, octopus, sea urchins and crabs. In the river mouths were titiri, a tiny whitebait, the most delicate of all kinds of river fish, and the sandy beaches were home to a variety of clams. A conch known as lambi repaid the difficulty of extracting the flesh, and the necessity of lengthy beating with a mallet, with a wad of meat possessing a unique and exquisite flavour. Still found in reasonable abundance today, the lambi's beautiful, labial pink shells are laid out for display on the bows of fishing boats moored along the public wharf at Pointe-à-Pitre. Lambi has the texture of squid or cuttlefish, and tastes like an extremely intense scallop. A divine flavour, I have to report, but regretfully, as there is no other readily available shellfish like lambi outside Caribbean markets, there is little point in giving a recipe, save to say I enjoyed it best as a fricassee, in which is conserved the lambi's own cooking juices, in preference to the lambi kebabs which, to my taste, accentuated the toughness and evaporated the juice.

All this seafood appeared on seventeenth-century French Caribbean tables in abundance. Having eliminated any serious Carib Indian competition for the precious stocks by killing them or driving them from the island, and enslaved Africans to gather and prepare this bounty for them, the conquerors settled in to enjoy what they still refer to as their *paradis sur terre*.

They took a hint or two on crab cooking from their Spanish rivals along the way. Back home, Galician cooks had always done a nice line with the large Spanish crabs they called centollos, and in the early days of Guadeloupe, when the Spanish anchored their caravels at Basse Terre to gather fresh water from the river Galion, they made a huge fuss of the white land crabs they found there. These they prepared in traditional Galician fashion, by mixing the finely shredded flesh with a piquant sauce and stuffing it back into the empty crab shell.

The French settlers followed suit, refined the dish, and gave the world:

Crabes Farcies (stuffed crabs)

> *C'est bon khé crâbe qui lacause li pas tini tête.'*
> It is because of his good heart that the crab has no head –
> OLD CREOLE PROVERB, MARTINIQUE

Chop a little fat bacon very finely and mix with bread, previously soaked in milk. Brown the mixture slightly in butter, with 1 clove of garlic, chives and chilli pepper, all finely chopped. Mix with the chopped and cooked crab meat, fill the shells with the stuffing, sprinkle with breadcrumbs, and put in a fairly brisk oven for 20 to 25 minutes. This is a most excellent dish, especially when made with some of the delicious West Indies crabs.

Recipes of All Nations, compiled and edited by Countess Morphy, London, 1935.

Rock lobsters were also stuffed, and often fricasseed. Then some bright spark came up with the idea of flaming rock lobster with rum, and combining it with chicken. Personally, I had never been entirely convinced about the idea of meat with lobster – until I was converted to it on Martinique. It is awesomely delicious. The delicacy of the chicken is such that the lobster is not over-whelmed in the same way as it is, for example, by steak in the similar American dish, Surf 'n' Turf. Maybe if we renamed this recipe Foam 'n' Feathers they might take more notice of it in California, but I wouldn't risk the wrath of the ALF by offering it as such in Britain.

Poulet à la Langouste
(chicken with rock lobster)

1 chicken, about 1 kg (2 lb), cut
  into eight pieces
juice of 1 lemon
4 cloves garlic, crushed
salt and pepper
1 small rock lobster, about 500 g
  (1 lb)
1 bouquet garni of thyme, bay
  leaves and parsley
1 teaspoon olive oil
1 tablespoon butter

3 shallots, chopped
3 large tomatoes, blanched, peeled
  and chopped
1 small green chilli, finely chopped
1 large sprig of fresh thyme
3 bay leaves
250 g (9 oz or 2 cups) fresh *pois
  d'Angole* (substitute fresh or
  frozen green peas)
2 tablespoons dark rum

Skin the chicken (optional, but you'll get a less fatty result). Sprinkle with the lemon juice, then with chopped garlic, salt and pepper. Leave to marinate while you prepare the rock lobster.

Plunge the rock lobster into plenty of boiling water, add the bouquet garni and salt, and barely cook – about 15 minutes. Allow to cool, then remove tail meat and cut into large pieces. Crack the shell and remove all meat from the pincers and legs.

In a large pot, heat the oil and butter, sauté the chicken and shallots until both are lightly browned, then add tomatoes, chilli, thyme and bay leaves. Cover and simmer gently for 15 minutes, stirring occasionally to prevent the chicken pieces sticking. Add the lobster pieces and cook for several minutes longer. Stir in the peas and heat through. Finally, heat the rum in a tiny pan until it fumes, set alight and pour over. When the flames have died down, remove and discard the bay leaves and sprig of thyme. Serve with plain rice.

SERVES 4.

Some early culinary influences on the French West Indies came from the most unlikely sources. The English islands, who gave them the recipe for punch, also contributed a type of scone. Still a popular Jamaican tea-time speciality, Johnny cakes (also called journey cakes) are a simple mixture of flour, butter and lard mixed with a little water, formed into little balls, flattened, and fried. In the Creole patois of the French West Indies they came to be called *danquite*, a corruption, oddly enough, of the English words 'don't quiet'. Made even smaller, the size of coins, these were eaten with aperitifs. (Made nowadays with the help of a little bicarbonate of soda, *danquites* are still a popular snack with Antillian dockers, who buy them from vans parked near the wharf and sprinkle them with various fruit juices such as soursop, passionfruit or sugar cane juice mixed with lime.)

One would not expect the austere, Calvinistic cookery of the Dutch to fire the imagination the French. Yet the marinated and poached whole fish known as *blaff*, today one of the most famous dishes of the French West Indies, was brought there in 1654 by Dutch refugees.

A mixed community of both Jews and Protestants, the Dutch had been driven from the Brazilian coast by the Portuguese, finding refuge on Martinique and Guadeloupe, subsequently on Marie-Galante, a small outer island of Guadeloupe. There, they introduced a new method of sugar refining, and also their simple method of poaching fish.

It has been suggested that *blaff* comes from the French *blafard* – pale (i.e. pale-skinned Dutch); alternatively – and rather jocularly – island cooks explain that *blaff* is the noise the fish makes when plunged into the boiling water to poach. However, the true etymology is that *blaff* derives from *braff*, a generic term used by this Dutch community for a mixed flesh and vegetable stew they ate back in Brazil, which was just as likely to begin with salt meat as with fish. The meat was boiled with bananas, sweet potatoes, taro and plenty of chilli.

In Martinique, Creole cooks retained this Dutch method of cooking salt meat and vegetables, which became *viande salée sauce chien*. The vegetables, however, they quickly separated from the fish. The difficulty experienced by speakers of the Creole patois in pronouncing the 'r' sound, meant that *braff* became *blaff*. Here is the dish as demonstrated to me by Roger Silvestre, a Martinique-born chef of twenty years' experience, who cooks at the Hôtel Diamant les Bains, at the beautiful seaside resort of Le Diamant, in the southern part of Martinique.

Blaff

1 kg (2 lb) whole fresh fish, scaled
   and gutted
juice of 2 lemons or limes
salt to taste
¼ fresh or dried chilli, chopped
1 onion, sliced
1 whole clove, bruised

3 whole allspice berries
½ fresh or dried chilli
1 tablespoon oil
2 cloves garlic, crushed
bouquet garni of thyme, parsley
   and chives

Several small fish are best, but if using a large fish, cut into steaks. Marinate the fish for 1–2 hours in the juice of one of the limes or lemons, salt, chilli and a tumblerful of water. If using whole fish, slash once on each side to let the marinade penetrate.

Bring to the boil 1 litre (1¾ pts) of water and add the remaining ingredients. Let the mixture boil for about 15 minutes. Add the fish and cook for about 10 minutes, depending on the size of the fish, keeping it at a low boil. Add the juice of the second lemon or lime before serving.

Serve with some of the onion and spices used for cooking the fish, and some of the cooking liquid.

SERVES 2–3.

I savoured this dish on the hotel's terrace, full of traditional Creole charm, with white-painted woodwork and tiled floors. A row of lush tropical pot plants fringed the open-air dining room, with tiny black birds and butterflies darting in and out. In the distance, a rooster crowed, competing only with the sound of the surf, and the swish of a cooling breeze, filtering through the coconut palms from the beach.

The next day in the hotel kitchen, I was shown a rather more elaborate seafood dish, typical of those which have been devised in the wake of tourism. It is a signature dish of the head chef Hubert Andrieu, also the owner of the hotel, built in 1945 by his father. Trained at the Ecole

Hotelière in Fort-de-France, Hubert took over the Diamant les Bains after returning from a job cooking at the Martinique pavilion at Canada's Expo in 1967.

Pavé d'Espadon Farci aux Crevettes
(swordfish steaks with shrimp and Creole sauce)

1 onion, finely chopped
3 cloves garlic, crushed
butter
1 teaspoon fresh thyme, chopped
small pinch of saffron
salt
250ml (9 fl oz or 1 cup) crème
   fraîche

3 swordfish steaks
25–30 prawns, shelled
60 small shrimps, shelled
cheese
chopped parsley

First make a Creole sauce. Sauté the onion and garlic in a little butter until translucent. Add thyme and saffron (previously toasted and ground with mortar and pestle and a little boiling water). Pour over crème fraîche, heat and season to taste with salt.

Sauté the swordfish steaks on both sides in a little butter. When lightly browned, transfer to the Creole sauce and simmer gently for 15 minutes. Briefly sauté the prawns and then the shrimps in butter.

To serve, remove the steaks from the sauce. Place on an ovenproof platter. Pile about 20 small shrimps on each steak, then 8–10 prawns. Sprinkle over the cheese and melt under the grill.

Ladle over the Creole sauce, sprinkle with chopped parsley and serve garnished with slices of lime, lettuce, carrots and potato (see plate 5).
SERVES 3.

At the opposite end of the scale from the Hôtel Diamant les Bains' Creole tradition and rustic charm is the modernity of Martinique's grandest hotel, La Batelière. The hotel is set in a vast, well-tended garden on the outskirts of Fort-de-France and it not only has its own swimming pool but also a small private beach. Its enormous lobby gleams with a small acreage of polished Italian marble. Despite such luxury the hotel prides itself on retaining an element of local flavour, however, and the rooms are decorated Creole style, with bright fabrics and wicker furniture.

Once a week the beachside restaurant/disco, Le Queens, puts on a buffet offering just about every classic Antillian Creole dish, from chargrilled lambi and the black pudding known as *boudin*, to the salt cod fritters known as *accra,* and the fish dish called *court-bouillon Creole.* Interestingly, the majority of the buffet's patrons are not tourists but local Martiniquans, mulattos and Afro-Caribbeans, who turn out respectfully in their smartest clothes, and take the opportunity to dance under coconut palms on a terrace beside the sea.

Here is the recipe for what is perhaps the French West Indies' most famous dish, as demonstrated to me by the hotel's chef, Jean Pierre St Aude.

Court-bouillon Creole

To the Creoles of Martinique and Guadeloupe, court-bouillon is the name of a dish, not the French herb-infused stock used for poaching. It is said not to be adequately spiced with chilli unless guests feel like taking their shirts off after eating it.

3 medium-sized whole fish, scaled
   and gutted
juice of 2 limes
1 onion, finely chopped
1 clove garlic, crushed
salt and pepper
50 g (2 oz) butter
1 tablespoon oil
4 spring onions, finely sliced
1 tablespoon tomato concentrate

3 chillies, chopped
1 sprig of thyme
3 cloves garlic, chopped
2 tomatoes, blanched, peeled and
   chopped
1 sprig of parsley, chopped
3 whole cloves, bruised
250 ml (9 fl oz or 1 cup) white wine
   or water

Marinate the fish for one hour in the lime juice, onion, first measure of garlic, salt, pepper and a tumblerful of water.

In a frying pan, heat butter and oil. Add spring onions, tomato concentrate, chilli, thyme and second measure of garlic. Sauté for 2–3 minutes.

Drain the fish and put in the frying pan along with remaining ingredients and simmer gently for 15 minutes. Serve with rice (see plate 6).

SERVES 6.

For all its abundance of fruit, vegetables, crustaceans and fish, the Antilles are not renowned for lamb or beef. In the past, there was a large trade in tough old cattle imported for slaughter from Puerto Rico or Jamaica, since much of the land is too hilly or mountainous for grazing. Only in the south of Martinique does the landscape become less stridently tropical, its low curving hills, known as *mornes*, succeeding one another like waves of the nearby sea. Small flocks of sheep and even smaller herds of Indian cows, with light grey coats and slender hooves, are enclosed by lush hedgerows and dark blobs of scattered trees.

The first French colonists on the migrant ships included livestock among their possessions, occupying the same precious deck space as their household furniture. But even today the Antilles are still not self-sufficient in either beef or milk, and while smallholders may run sheep, they are just as likely to keep goats, known not by the usual French name of *chèvre* but as *cabri*. The meat is greatly sought after for curries.

Lamb emerged very early as a grand occasion meat in the Antilles. A common eighteenth-century Martiniquan cane plantation recipe for a pit-roasted whole sheep called for a stuffing reminiscent of the Roman Empire's last days, with onions, spices, orange juice, and assorted birds like ortolans, thrushes and sandpipers. In the cross-fertilization which colours the cooking of France's former empire, the modern Antillean version of this dish is likely to be *méchoui*, the whole roasted lamb beloved of the French in Algeria (see page 208).

No part of the animal was wasted, as can be seen in a Martiniquan dish traditionally associated with family festivities – *pâté en pot*. Comprising all the unmentionable parts of a sheep – lungs, head, tripe, heart, belly and feet – the meat is minced, heavily spiced and stewed, the end result being akin to a runny haggis minus the oatmeal. Its title notwithstanding, the dish is less of a *pâté* than a *patée* – a word which means a pulpy consistency, and which probably is the derivation of the name. (Although to confuse matters, Dr André Nègre, in his *Antilles et Guyane à travers leur cuisine*, suggests the title ought to be written *patte en pot* – a reference to the *patte*, or hoof, which is an integral ingredient.)

In rural areas throughout the Antilles, a pig or two is very common-ly seen rooting about for sustenance in sandy backyards. The Antillean pig has ugly blackish hair, and is called *cochon planche* in order to distinguish it from its fatter cousins – appropriately, for almost always it is as thin as a plank.

Yet there can be no doubt that in the Antilles, as in France itself, *le cochon* is king. At grand plantation dinners during the colonial era, a whole roast suckling pig was considered a necessary symbol of largesse, paraded in its entirety around the dining room of the planter's mansion and presented before each guest for an 'ooh la la', before being returned to the kitchen for dismemberment.

At Christmas, various parts of the pig appear on the table in many guises. First, there is *boudin* – the black pudding so dear to the Creole heart, mostly prepared by professional charcutiers nowadays. Made from a base of pig's blood, milk and breadcrumbs (sometimes also a little cassava meal) the small sausages are distinguished from their metropolitan French counterparts by more assertive seasoning, not only with onion, spring onion, garlic, thyme and parsley, but with island spices – allspice, cloves and chillies.

Prime pork fillet is minced to fill pastry patties for Christmas, and it is not at all uncommon to feature a roast suckling pig or pork ragoût. On top of all this, there is the glazed leg of ham.

The idea of decorating a Christmas ham with pineapple, now wide-spread throughout the western world, probably owes its origin to the *jambon à la Creole* of the French Caribbean. Nowadays this garnish tends to be rather derided by supercilious foodies, at least in its debased form using tinned pineapple rings and glacé cherries. However, the original recipe calls for fresh pineapple rings fried in butter, an altogether different proposition, and for dark rum – not brandy – to be mixed with brown sugar for the glaze.

Poultry is equally a festive and an everyday dish in the Antilles. It may feature as part of a meal following a child's first communion, or as a fricassee at Easter.

Cock-fighting and its associated betting is still regularly practised at officially sanctioned pits throughout the French West Indies. The deceased victims of the ring, tough, wiry old roosters, traditional-ly go into *court-bouillon mulâtre* – marinated in lemon juice, stewed, and mixed at the last minute with cooked pork, tomatoes and bananas.

Provided they are not too ripe, bananas complement the sweetness of chicken very nicely indeed.

Poulet aux Bananes
(chicken with bananas)

1 chicken, about 1.5 kg (3–3½ lb)
1 large onion, sliced
1 teaspoon dried sage
1 bay leaf
salt and pepper
¼ teaspoon ground cloves
¼ teaspoon ground nutmeg

1 small dried chilli, chopped
juice of 1 lime or lemon
2 under-ripe bananas or plantains,
   peeled and sliced
3 tomatoes, skinned,
   de-seeded and chopped
2–3 tablespoons cornflour

Skin the chicken and cut into pieces. Place in a pot with 1.5 litres (2½ pts) of water, bring to the boil, and skim off the scum. Add the sage and bay leaf and simmer for 10 minutes.

Remove the chicken. Cut away the breast bones and return them to the pot to help flavour the cooking liquid. Boil the cooking liquid vigorously until reduced by three-quarters. Strain off the resulting stock, season to taste with salt and pepper, then return to the pot with the chicken pieces, the cloves, nutmeg and chilli. Gently simmer for about 8 minutes. Add citrus juice, bananas and tomatoes and cook for several minutes longer. Finally, thicken the broth by stirring in cornflour mixed to a paste with a little cold water.

SERVES 4.

Lafcadio Hearn tells us chicken was also the base ingredient of *poule-epi-diri*, a simple, now largely forgotten Antillean version of the famous Spanish New Orleans dish, jambalaya.

Hearn, still honoured in New Orleans as the author of the world's first Creole cookbook, also lived in the French West Indies in the 1880s, spending much of his time in Fort-de-France (where there is now a car parking building named after him). In the book he subsequently wrote, *Two Years in the French West Indies*, he noted that Martiniquans thought *poule-epi-diri* to be such a delicacy that 'an over-exacting person, or one difficult to satisfy, is reproved with the simple question, *'Ca ou le nco – poule-epi-diri?'* (What more do you want – chicken and rice?).

Rather more elaboration, however, went into the dressing of game birds, particularly if rank flavours needed to be disguised. The flesh of wood pigeons, for example, acquired a faintly bitter flavour if it had been eating the nuts of the gum tree.

Until the twentieth century, the Antilles sported game animals in wide variety, if never in high numbers. From June to October the French kitted themselves out with hip flasks and exaggerated feathered caps for the bird hunting season – turtle dove, ortolan, wild duck, rail, teal, snipe, plover, partridge. Even a rare species of yellow-footed thrush was among those shot and prepared for the table in traditional French ways.

Racoon was reported to have a rather gamey flavour, calling for a heavy disguise of spices, but the manicou, a type of opossum, had finer tasting flesh and was relentlessly hunted. But providing the best hunting of all was the poor agouti, a harmless, shy, herbivorous rodent, whose unfortunate head gives it the look of an innocent rat (if such a thing is possible). Agouti hunting was done with dogs, who risked having their eyes gouged out when one was cornered. Nevertheless, the animal was hunted virtually out of existence by the end of the 1920s. Today only a few survive on La Désirade, an outlying island of Guadeloupe, while the racoon is a protected and endangered species.

The flesh of the Martiniquan agouti was 'good and easy to digest', reports a seventeenth-century Dominican monk, Jean Baptiste Labat. As for the wood pigeon, he had very firm advice:

'Wood pigeon can be eaten half-cooked and therefore still a little bloody; doctors have been wrong in recommending meat be roast or boiled so hard that hardly any of its juice is left.'

Unlike so many highly opinionated people who are irritating in their unfailing tendency to be correct, Father Labat's contentiousness is easily forgiven by readers of his massive six-volume memoirs (*Nouveau Voyage aux Isles de l'Amérique par le Rev. P. Labat,* Paris 1772) because his immensely witty, garrulous nature always shines through.

Born in 1663 of a bourgeois family near Bordeaux, he entered holy orders at the age of twenty-two, and after an early career as a teacher and a military chaplain, left with a mission for Martinique in 1693, staying for about twelve years.

Grabbing every opportunity to join a voyage around the Caribbean, he comes across as a swashbuckling, epicurean French counterpart of Samuel Pepys, involved in every sort of classic high seas adventure, whether being captured by pirates, haggling over the price of their loot, or firing cannons against the English. Religious duties, it seemed, came well down on his list of priorities – certainly well below his duty to eat and drink well. This much is evident from his portrait, depicting a fat, moonfaced priest, with large gleaming eyes and a comical curl to his lip, worthy of a character from Chaucer or Rabelais. Labat, indeed, is the Caribbean's best guide to all things edible back in the seventeenth century, his memoirs cataloguing every fruit, vegetable, animal, fish, crustacean and insect – along with recipes for cooking them.

Father Labat's Barbecued Whole Pig

According to the sacred rites, this sacrifice takes place on a wooden grill: push four forks into the ground to mark out a square of about 1.5 metres each side; lay four cross-beams to connect the forks, with little poles between, and securely lash everything together: here is your grill.

Lay the pig on the grill, belly up and cut open, generously filled with herbs, spices, cloves, nutmeg, lime juice . . . in the face of so many spices, I don't think sage should show itself; however, this remains to be tried. Venture forth with 50 chives, a large handful of parsley, 30 bay leaves, 20 sprigs of thyme, 20 cloves, half a nutmeg and the juice of 50 limes.

One day Labat put this recipe into practice, on a picnic he provided for some fellow priests. Since all guests had to act the part of buccaneers, no metal implements, plates, dishes, spoons or forks were allowed. 'Even tablecloths are forbidden,' Labat rules, 'they are too much at variance with buccaneer simplicity.'

Having prepared the grill and the pig according to Labat's recipe, the priests cooked it over the embers, said a blessing 'and sat down at a table so solid that nothing but an earthquake could have shaken it, for our table was the earth itself.'

Providing his guests with napkins and bread, Labat concedes, was really against the rules – 'for real buccaneers don't know the meaning of napkins and use only baked plantains for bread.' In the interest of authenticity, however, they did forgo the normal seventeenth-century practice of diluting their wine with water:

I do not think it necessary to inform the reader that one of the essential things in a *boucan* is to drink frequently. The law compels it, the sauce invites it, and few err in this respect. But since man is frail and would often fall if he had no one to remind him of his duty and correct him, the master of the *boucan* has to watch his party. Should he find any one idle or negligent he must at once call everybody's attention to the fact. The delinquent must then do penance by drinking from the large calabash, no mean punishment since this calabash is always kept full of wine.

A similar list of seasonings goes into another of Labat's barbecuing recipes, for a delicacy which has long disappeared from the French West Indies – turtle. Specifically, it was the plastron that was eaten – three or four fingers' breadth of fatty flesh which clung to the ventral part of the shell. The shell was placed on the embers, the cavity sprinkled with spices, and the meat pricked from time to time during cooking to ensure even penetration of the cooking juices. Armed with knives, buccaneers would simply sit around the cooked shell and tear off bits of flesh.

Labat had first-hand experience of such fare – he once sailed on a pirate ship from Martinique to St Thomas. Bad weather blew the vessel off course, forcing it to put into a tiny eastern Caribbean island for repairs. There, Labat was astounded to meet two English women from Barbados, who had been abandoned there with their servants by another ship, similarly beset while en route to Antigua.

Obligingly, the pirates dropped them off at their destination once their ship was seaworthy again – but not before Labat had spent several days on the island swapping recipes with the English women. He showed them how to barbecue a turtle, while they taught him how to cook a brisket of Irish beef, pâtés, turtle steak and ragoûts.

'Our two ladies took charge of everything in connection with the culinary department and performed wonders,' Labat recalled. 'I could write a volume on the subject, telling how to serve 125 dishes at no cost on a desert island in magnificent style.'

Not all women of that era would have been so able. Indeed, such was the life of utter indolent luxury lived by the island-born white wives of the planters – then called Creoles – that they were the envy of Europe. 'Beautiful as a Creole' and 'rich as a Creole' were common catch-phrases. Throughout Europe, Creole women were thought to possess an alluring, languid grace, and they attained the highest social circles. Madame de Maintenon, for example, who became the last wife of Louis XIV in 1684 and died in the palace of Versailles, had been brought up on the tiny island of Marie-Galante, off Guadeloupe. Then of course, there was Napoleon's wife, Josephine, daughter of a prosperous sugar planter in Martinique.

Josephine retained a lifelong passion for the tropical fruits of her childhood, and when she lived in Paris, wrote home to her mother for supplies of guavas, mangoes, oranges and bananas. It is also claimed that Napoleon, in exile at the end of his life on St Helena, could only have his appetite roused by a dish of banana fritters marinated in rum – possibly because it reminded him of his lost empress.

Whether this was a recipe Josephine brought from Martinique is not known. What is almost certain, however, is that Josephine, along with virtually every other plantation mistress of her era, never sullied her hands by actually cooking this or any other dish. There was, after all, a large retinue of slaves to spare them any exertion at all save gossip. Possibly the mistress scarcely visited the kitchen at all, since it was often a separate building placed some distance from the house, in order to minimize the fire risk.

Hung along the brick walls of the cookhouse would be rows of battered casserole dishes of varying size, often locally made. Invariably there would be a special pan for cooking *blaff*, and a tall cylindrical pot known as a *fait-tout*, used for all types of soups and ragoûts.

In the middle of the room stood a huge work table, roughly hewn by machetes from local timber; in the corner, a battered old chair or stool perhaps demoted after long service in the master's study.

The stove itself would be a sturdy construction of brick, with five or six openings in which to place glowing charcoal. The sinks and benches would also be of brick. Large sideboards, their doors covered in grilles, held expensive ingredients such as vanilla pods, cocoa pods, refined sugar and flavoured rums for desserts. Shelves contained scales and sets of tin measuring cups.

A number of specialized implements would also be found there, such as a hand-grinder for coffee, a tin *cafetière* for filtering coffee once made, and a wide, flattish cauldron used for deep frying (and also to roast green coffee beans). Calabashes, dried in the sun and cut in half, served for bowls, and there would be a mortar and pestle, made either of wood or stone.

There were also several hangovers from the ancestral African kitchen: a large wood-fired earthenware pot, known as a *canari*, and a giant swizzle stick known as a *baton lélé*. Cut from a tree, it comprised a straight stick, ending in a wheel of amputated concentric twigs. The implement has two main uses – to mix punches and to make vegetable purées.

In African hands, traditional French recipes were being adapted to local ingredients and African techniques. Spices and chillies were used much more frequently, not only, as has so often been suggested, to disguise the flavour of rank meat and fish, but also for their own sake, for pleasure. What in Europe had been a mainly protein and carbohydrate diet, no longer seemed so appropriate in the sweltering heat of the tropics, and African cooks were only too happy to lighten up the masters' meals in ways that were familiar – by adding green vegetables. It has even been suggested that this input of green vegetables into the slaveholders' diet saved countless numbers from nutritional deficiencies.

Those who cooked in the kitchens were, of course, the fortunate few. Theirs were the easiest jobs, coveted not only with respect to food, but also clothes and lodgings. In particular, the nanny, or 'Da', who might combine child-minding with some cooking, occupied a position of great prestige in many planters' homes. Below her was the class of slaves with trades, such as blacksmiths, coopers, carpenters and gardeners; while at the bottom of the scale were the field labourers, required to rise before sunrise and labour until nightfall with only a hat of felt or straw to protect them from the tropical sun.

Their diet differed very little from that which they had endured on the slave ships during the notorious Middle Passage, the voyage across the Atlantic from West Africa to the Caribbean. In most instances, at least after the early stages of the trade, there was enough to eat on board these ships, not out of humanitarian concerns but simply to serve the self-interest of the captains, who were partly paid according to the number of slaves landed alive and saleable. The same motives explain regular exercising of slaves and the scrubbing and disinfecting of their quarters with lime juice or vinegar.

Slaves were usually fed two meals a day, set out in little tubs, around which ten or so might be assembled and issued with wooden spoons. Since slavers had learned by the early 1700s that slaves fared better when given traditional foods, their diet varied according to nationality or tribal origins. However, typical foodstuffs were pulses such as black-eyed beans, rice, ship's biscuits, barley and yams. Corn was fried into cakes, while flour was mixed with palm oil and water and seasoned with pepper as a sort of gravy. Occasionally salt fish or meat might be provided, and a mouthwash of lime or vinegar would often be given at the morning meal, in order to ward off scurvy. The daily supply of water, perhaps the most crucial factor in the slave's survival, was set down by the French government in the first half of the nineteenth century at three litres (about five pints) per slave, but in some cases only a quarter of this was actually issued.

As early as 1685 the government of France had set down the legal status of both slaves and owners in the *Code Noir,* or Black Code. It was a double-edged sword, granting the slaves some rights but forbidding them to own property or to bear arms, and detailing the most horrendous punishments for various offences, such as flogging, branding, the cutting off of ears or buttocks, and death.

As regards diet, Article 22 provided that 'slaves ten years and above be given two and a half measures of manioc flour or three cassavas weighing two and a half pounds each (or the equivalent) with two pounds of salt beef or three pounds of fish or other viands in like proportion, and for children under ten years, half the above ration.' Article 23 forbade giving rum instead of such rations, a common practice since rum was cheaper and a tipsy slave was better able to work on an empty stomach. Article 24 granted slaves the right to complain if they were not properly nourished – a legal nicety, surely, since the same code stripped them of their right to be a party or even a witness in both civil and criminal cases.

The mass of plantation slaves ate whatever their owners found economical. This almost never meant meat and very rarely fish. Fresh fish, of course, surrounded the islanders on all sides, but in the words of one early traveller to the Caribbean, the planters 'tend their profits so much they will not spare a Negro's absence so long as to go to the Bridge and fetch it.'

Morue – a salt fish, occasionally mackerel but usually cod – was far more convenient. Very familiar to French slave keepers (medieval Bretons had founded the international salt cod trade), it did not spoil in the tropical heat, and came down from New England in the same ships that carried back rum and molasses. Usually only second-rate salt cod reached the French West Indies, since the best quality went to Europe.

Over the centuries, *morue* formed the main source of protein for the Afro-Caribbean population – 'a dish of daily penitence, effectively', noted Marie Eugénie Bourgeois in her 1961 cookery book. 'It provides for the mother of the family who can not afford meat or fresh fish, only appearing on middle class tables on a Friday, for religious reasons.'

At the most rudimentary level, the fillets of salt cod were simply soaked to remove the excess salt, then grilled on both sides over hot coals and eaten with cassava flour boiled with water, oil and lemon juice, perhaps with a slice of avocado mashed with chilli. But by Madame Bourgeois's time, only 'woodsmen, fishermen, field labourers and old mountain dwellers' still favoured such a coarse concoction. On the other hand, the tiny salt cod fritters known as *accras de morue* are equally at home in the basket of a street seller or on the silver platter of an elegant cocktail reception among wealthy Creoles. They are also the common accompaniment to rum punches served as aperitifs in Martiniquan and Guadeloupian restaurants.

Morue is also shredded and marinated in vinaigrette, or made into soufflés, pilafs and Provençal-style *brandades*. However, while it is still readily available at markets on the islands, *morue* is not the staple it once was, since its price has risen sharply in accordance with the world-wide depletion of cod fish stocks – so much indeed, as to be beyond the reach of poorer households.

While many of the staple foodstuffs eaten by the slaves were native to the New World, they were nevertheless very familiar, due to the radical change in the diet of the African continent that had taken place from the mid-sixteenth to the end of the eighteenth century, when Europeans introduced coconuts, sweet potatoes, maize, cassava, pineapples, guavas and peanuts. Other staple vegetables from the slave era, such as yams, are native both to Africa and the Caribbean.

Yams come in a great variety of shapes and sizes, but the most important in the French West Indies is a variety of taro known as *chou de chine*. Many Europeans find it difficult to get excited about taro root, which does not exactly burst with flavour. Nor, for that matter, does another great staple from the slave era – breadfruit.

When James Cook first saw breadfruit growing in Tahiti, he considered it would be good for slaves in the West Indies, despite describing its taste as 'completely flavourless' and 'as disagreeable as that of a pickled olive generally the first time it is eaten'. Captain William Bligh was sent to fetch saplings from Tahiti, and it was his action of reducing the crew's rations of drinking water to keep these plants alive that ultimately triggered the mutiny on the *Bounty*. His second attempt to introduce breadfruit to St Vincent and Jamaica was successful in 1792–3. From there its cultivation spread through the Caribbean. Runaway slaves in the French West Indies largely lived off the breadfruit from wild trees in the hills, and indeed, such abundance aroused the prejudice of some white colonists.

'I'd like to see them all cut down, every one of them, and burnt,' a civil engineer told the English travel writer Patrick Leigh Fermor in the late 1940s. ' "It's the bloody breadfruit that keeps the black alive without working. It lets them grow fat without doing a hand's turn, takes away all their incentive to work. That's what puts them beyond our control," he held up two hands, with the fingers crooked like claws through which the whole of the Negro world was slipping. "And who's to blame for that? You, sir." A claw was placed on one of my shoulders in a conciliatory gesture. "Not you directly, but your Bligg!" ' – by which he meant Bligh.

Breadfruit comes in both knobbly and smooth varieties, some the size of footballs. As with the taro, it tastes rather like a dense potato, which makes a reasonably acceptable substitute for both breadfruit and taro in certain recipes, such as this classic soup from Guadeloupe. As its name suggests, this dish was brought from the Congo, not by slaves but by *les Congos,* workers recruited in this part of Africa from 1854, following the abolition of slavery. It is however, a soup in name only, being more of a liquid stew, with all its constituent vegetables chopped but kept intact.

Soupe à Congo

Vie cannari ka fe bon bouillon – Old pots make the best soup –
OLD CREOLE PROVERB, MARTINIQUE

500 g (1 lb) taro (or substitute
   potatoes), peeled and cubed
1 sweet potato, cubed
500 g (1 lb) green beans, sliced
500 g (1 lb) mixed dried beans
   (e.g. kidney beans, dried broad
   beans), soaked overnight
250 g (8 oz) carrots, diced
250 g (8 oz) *giraumon* (substitute
   pumpkin)

½ cabbage, cut in thick slices
4 leaves sorrel (optional)
4 cloves garlic, whole
3 medium onions, chopped
2 small red chillies, chopped
2 cloves
200 g (7 oz) bacon or lard,
   chopped

Place all ingredients except bacon or lard in a pot, cover with about 2.5 litres (4½ pts) of water, cover and gently simmer for 1½–2 hours. About 30 minutes

before the end of cooking, simmer the bacon or lard in a little water and add to the soup before serving. Season to taste with salt and pepper.
SERVES 8.

To Europeans brought up on bananas, the first taste of a plantain can be disappointing; there is none of the sweetness or intensity of flavour, and in order to be properly appreciated, plantains must be regarded as a substitute for potatoes, or more specifically breadfruit, to which they bear a passing resemblance both in flavour and texture.

With the inexplicable Creole penchant for substituting one common name for another, a plantain in the French West Indies is known as a *banane*, while a banana is known as a *figue* (fig), a reference to the banana leaf which according to one interpretation of Genesis, was the actual leaf used to cover Adam's anatomy, with a great deal more modesty, one assumes, than the puny fig leaf of mythology.

Bananes Vertes aux Epinards
(plantains with spinach and lemon)

2 large plantains, approx. 750 g (1½ lb)
salt
1 kg (2 lb) spinach

¼ teaspoon fresh green chilli, chopped
juice of 2–3 lemons

With a small sharp knife, peel the plantains and cut into rounds. Gently boil in salted water for 30 minutes. Drain.

Wash the spinach and remove the larger stalks, then place in a pot with just the water remaining on the leaves, with the cooked plantains and chilli sprinkled over the top. Steam for about 5 minutes, then drain everything in a colander, pressing down gently to remove excess moisture. Transfer to a serving dish, sprinkle liberally with the lemon juice, and serve hot.
SERVES 4.

'The potager, fringed in brushwood,' wrote Quérillac in 1931, 'is the precious resource and the greatest pride of the lonely exile. Tomatoes grow wonderfully well; radishes and salad greens are watered with tender care. Aubergines always prosper and the indigenous people themselves have learnt to cultivate turnips and carrots.'

Such vegetables were, of course, introductions of the colonizing French, along with flavourings of thyme, bay leaves and garlic, which are today so central to the French West Indian diet. Today, tomatoes, carrots and cabbages are grown in the north of Martinique, not far from Mount Pelée, because of the good volcanic soils. However, unlike yams, sweet potatoes, avocados and tropical fruit, these European vegetables are difficult to grow, and today many are imported.

Tomates aux Aubergines
(tomatoes with aubergines)

2 large aubergines
2 red peppers
2 medium onions, finely chopped
3 tablespoons olive oil
1 level teaspoon ground mace
2 teaspoons fresh oregano,
    chopped

2 cloves garlic, crushed
8–10 capers
black pepper
salt
10 medium tomatoes

Cut a slit in the aubergines and place under the grill with the red peppers. Grill until the aubergines deflate and turn soft, and the skin of the red peppers blackens on all sides.

Remove the aubergines, allow any thick oily juices to drain off (they may be bitter) then scoop the pulpy flesh away from the skin. Discard the skin. Finely chop the flesh and set aside.

Meanwhile, place the grilled red peppers in a tightly wrapped paper bag. Remove when they have cooled a little, peel, discard skin and seeds and chop the flesh finely.

Preheat oven to 190°C (375°F/Gas 5).

Sauté the onion in the olive oil until they turn translucent, then add mace, oregano, garlic and capers. Season to taste with black pepper and salt.

Blanch, peel and chop the tomatoes.

In a greased ovenproof dish, spread a layer of onion mixture, then the aubergines, red peppers and finally the tomatoes. Cover and cook for 15 minutes.

SERVES 6.

Introduced from Mexico in the eighteenth century, the christophene found special favour in the French-speaking islands. Also known as chayote, chocho, choko and, in Louisiana, mirliton, it spread through the French-speaking world, turning up in colonies as far apart as Algeria and Réunion. By the 1920s, its cultivation was widespread in the south of France.

Christophines Farcies
(stuffed chayotes)

4 christophines (chokos, vegetable pear)
5 tablespoons butter
2 medium onions, finely diced
100g (3 oz or ½ cup) breadcrumbs
1 teaspoon fresh thyme, chopped
1 teaspoon salt
175g (6 oz or 1 cup) ham, finely diced
1 tablespoon parsley, chopped

Boil the christophines for 10 minutes, remove and slice in two lengthways. Scoop out and discard the central seed. Scoop out the flesh and chop.

In a saucepan, melt the butter and fry the onions until translucent. Add chopped christophine flesh and remaining ingredients, stir well, then pile the stuffing into the empty shells. Bake at 160°C (325°F/Gas 3) for 15 minutes.

SERVES 4.

Gratin de Christophines

3 large christophines
40 g (1½ oz) butter
3 shallots, chopped
2 cloves garlic, chopped
salt and pepper
30 g (1 oz or ¼ cup) flour
500 ml milk
75 g (3 oz) gruyère cheese, grated

Cut each christophine in two lengthways, then steam for 15–20 minutes. Peel, remove central seed and cut into cubes while still hot. Arrange in a flat ovenproof dish.

Melt the butter, add the shallots and garlic, and sauté until softened but not brown. Sprinkle over the flour, little by little, and stir it in. Stir for 2 minutes, then add the milk, stirring in a little at a time. Season with salt and pepper. Bring to the boil, continuing to stir, then pour over the christophines. Sprinkle the gruyère over and flash under a hot grill.

SERVES 4.

Christophine Vinaigrette

Provided the christophine is nice and fresh, this is the perfect way to exploit its potential as a raw vegetable. It should be served within 15 minutes of making it, otherwise the christophine begins to turn soggy and expel the vinaigrette it has just absorbed so cooperatively.

2 medium christophines
2 tablespoons white wine vinegar
¼ teaspoon salt
60 ml (2 fl oz or ¼ cup) extra virgin
   olive oil

½ teaspoon fresh chilli finely
   chopped
1 large clove garlic, crushed

Peel the christophines, quarter them, remove the seed, and grate on a grater, using long strokes to obtain long strands of christophine. Strain off the liquid and gently squeeze the christophine to remove any excess liquid.

Make a vinaigrette by mixing the salt and vinegar. Stir in the olive oil, then the garlic and chilli. Mix the vinaigrette through the christophine just before serving.

SERVES 4.

Haricots Rouges Consommés
(consommé of red kidney beans)

500 g (1 lb) red kidney beans
5 whole cloves, bruised
bouquet garni
2 onions, quartered
125 g (4½ oz) smoked pork belly
   (or bacon scraps), cubed

4 cloves garlic, crushed
3 tablespoons extra virgin olive oil
3 tablespoons white wine vinegar
salt and pepper

Cover the beans with 2–3 cm (1 in) of water and soak for at least 3 hours. Bring to the boil and boil vigorously for 10 minutes, then add bouquet garni, pork belly, cloves and onions. Cover and simmer for 40 minutes. When the beans are soft, season to taste with salt and pepper, add the garlic, and boil with the lid off for another 10–15 minutes. Mash some of the beans with a potato masher until they begin to thicken the liquid. Add olive oil, vinegar, salt and pepper to taste.

SERVES 5–6.

While kidney beans are native to the Americas, with the slaves came native African dried beans (known, confusingly, as *pois* – peas) such as pigeon peas and black-eyed beans (known as *pois d'Angole*) . With vegetables such as okra and a variety of leafy greens they went into a famous ancestral soup from West Africa. This came to be known throughout the entire Caribbean as callaloo, or calalou.

Calalou

According to Père Labat, 22 species of green leaf are needed for a calalou. Certainly the range available to Caribbean cooks is astounding, and many of these are rather difficult to obtain elsewhere. However, an approximation of calalou can be made with spinach.

1.5 kg (3 lb) taro leaves, spinach or swiss chard
1 medium aubergine, peeled and sliced
250 g (8 oz) okra (about 30), sliced
4 tablespoons peanut oil
250 g (8 oz) salt pork, cubed
3 green (unripe) bananas, peeled and sliced

3 spring onions, sliced
5 cloves garlic, chopped
1 teaspoon fresh thyme, chopped
½ teaspoon ground cloves
½ green chilli, chopped
3 tablespoons white wine vinegar
salt and ground black pepper
400 ml (14 fl oz) tin coconut cream

Soak the leaves in a sink of cold water, swishing them about to loosen any dirt. Remove stalks then chop them roughly and place in a large pot with the aubergine and okra. Add 1.5 litres (2½ pts) of water, bring to the boil, reduce heat, cover and cook until tender but still green.

In a large casserole dish, heat the oil and sauté pork, bananas and onions. Lower heat and simmer until bananas are tender, then add garlic, thyme, cloves, spring onion, chilli, vinegar, salt and pepper. Cook a minute longer. Pick out the pieces of pork and reserve. Mix the rest with the greens and their liquid.

Traditionally the mixture is now forced through a sieve and then whisked with a *baton lélé* until it forms a light fluffy purée. More or less the same effect, however, can be achieved with a food processor or blender. Process in several batches.

Return to the pot along with the pork and the coconut cream and reheat gently before serving.
SERVES 6–8.

Calalou is traditionally associated with picnics, one of the most popular Creole pastimes.

'On these occasions, they arise with the sun and are away early in the morning,' wrote Quérillac:

> Whether on horseback or on foot, the convoy proceeds leisurely along the bluffs above the raging torrent. A troupe of negresses follows, carrying on their heads, balanced on pads of coiled rags, broad, heavy baskets of food. The groom boys, ever anxious to limit their efforts, are hanging by the tails of the nags. They allow themselves to be carried and lulled to sleep, occasionally plucking leaves from plants along the way . . . Laughing, singing and chatting merrily, they thus reach the elected spot: the banks beside a pool, dug even for a king . . . The women change into bathing costumes. Meanwhile the men and boys frolic about in the limpid water, playfully squeezing each other.
>
> And so the bathing begins – soft, deliciously restful, since it takes place in one of a number of warm rivers, such as the 'Bains Jaunes' of Guadeloupe, the water of which is so tepid that one can remain in it for several hours without feeling tired.
>
> The servants busy themselves around the big baskets, unpacking silverware, glasses, wines and food. The picnic blanket is soon laid beside the pool, on the banks alongside the swimming hole, so one can dine in the water as well as on the grass. Large leaves serve as plates and platters, from which each helps himself. And no spectacle is more curious than that of these bathers, immersed up to their necks, but holding their right hand out of the water with a chicken leg, a glass, a piece of fruit or a *mordant* – that is, a crab pincer.
>
> Here, the 'steaming calalou' is de rigueur. So one always remembers to bring among the provisions, the necessary ingredients.
>
> Upon arrival, the cooks were sent to find three large stones. These are laid out as a fire grate, in which is lit a bright fire. A 'canari' placed over this improvised fireplace serves as a stock pot, in which all the essential elements of a calalou have been placed.

This scene is not greatly changed today, save that the participants in the picnic are more likely to be Afro-Caribbean than white. And rather than have young people play guitars, accordions and banjos under the mango trees as in former times, zouk music will be typically blaring forth from a ghettoblaster. On a grassy area, or by the beach, a net might have been set up for a game of volleyball. And along with all the other food brought along in giant plastic and polystyrene chilly-bins, the calalou will probably have been brought ready-made, in a thermos flask.

Another picnic tradition persists on the Monday following Easter, when families and friends gather on the beaches to light fires, cook and eat a traditional dish, *matété de crabes.*

This dish is said to be descended from *ago glain*, a dish from the former kingdom of Dahomey (modern Benin) in West Africa. On Guadeloupe, the dish is sometimes cooked with cassava meal and is called *matoutou*, a reference to a large watertight platter which the Caribs formerly constructed from reeds and fan palms.

Matété de Crabes

2.5 kg (5–5½ lb) crabs, preferably land crabs (substitute mud, sea or swimming crabs)	6 chives, finely chopped
	500 g (1 lb or 2 cups) long-grain rice
2 tablespoons butter	1 large sprig of fresh thyme
2 tablespoons olive oil	(or ½ teaspoon dried)
2 cloves garlic, crushed	1 bay leaf
1 small onion, finely diced	1 chilli, chopped
2 spring onions, chopped	sprig of parsley, chopped

If the crabs are alive, kill them by stabbing a knife between the eyes. Remove the claws, then open the carapace, remove and discard the digestive bags and other inedibles from each shell.

In a large pot, add the crab pieces to the butter and oil, along with garlic, onion, spring onions and chives. Fry for about 10 minutes. Add the rice, thyme, bay leaf and chilli, and enough water to barely cover. Place a lid on the pot, bring to the boil, lower the heat and simmer until the rice has almost cooked. Remove from the heat and leave with the lid on, until the rice is cooked as the water is absorbed. Just before serving, mix through parsley and make sure the crabs are well exposed.

SERVES 6.

A variation on *crême anglaise*, known as *chaudeau*, is also associated with a specific event – a child's first communion.

Chaudeau

1 litre (1¾ pts or 4 cups) milk
100 g (4 oz or ½ cup) sugar
zest of 1 lime
1 vanilla pod, split down the middle

1 cinnamon stick
4 large eggs
2 teaspoons orange flower water
  (optional)

Place milk in a heavy saucepan with sugar, lime zest, vanilla pod and cinnamon stick. Bring almost to the boil, then remove from the heat.

In a bowl, lightly beat the eggs and pour in some of the hot, sweetened milk. Continue beating. Now pour the egg mixture back into the milk in the saucepan, beating continuously.

Return the saucepan to the stove, and over a low heat, continue to stir for 15–20 minutes, until it thickens sufficiently to coat the back of a spoon. At no point allow the mixture to boil, or it will curdle. Remove and discard the lime zest, vanilla pod and cinnamon stick. Stir in the orange flower water (if using) before serving.

SERVES 6.

In former times, children were shut away together for three days prior to their first communion, without any contact with the outside, and not allowed back with their parents until the day after the ceremony. In order to ease the separation, the parents would take along cakes and *chaudeau*, and after the children had come out from their mass, would feed them these treats along with a cup of hot chocolate. Over time, this in itself evolved into an elaborate ceremony, involving multi-tiered Savoy cakes, nougats and sweets. Quérillac wrote in 1931:

For the children, there are *traits* – immense wooden platters – stacked with gigantic Savoy biscuits, nougats, pyramids of macaroons, biscuits, sweets of all sorts and a monumental pot of *chaudeau*. Everything is ornamented with flowers, embroidery and lace work, enhancing the elegance and the refinement of the presentation.

When the church bells announce the end of the mass, the servants – who have been waiting for this signal – place the platters on their heads, and join together in procession along the streets to the cathedral, where they wait under the porch for the children to come out.

It is difficult to imagine just how picturesque this spectacle is: the pretty mulattos, the brown *cabresses* [coquettes], the sombre negresses, clothed in ample dresses of striking colours, pinched at the waist, puffed out like baskets over white starched and embroidered petticoats: the silk neckerchiefs, the madras turban, running the full gamut from red, green, yellow, violet . . . the 'chou pastry' necklaces; golden sparkling rings, raised tier upon tier on their chests, the platters bursting with the whiteness of linen and porcelain. It all shimmers under the splendid tropical sun which endows everything with a lustre and an incomparable colouring.

The vanity of this festival! . . . Not just one, but many platters are paraded by the rich families. And this never fails to incite the envy of the under-privileged. The poor don't hesitate to run into debt and go without for long periods in order to present a *trait*, decorated with dignity, and giving them the appearance, in the final analysis, of being richer than they actually are.

The contemplative nature of this gathering of communicants is thus lost, alas! How is it possible, I ask, to maintain a sense of humility in the face of such exhibitionism? All piety aside, a child can not resist a fit of pique if a neighbour's platter is more beautiful than their own, or the satisfaction of noting that theirs is more sumptuous.

As in New Orleans, the onset of Lent is preceded with a huge carnival, involving parades, floats, music and much dancing. Participants coat themselves with molasses and powdered charcoal, and these *nègres gros sirop* march in procession, followed by a crowd, who buy street food along the way, such as tarts, little pastries and meatballs. The day before Ash Wednesday is Mardi Gras, the Devil's day, and everybody wears red for the occasion. On this day, *crêpes* and fritters are eaten.

But the highlight of the culinary year in Guadeloupe occurs in the second week of August, with the Fête des Cuisinières – or Feast of the Women Cooks.

Founded as a culinary association in Pointe-à-Pitre on 4 July 1916, Le Cuistot Mutuel association holds the Fête to honour the Christian martyr St Lawrence. The reason? His fate in AD 258, was to be grilled alive over glowing charcoal! Thus, the emblem of the association is a grilling basket (only containing a fish rather than a saint), flanked with the letters SL.

The week-long festival begins with a remembrance mass for the souls of the departed *cuisinières*, continues with a number of food-centred activities, and culminates with a street parade.

The big day begins with a mass in the Cathedral of St Peter and St Paul in Pointe-à-Pitre, attended by all the *cuisinières* dressed in traditional Creole finery – a Madras turban, a scarf, a small tonnage of gold chains, brooches and earrings, a V-shaped bodice and a dress made from a bright new fabric, chosen each year by the association. Nowadays a few males have been accepted as members, while in recent years Martinique has formed its own association, Le Cordon Madras, which sends a delegation to the festival.

The *cuisinières* will have been up early that morning, putting the final decorative touches to grand platters of lobsters, crabs, coiled mounds of boudin sausage, multi-layered cakes and other Creole specialities, both traditional and modern, sometimes placed in baskets to which are tied miniature cooking implements (pots, sieves, egg baskets), and taken into the cathedral where they are laid in front of a statue of Saint Lawrence.

After the service, the food is carried out again and paraded through the streets by the *cuisinières*, amid much singing, dancing and ringing of bells by the 'mistresses of ceremonies', to a feasting hall where, for a nominal fee, the food is shared with all. Finally, a band strikes up the béguine, mérengué and mazurka, and the dancing begins, the elderly often showing as much spark as the young, even dancing with each other when there are not enough men to go around.

Among the dishes at this feast will be one which originates outside the Creole mainstream – curry, or as it is called in the Antilles, colombo. This is the legacy of some 70,000 Indians who arrived in Martinique as plantation labourers between 1852 and 1865 following the emancipation of the slaves. Derived mainly from the French territories in south India, *les coolies* were low-caste Hindus, mostly of Tamil ancestry, who never went on to prosper as shopkeepers or merchants as their compatriots did elsewhere. Indeed, all but four or five thousand either migrated elsewhere or died of disease, the remainder staying on as sugar plantation labourers in the north of Martinique or southern Guadeloupe, or as street sweepers in the cities. Their descendants are still referred to as coolies, although understandably they now object to the name.

But if the economic impact of the Indians was small, their culinary influence was huge: various colombos of pork, beef, *lambi* and especially of the goat meat they refer to as *cabri,* are among the most popular dishes of the modern French West Indies.

While the etymology cannot be proven, it is tempting to identify Colombo, the capital of Sri Lanka, as the origin of colombo – a name which refers both to the finished dish and the distinctive curry powder which goes into it.

Colombo powder or paste is not so much a curry powder in the Anglo-Indian sense, as a variation on a traditional southern Indian spice masala, comprising mustard seeds, turmeric, saffron, chilli, ground roasted rice, garlic, and sometimes tamarind and black peppercorns.

Colombo de Porc
(pork curry)

This curry clearly shows the influence of the French kitchen, with products such as olive oil and thyme, as well as employing a local spice, the *bois d'Inde,* or bay rum berry, very closely related to allspice.

1 kg (2 lb) pork loin
2 tablespoons olive oil
2 tablespoons butter
1 medium onion, sliced
3 shallots, minced
3 cloves garlic
2 large branches fresh thyme or 2
  teaspoons dried
1 tablespoon colombo powder
  (substitute curry powder)
1 teaspoon ground *bois d'Inde*
  (substitute allspice)

1 tablespoon white wine or cider
  vinegar
salt and pepper
1 habanera-type chilli, pricked with
  a fork
1 chayote, cut into 2–3 cm (1 in)
  pieces
1 small aubergine, cubed
3 medium tomatoes blanched,
  skinned and roughly chopped
parsley, finely chopped

With a small sharp knife, strip the pork loin of excess fat, and cut into cubes.

Heat the olive oil, add the butter, then the pork, onions, shallots and garlic. Stir-fry until the meat is browned all over, adding the thyme and spices part way through. Reduce the heat, cover tightly, and simmer for 30 minutes.

Add vinegar, chilli, chayote, aubergine and tomatoes with 3 tablespoons of water. Very gently simmer for a further 20 minutes, covered tightly to trap in the steam and pan juices. Uncover and simmer to reduce the liquid down to a thick sauce.

Just before serving sprinkle with chopped parsley.

SERVES 4.

While they never sustained the numbers necessary to re-create India in miniature, there still exist some pockets of Hindu culture in the Antilles, such as at Capesterre in Guadeloupe, where religious festivals are accompanied by feasting, the communal meals presented on banana leaves, laid south Indian fashion, on the ground in front of each guest. Besides colombos of goat and chicken, there are curries referred to as *moltani*, their molten qualities assuaged in a peculiarly local fashion, with mouthfuls of a bland, sweet purée made from an esteemed local variety of pumpkin known as *giraumon*.

A small Chinese community has existed in the Antilles for over a century, but they never had the commitment to the land shown by other ethnic groups, and today have been largely dispersed due to migration. More influential, especially in the culinary sense, are the Vietnamese and Laotian wives of former French colonial soldiers, who settled in the Antilles following the eviction of the French from Indo-China. From them comes the modern taste for *nems* (spring rolls), for *chavo* (a crêpe filled with bean sprouts, mushrooms, hard-boiled eggs and various meats) and *chua-chua* (a crab and egg soufflé). Even the ubiquitous noodle soup known as *soupe chinois* is more likely to have been Vietnamese than Chinese in origin.

To be sure, other globalizing influences have been at work on Creole food in the Antilles. The elderly may complain that the younger generation no longer possesses the patience to cook certain Creole dishes, and mulatto cooks such as Marie-Yvonne Andrieu of the Hotel Diamant Les Bains mourn the gradual disappearance of old dishes such as *migan* (a purée of breadfruit and other vegetables) and *riz doux* (sweet rice). Mme Andrieu also bemoans the *arrivistes* from France who open restaurants in order to take advantage of a 1993 law allowing French investors five tax-free years in Martinique. Such people, she says, operate 'Creole' restaurants without being able to cook authentic Creole food. Yet despite the introduction of supermarkets, of kitchen appliances and convenience foods, the Creole food in the Antilles is proving remarkably resilient. It has even resisted Americanization: true, there are now four McDonald's outlets in

Martinique, but Pizza Hut has had a remarkably hard time of it in the French West Indies.

ST MARTIN AND ST BARTHÉLÉMY

Partitioned in 1648 between the Netherlands and France, the island of St Martin retains its Dutch and French sides to this day, although there are no customs formalities, and traders and tourists cross the border without noticing more than the view.

It is, however, impossible to not notice that what natural beauty the island may once have possessed has now largely disappeared beneath a layer of concrete; St Martin has been well and truly discovered by tourists from America and Europe, and today the most beautiful beaches are fringed by seemingly uncontrolled developments of hotels, restaurants, condominiums and boutiques.

For the island's cuisine, tourism has proven a double-edged sword. On the one hand, there has been an explosion of extremely expensive fine restaurants, serving oysters and sole flown in fresh from Paris, ready to be transformed into sophisticated dishes by expatriate French chefs. In addition, there are now a number of good Vietnamese and Chinese restaurants.

On the other hand, the influx of tourists from the mid-1960s meant that large-scale agriculture – always a challenge in the parched landscape which often suffers from drought – was abandoned. Today nearly all the produce for sale on St Martin is imported from faraway Guadeloupe and the neighbouring islands of St Kitts and Dominica. Fishing, which previously had been small-scale and only semi-commercial (often much of the catch might be given away to family and friends), has today turned fully professional. Despite the sea around St Martin being full of kingfish, blackfish, red snapper, goatfish, groper and tuna, retail supplies are still scarce and the fish very expensive.

Not that the islanders, who today enjoy one of the highest standards of living in the Caribbean, would be nostalgic for the old way of life, where people lived in thatched huts and subsisted on cassava bread, potatoes, milk, fish and pulses, as well as maize, which each family would pound into cornmeal with a huge pestle and mortar carved from a tree trunk.

Something of the old colour is still to be seen on a Saturday or a Wednesday, market days in Marigot, the main town in the French side of the island. A mixture of open and umbrella-shaded stalls operated by brightly clothed women offer the usual Caribbean foodstuffs – cassava, breadfruits, chayotes, mangoes, bananas, plantains, soursops and papayas.

Poulet à la Papaye
(chicken with papaya)

1 chicken, about 1.5 kg (3–3½ lb)
1 lime
2 tablespoons butter
1 tablespoon olive oil
400 ml (14 fl oz or 1½ cups) chicken stock
pinch of dried thyme
2 teaspoons cornflour
300g (10 oz or 2 cups) diced fresh papaya
1 tablespoon fresh mint leaves, chopped

Cut the wings from the chicken. Remove the skin of the chicken and discard, along with any fat. Bone the chicken and use the carcass and leg bones to make stock. Slice the legs and breast into two, rub these pieces with the cut lime, and leave for 15 minutes.

Heat the butter and olive oil, sauté the chicken, turning once or twice, for 5 minutes.

Pour over the stock, add the thyme and cook, covered, on a low boil for 10 minutes, or until the chicken is cooked through.

Mix the cornflour with a little cold water, add to the pot and bring to the boil in order to thicken the broth.

Several minutes before the end of cooking, stir in the papaya pieces and heat them through.

Serve sprinkled with chopped mint.
SERVES 4.

Crêpes de Giraumon
(pumpkin pancakes)

1 kg (2 lb) *giraumon*, pumpkin or winter squash
100 g (4 oz or 1 cup) flour
70 g (2½ oz or ¾ cup) sugar
½ teaspoon salt
½ teaspoon baking powder
1 teaspoon ground cinnamon
¼ teaspoon grated nutmeg
½ teaspoon pure vanilla essence
2 eggs
500 ml (scant 1 pt or 2 cups) milk

Bake or microwave the pumpkin until soft. Cut into rough pieces, place in a food processor with remaining ingredients and purée to a smooth batter. Add a little more milk if the mixture seems too thick.

Heat a little oil in a large frying pan and add the mixture, a ladleful (about 2 tablespoons) at a time, to form pancakes. Fry until golden on both sides. Drain on a paper towel.

SERVES 4–6.

From Guana Bay Point on the Dutch side of the island, there is a view of nearby St Barthélémy. This tiny island came to prominence in the 1990s as a preferred destination of the rich and famous. Certainly the exorbitant cost of both food and accommodation serves to deter the backpacker market, although the restaurants are among the finest in the Caribbean, with many bringing out French chefs from metropolitan France to cook for the season.

Traditional French food rules on the island, with several good bakeries turning out excellent French bread. While Creole food is to be found, it does not have nearly the status or prominence as on other islands, due to St Bathélémy's peculiar history. It was never a sugar-producing island, so never had large-scale importation of African labourers, and the African community forms only a small percentage of the total population. Most of the island's inhabitants trace their ancestry back to Brittany, Normandy and Poitou, together with a small number of Swedish descent. Even today, in the village of Corrossol, some of the elderly women can be seen wearing their traditional Breton costumes, consisting of a long black dress and a starched bonnet known as a *quichenotte* (a corruption of 'kiss-me-not'), said to have been adopted to protect women from the unwanted attention of British sailors in the nineteenth century.

HAITI

Haitian cooking mirrors the island's unique history as the Caribbean's first black republic, formed in 1803 after a long and bitter slave uprising against the French.

Despite the fact that the overwhelming majority of the population is of African ancestry, French culture has always been determinedly upheld by the mulattos, descendants of unions between French slave owners and their slaves, who until the notorious era of Papa Doc

Duvalier and his son, held much of the political and economic power on the island. Even today, one per cent of the population possess 40 per cent of the wealth, and as a result there are a number of quite good French restaurants serving cuisine bourgeoise along the lines of flambéed lobster and *escargots bourguignonne*.

The real point of interest in Haitian cooking, however, lies in the mass of the population, most of whom are illiterate, and a cuisine derived from adapting the island's produce and seafood to a blend of African cooking, with subtle French touches. Not all of it is especially appealing, such as *tum tum*, a mush of pounded cornmeal or breadfruit. Nor might too many tourists be willing to sample *tasso*, or strips of goat meat slit down the middle and filled with salt and pepper, then placed on the iron roof of the peasant's hut to dry in the sun (and possibly to provide a convention centre for the local fly population). The meat is taken indoors at night, and the process repeated until the meat is dry and hard. When needed, the meat is soaked in water and then fried and served with avocados and boiled plantains.

Equally unmentionable are the beef liver, kidney, intestines and head which are boiled into *bouillon palan*, a sort of haggis incorporating local fruit and vegetables such as bananas, yams, sweet potatoes, and a vigorous form of local watercress, which has a size and a peppery acidity all of its own. As on the other French islands, *boudin* is also popular.

The most famous pig product of Haiti, however, is a dish of pork chunks cooked with a tangy sauce, known as *griots de porc*. It is not a dish you are likely to encounter at the after-service functions which American fundamentalist missionaries use as a means of attracting a congregation from the Haitian populace. At those gatherings, the participants are likely to be dining on hamburgers and Coke. Over at the rough and ready open-sided voodoo temples known as *hommfors*, meanwhile, a rival congregation is busily tucking into *griots de porc*, made from a pig which has been sacrificed to Azaka, the deity of the hunt and the wilderness. For make no mistake: griots de porc has its origins in the Voodoo faith, even if the dish may nowadays be served in hotels and at dinner parties of the wealthy and respectable, where mention of the word Azaka in front of foreign guests would be the cause of severe embarrassment.

Griots de Porc
(pork cooked in caramelized orange juice)

500 g (1 lb) lean pork (loin or shoulder)

400 ml (14 fl oz or 1½ cups) freshly squeezed Seville orange juice (or substitute half sweet navel orange juice and half lemon juice)

1 large onion, finely chopped

2 cloves garlic, finely chopped

pinch of dried thyme

1 small fresh hot red chilli, finely chopped

¼ teaspoon salt

few grinds of black pepper

Cut the pork into 2–3 cm (1 in) cubes. Mix remaining ingredients into a marinade, pour over the pork cubes in a non-reactive bowl (china, enamel or plastic) and marinate overnight in the refrigerator, or for at least 2 hours at room temperature.

Transfer to a heavy cooking pot, bring to the boil over a medium heat, and cook uncovered, until the liquid has nearly all evaporated away, leaving a thick sauce. While in Haiti this is traditionally eaten with *banane pesé*, (made of plantains boiled, shaped into cakes and fried), rice does nicely also.

SERVES 4.

In many ways Haiti may be the island of rum and roosters, where the chickens tend to be small and tough, often as not simply pan-fried and served with or without a sauce. For this dish, however, the luxury of a poussin is called for. If you cannot find a very young chicken, substitute half a fully grown chicken. While Haitian cooks would never skin the lean young chicken they had allowed to range freely in their backyards, you should remove the fat of a fatty battery-raised supermarket chicken. This is not only healthier, but also more aesthetically pleasing, as the skin of a chicken braised in liquid tends to take on an unpleasantly flabby texture.

Poul'cocotte aux Aubergines
(chicken with aubergine)

1 poussin, about 500 g (1 lb), or half a chicken

2 tablespoons oil

6 whole cloves

3 rashers streaky bacon, cut in half

200 ml (7 fl oz or ¾ cup) chicken stock (or 1 stock cube dissolved in 200 ml water)

1 large aubergine, finely diced

1 small red pepper, finely diced

2 cloves garlic, crushed
1 thumb or knob fresh ginger,
   grated

juice of 1 lemon
2 teaspoons hot pepper sauce
1 teaspoon angostura bitters

Skin the poussin or chicken. If using a poussin, truss. Set aside.

In a heavy pot, heat the oil with the whole cloves until very hot, add the bacon and fry over a high heat to rend out as much fat as possible. Remove the bacon and set aside. Pick out the cloves and discard. Brown the chicken on all sides in the bacon-and-clove-flavoured oil. Remove the chicken and set aside.

Add remaining ingredients, cover the pot, bring to the boil, lower the heat and simmer for 10 minutes. Add the chicken and cook gently for a further 30 minutes, turning several times during cooking. A couple of minutes before serving, return the bacon to the pot to heat through. Serve with fried sweet potatoes and a green salad.

SERVES 2.

During the wet season in the mountainous areas of Haiti, a type of mushroom is to be found, eagerly sought after by cooks. Known as *djon-djon*, it lends its name to this dish. Tiny and black, it has an inedible stem, and is valued for the flavoursome dark brownish black juice it secretes during cooking, which wafts its mushroom aroma through the whole dish. To offset the mushroom's delicious flavour it is combined with a bland vehicle, rice.

The mushrooms are sometimes sun-dried before use. While the djon-djon is not found outside Haiti, its closest relation is the black chanterelle. Failing that, use ordinary wild field mushrooms or fresh, juicy cultivated portobello mushrooms for this dish.

Djon-djon
(Haitian rice)

1 tablespoon clarified butter
50 g (2 oz) salt pork or streaky
   bacon, finely chopped
250 g (8 oz) *djon-djon* or fresh
   portobello mushrooms, finely
   chopped
1 small red pepper, chopped
4 spring onions (green tops
   included), chopped

4 cloves garlic, finely chopped
2 teaspoons chopped fresh thyme
500 g (1 lb or 2 cups) long-grain
   rice, rinsed
½ teaspoon salt
few grinds of black pepper
750 ml (1¼ pts or 3 cups) chicken
   stock or water

Heat the butter and quickly sauté the salt pork or bacon; add the mush-rooms and sauté for several minutes longer. Add the pepper and spring onions and sauté for 1 minute only. Add the garlic, thyme and rice, season with salt and pepper, stir thoroughly, then pour over the chicken stock or water. Bring to the boil, reduce heat to medium low, cover the pot tightly, and leave for 10 minutes. After the liquid has been absorbed by the rice, turn off the heat and leave for another 5 minutes with the lid on. Serve immediately.

SERVES 4.

FRENCH GUIANA

Sandwiched between Surinam and Brazil, French Guiana remains an obscure corner of northern South America, perhaps best remembered for Devil's Island, the former French penal colony off its shore.

Sparsely populated, with a population of only about 150,000 spread out over its humid rain forests and savannahs, Guyane (as it is known to the French) may be an Overseas Department of France, but appears largely forgotten even by the French themselves: the Maison du Tourisme de la Guyane in Paris has long since closed its doors through lack of demand, as tourists seek cheaper, more comfortable holiday alternatives elsewhere.

For all that, the territory possesses a fascinating cuisine, a mosaic of African, Creole, French, Brazilian and Haitian, with smaller inputs from minorities such as Vietnamese, Chinese, Moroccans, Algerians, Lebanese, Tahitians, Mexicans and Amerindians. It is a cuisine made all the more extraordinary by the variety of wild food at the cook's disposal. True, the majority of staples such as milk, sugar, rice, even bananas, must be imported at vast expense, and the only market gardening of note is carried out by Laotian immigrants near Cacao.

Yet the abundance of fish is astounding, whether from the sea, from the twenty-plus rivers which run to the Atlantic, or from vast, stagnant, brownish-black ponds and creeks, in which lurk prehistoric fish such as the attipa, whose joined cartilage gives it the appearance of a medieval suit of armour. The notorious piranha receives its come-uppance in the cooking pots of the humans who count among its victims, appearing at the table as a French West Indian style *blaff* (see page 11), as a *touffé*, (i.e. 'smothered' – stewed with veg and spices in a wet gravy) or *au vert* (poached within minutes of leaving the water).

Other bizarre fish include the grondin (locally known as the *grondé*) which emits grunting sounds when freshly landed; the petite gueule, which must be cleaned of its coating of mucous slime before cooking; and the lubine, whose flesh emits a strong odour of urine. Prized species include the acoupa, the fleshy carangue, the croupia and the parasi. Shark flesh is particularly favoured for smoking – grilled over live embers, over which are thrown the fried outer fibres of coconut husks and the waste fibres of sugar cane. Fried shark was once a popular item sold by hawkers on the left bank of the Canal Laussat in Cayenne. They laid their wares on the ground, their cries and the aromas from their food mingling with those of their competitors – Indonesian satay, shrimp fritters, vanilla-scented mullet eggs, even turtle eggs.

Salted, sun-dried mud-fish is a specialty of Kourou, a town built on the ruins of the infamous Centre Pénitentiaire de Kourou, where Alfred Dreyfus was imprisoned. Known as *tètèouèlè* (derived, it has been suggested, from the suffix of *dégustait* – since it tastes so good), it is seen hanging like a ham in the dry parts of Guyanese dwellings. To prepare the dried fish, it is soaked overnight in water and spices, then prepared as a famous Guyanese dish – *la pimentade.*

Nowadays, *pimentade* is essentially the same dish as the *court-bouillon* of the French West Indies (see page 13). However, before cultivation of the tomato began in the penitentiary centres of Kourou and St Laurent-du-Maroni around 1900, the *pimentade* was coloured red with annatto butter – the so-called *roucou*, or annatto powder mixed with lard or butter, which Dutch merchants had made into a trading commodity.

Daube de Poisson
(daube of fish)

Daube is another example of the Creole cook's appropriation of a classical French term. For whether it is applied to a French West Indian dish of bananas, cooked for 10 minutes with herbs and spices, or to this dish of fish, which also receives brief cooking, the Creole *daube* scarcely fits the conventional understanding of a slow cooked casserole, in which meat is cooked in red wine for anything from 5 to 12 hours.

1 large fish, filleted	2 cloves garlic, crushed
juice of 2–3 lemons	1 small red chilli, chopped

salt

oil for frying

2 tablespoons smoked lard (or
substitute finely chopped *speck*)

1 large onion, finely chopped

2 tablespoons tomato concentrat

salt and pepper

Slice the fish fillets into thick strips and sprinkle with lemon juice, garlic, chilli and salt. Leave to marinate for about an hour. Wipe dry with paper towels.

Heat the oil in a large pan and fry the fish fillets on both sides, until lightly coloured but not properly cooked. Remove and set aside.

In the oil remaining in the pan, heat the lard (if using speck, fry to render out the fat) then add the onions and fry until transparent. Add the tomato concentrate and 125 ml (4 fl oz or ½ cup) of water, mix through, add salt and pepper to taste, then place the fish over the sauce and cook, covered, for another 6–8 minutes.

This can be served with any of a number of starch accompaniments – plain rice, cooked cassava meal, boiled bananas, boiled vegetables or fried bananas.

SERVES 4.

Freshwater crabs are caught by lowering a stick into the water – the crab grabs the wood, and is itself grabbed in turn. Mangrove crabs are attracted by a bait of rotten fish, but require deft handling once landed, for if you miss the opportunity to grab the crab by its formidably powerful claws, the crab will not miss you. Wild dogs also catch these crabs by lowering their tails into the crab holes, then lifting them out, yelping with pain with a crab attached, which is then crushed and eaten. During the summer months, small shrimps are caught and dried for rainy days, while freshwater crayfish are sometimes caught and kept for up to eight days, fed on salad greens and coconut, which are said to add flavour to the flesh. They are commonly made into bisques and soups, but during festivals at Cayenne, street stalls sell them grilled as kebabs.

Mussels are rare in the wild (though mussel farms have now been successfully established) but other shellfish, such as the conical mantouni (*Littorina littorea*) abound near river mouths, and cockles are plentiful on the sandy beaches. There is also an aquatic form of snail, gathered by hand from lakes and springs. They are washed and disgorged French style, with vinegar and flour, then simmered in wine and broth and served with Breton-style butter, flavoured with shallots, garlic and parsley.

The Gallic passion for frogs' legs also finds full expression in Guiana, where the frogs are so big their legs are comparable to a young chicken. The Guyanese frog resembles one of the edible species found in France, the rousse (*Rana temporaria*), both in appearance and in the flavour of its flesh. The favoured method of catching such frogs is to dangle over the surface of a pond a red rag attached to a stick by a length of string, and wait for the frog to pounce and attach itself to the rag.

The canny buyer of frogs' legs at a Guyanese market knows by examining the shin bone whether the seller is trying to pass off toads' legs as frogs'. It is as well to be careful; the skin of the toad known as the *batracien*, for example, is so toxic that the Indians of Brazil used it to poison their arrow heads.

As with snails, the favourite Guyanese preparation of frogs' legs is *à la française*. Cooks marinate the legs in a little vinegar, salt, pepper and chopped parsley, then briefly fry them in oil, treating the tender white flesh of the thigh with particular reverence.

But while the French palate is not at all shocked by snails and frogs, iguanas often do present a fresh challenge to the neophyte recently arrived from mainland France – particularly as presented on the average market stall. In front of rusty scales on a sack draped over a wooden crate, the decapitated bodies lie with their reptilian legs splayed apart, their underbellies slashed, gutted and opened to expose great lumps of bright yellow fat. If you inspect the carcass carefully, you will notice that the male carries a double penis, which no doubt explains the iguana's supposed aphrodisiac qualities (sure, sure). But the Guyanese are insistent: skinned, carefully stripped of its musk glands and made into a fricassee, the iguana is said to have all the finesse and *saveur* of chicken. (Isn't it funny how every bizarre creature is said to taste of chicken?) As early as the seventeenth century, the Reverend Père du Tertre wrote: 'I would be so bold as to say it is one of the best things to eat in the Iles, when it is well seasoned.'

The meat of cayman crocodile also has its aficionados. Indeed, a Guyanese custom connected with its consumption has grown out of an incident in 1894, whereby gold was found in the vicinity of the burial spot of a cayman which had been shot for sport. As the bringer of such good luck, the deceased cayman was disinterred twenty-four hours later, honoured with the title Monsieur Frédérick de Lafond, wrapped in leaves and cooked Galibi Indian style, with each participant bringing a glass full of gold nuggets in order to cover the cost of the liquid refreshments. Today, the custom has evolved into an elaborate high society banquet, with the head of a smoked cayman as a centrepiece, wreathed in parsley. An orator, dressed in lawyer's robes, enters the room and recites an oratory, climaxing with the pouring of alcohol over the cayman's head and lighting it for a ritual 'cremation'.

While threatened Guyanese creatures such as the dugong are now protected, the array of game lined up for sale in Guyanese markets would still horrify an environmentalist: armadillos, for example, hacked in two from top to tail, little black hocco birds, fillets of anaconda. Nevertheless, hunting is such a part of the Guyanese way of life that they think nothing of it. Game provides an almost daily part of the diet in remote areas, and the Guyanese have long been renowned for their skill in tracking and trapping. The Amerindians practised it for survival, it was always the favoured sport of the Guyanese elite, and today in the communes of the interior there is not a settler without a gun.

On the savannah game birds abound, some favoured more than others. The little coq de savanne, for example, is usually rather dry and sinewy, whereas guinea fowl is prized for its flesh which is reminiscent of domestic pigeon. Quails are similar to their counterparts in Europe, while dove is said to be the tastiest bird in French Guiana (provided one does not eat it between December and March, when it eats a bitter grain, the flavour of which permeates its flesh).

Woodcock is such a popular game bird that its hunting is regulated. Its flesh is said to be most delicate and at its best on return from having spent the summer in the temperate climate of Hudson Bay. Père Labat recommended that in order to successfully grill woodcock on skewers, the feathers had first to be plucked without damaging the skin.

Godwit and ibis, having strongly flavoured flesh, are marinated in lemon juice, salt, pepper and thyme.

Of forest birds, the jet black hocco is the most prized, especially when young and tender, but even tough old birds, weighing perhaps 4–5 kg (around 10 lb) each, are turned into salmis and pâtés. The agami, or trumpeter, is perhaps not as favoured, and the partridge is considered rather a dry-fleshed bird. So too is the flamingo, but since the flavour of its flesh is said to recall pheasant, it too is hunted remorselessly, along with the strikingly big-beaked toucan, which when shot young, is roasted, fricasseed or put into soups. Not even the parrot is spared a sentimental thought: it too is shot and made into soup.

The tapir, once stripped of its musk glands, is smoked, stewed, even grilled as a steak. According to Dr André Nègre, a well-marinated steak might be mistaken for beef. Sloth, on the other hand, is likened to a fattier version of mutton. Jaguars and pumas are shot less rarely, not for any environmental reason, but because their flesh is malodorous. Perhaps most distressing of all, at least to Anglo-Saxon eyes, is the sight of monkey meat at Guyanese markets.

As in the French West Indies, the agouti has always been highly prized for the table in French Guiana, but is rarely eaten these days, having been hunted virtually to extinction by the 1930s. A type of opossum, the pian, which ravages pineapple plantations, is caught by a novel method: some pieces of pineapple are soaked in rum and set out as bait, and while the hunter keeps watch, along comes the pian, eats the pineapple, and rolls over, belly up, stone drunk! For the cook, this method of capture has the advantage that the meat comes ready-marinated.

As for pineapples, the largest, and also the most sought-after Guyanese variety is the Maipouri, so juicy and sweet (as only a ground-ripened tropical pineapple can be) that it is generally eaten as is, cut into rounds or slices, and served in its own juice. A lesser variety would be made into a tart.

Tarte à l'Ananas
(pineapple tart)

Pastry
250 g (8 oz) flour
125 g (4½ oz) butter
½ teaspoon salt

250 g (8 oz) crème fraîche
5 eggs
125 g (4½ oz) sugar
½ teaspoon vanilla essence

Filling
1 ripe pineapple

To make the shortcrust pastry, sift flour on to a flat surface, work in slightly softened butter and salt, and add just enough water to create a pliable dough. Refrigerate for 30 minutes, roll out and line a 25 cm (10 in) tart dish. Refrigerate for another 30 minutes, cover with foil or a cooking sheet, sprinkle over haricot beans (or small coins) in order to prevent the pastry rising, and bake blind for 15 minutes at 200°C (400°F/Gas 6).

Meanwhile, prepare the filling. Peel the pineapple, remove all 'eyes' and cut lengthways into four wedge-shaped quarters. Remove the stringy core by cutting off the pointed end of each wedge. Cut the pineapple into small pieces on a plate, retaining the juice.

Beat together the crème fraîche, eggs, sugar and vanilla essence. Pour this mixture into the baked pie shell, add the pineapple pieces, and sprinkle the top of the pie with the excess pineapple juice. Bake at 200°C (400°F/Gas 6) for 15–20 minutes until set.

A common use for pineapple skin is to steep it in a bowl of water for several days, covered in muslin, until the mixture ferments and turns into a refreshing 'pineapple beer.'

Other fruits, such as soursop, guava, melon, cashew apple and ambarella, are commonly juiced or made into jams and sorbets. The tamarind pod is made into jellies, jams and mixed with other fruits into sorbets but, much to the loss of Guyanese cuisine, it is not put to savoury uses as in South-East Asian cooking. For the sour element in their cuisine, the lemon must suffice.

Poulet au Citron
(lemon chicken)

1 chicken, about 1 kg (2 lb)
50 g (2 oz or ½ cup) flour
3 tablespoons oil
juice of 5 lemons
4 cloves garlic, crushed

salt and pepper
3 teaspoons chopped fresh thyme
3 bay leaves
5 cloves, ground

Wash the chicken, pat dry with paper towels, then cut into eight pieces. Place with flour in a plastic bag and shake to coat the pieces on all sides.

Heat the oil in a large pot, brown the pieces of chicken on all sides, then add the remaining ingredients, plus 125 ml (4 fl oz or ½ cup) of water. Cover tightly and simmer on a low heat for 45 minutes.

SERVES 4.

One very important South-East Asian introduction is the mango. The grafted varieties such as the Reine-Amélie, the Divine and the Freycinette, generally have the finest flavour, though the non-grafted Saint-Michel also has its devotees, despite its strong odour of turpentine (which can be minimized by picking the fruit green and leaving it out in the light and air for a few days, wrapped in a cloth).

Part of every Guyanese childhood involves a game of throwing stones at green mangoes on the tree, gathering the direct hits, and taking them home to slice and dress into a *calalouangue*.

The sonorous name suggests African origins, and indeed, the *calalouangue* bears close resemblance to the *rougail* of Réunion (see page 59) except that it is served alone as a hors d'oeuvre, rather than as a side dish to a main course of meat or fish with rice.

Calalouangue

The ideal mango for this dish is in a state somewhere between green and fully ripened.

4 greenish mangoes, peeled and
  sliced thinly
2 cloves garlic
1 small onion, chopped

1 red chilli
salt and pepper to taste
juice of 1 large lemon
2 tablespoons oil

Pound to a paste the garlic, onion, chilli, salt and pepper with pestle and mortar, or in a food processor. Toss this mixture with the mango slices and sprinkle with lemon juice and oil.

For festive occasions, a 'fruit basket' is carved from a large oblong melon, handle and all, then filled with cubes of various tropical fruits (lychee, guava, ambarella, papaya), doused with rum and a dash of strong China tea, then placed in the centre of the table.

In the past, a common sight around the entrances of schools in French Guiana was the itinerant sweet-seller, with a tray full of little cakes and sweets, one hand at the ready with paper to wrap the purchases, the other nonchalantly waving away the flies trying to settle on the merchandise. Nowadays, these hawkers and their wares have virtually disappeared, along with most their wares, although some are still commercially available, such as *le bédégouel*, a spicy gâteau beloved of children, little choux pastries known as *carolines*, galettes called *sispas*, plus a number of sweets of Algerian inspiration, such as 'cigars' made with flour, honey and ground peanuts.

Docono or *dokonon*, a famous Guyanese dessert of African origin is usually cooked with ground fresh corn, sometimes with cornmeal or even semolina as suggested here.

Docono

On a low heat, cook coarse semolina in sweetened [coconut] milk, stirring continuously with a wooden spoon. Halfway through cooking, add sliced bananas, vanilla and cinnamon.

Once cooked, pour the mixture into bowls and carry to the table hot, or allow to cool and serve iced.

Cuisine Coloniale: Les Bonnes Recettes de Chlöe Mondésir, collected by A. Quérillac, Paris, 1931.

Unfortunately, French Guiana's national dish, a soup-stew known as *le bouillon d' aouara*, is rarely tasted outside the country itself, due to the unavailability of its key ingredient. This is the date-like drupe of a spiny palm, the aouara, which for some unknown reason only bears fruits in America when grown in the Amazon basin. The fruits are left to fall to the ground, gradually ripening to a deep crimson colour, at which point they are processed into a red paste which resembles tomato concentrate. It takes 50 kg (around 1 cwt) of these drupes to make just 1 kg (2 lb) of paste, the sole seasoning of the bouillon which takes its name.

Originally from the West African state of Guinea, *bouillon d'aouara* is a baroque collection not only of eight or so different vegetables, but of everything furred, scaled or feathered – pork, beef, smoked fish, crabs, shrimps, chicken and, in previous centuries, game. Perhaps most remarkable of all, it is one Guyanese recipe which contains no garlic, onions, cloves or allspice.

All foreigners who eat *bouillon d'aouara*, it is said, gain honorary citizenship of French Guiana, for having once tasted this dish, it is inevitable they will one day return for more.

2 The Indian Ocean

Despite having evolved on opposite sides of the world, there are startling and quite fundamental similarities between the Creole cuisine of the French West Indies and that of the Francophone islands of the Indian Ocean – Réunion, Mauritius, Madagascar, the Seychelles and Comoros.

In both regions, the Gallic-African fusion is reflected in a passion for tomatoes, garlic and chilli, and a willingness to allow tropical spices and French herbs to coexist in the same dish. Both regions also share a marked taste for salt fish, for pork above other meats, and an inherited taste for *boucanage*, or smoked meats. For daily subsistence, there is a common reliance upon pulses and leafy greens, supplemented with rice, maize, root vegetables such as taro, and a steady supply of tropical fruits. As a consequence of the sugar cane industries in both regions, rum is the shared national drink.

On the other hand, Spanish influence, so obvious in the Caribbean, is largely absent in the islands of the Indian Ocean, where that of India looms correspondingly larger. Turmeric and ginger, used only rarely in the Creole cooking of the French West Indies, are, along with chillies, the most important aromatics in the islands of the Indian Ocean. Indeed, Indian origins can be traced for the four basic classes of dishes which all these Indian Ocean societies share in common: curries of meat and fish, the fresh chutneys known as *rougails*, the green vegetable dishes known as *brèdes*, and the pickled vegetables known as *achards*.

RÉUNION

Réunion remains the most thoroughly French of all the islands of the Indian Ocean, a French overseas department with close ties to its motherland.

Officially claimed by the king of France in 1649, the island had been a convenient stopover for European navigators since the beginning of the previous century. These sailors left behind animals which, having turned wild in the intervening century, provided a convenient source of food. In his memoirs of 1687, Père Bernadin recalled:

Beasts like cattle, pigs, goats and land tortoises form the everyday diet of the people of the island. Sea turtle (which is a great enlivenment for ships' crews) is fairly common, as is fish, both salt and freshwater . . . Poultry like parrots, peewits, turtle-doves, pigeons, flamingos, ducks, teals, curlews, capons, turkeys and all the rest are in great abundance there.

In the absence of refrigeration, however, meat had to be taken up into the cool of the hills on the day the animal was slaughtered, since it would not keep much more than a day in the tropical heat. Because cattle were used for provisioning ships, for a long time the settlers were forbidden to kill them, although wild goats and pigs were fair game, as were the 'heavenly manna', tortoises. Writing in 1703, Monsignor de Tournon tells us the flesh was 'very good and similar in flavour to veal', but just five years later, their population had been completely wiped out in the inhabited regions of the island. As early as the mid-seventeenth century, the same fate had befallen the sea turtle, although with the advent of aquaculture since the 1980s, turtle meat is once more available. Wasp larvae, quails, hares and tenrec, a small hedgehog-like animal, were also eaten by these early followers of the beachcomber's existence.

To these products of hunting and gathering were progressively added those of agriculture. Creoles of European origin quickly established pigs, both the European varieties and the smaller, leaner black Chinese breeds, as the favoured farm animal. It was the Creoles, also, who established a tradition of charcuterie, even if such products as *saucisson* and *andouille* are rather different to the products of the same name in metropolitan France.

Such products are still occasionally made on farms following the slaughter of a pig, when members of an extended family or community gather together for the Fête du Cochon. It is a tradition with deep roots in rural France, when pigs, fattened on acorns, would be slaughtered in the autumn and turned into hams, sausages and terrines to tide the villagers over for the winter. These festive occasions have strong parallels among the Cajuns of Louisiana and the *habitants* of Quebec, although the tradition has virtually died everywhere since the advent of domestic freezers.

In Réunion it was usually a family affair, each person with his or her role clearly defined, working all day from early morning to early evening. The patriarch, his sons and sons-in-law would slaughter the pig, singe the hairs over a fire made of screwpine straw, shave the skin and cut up the meat, while the women would collect the liver and kidneys in baskets made of woven banana leaves. Along with the membranous peritoneum that lines the inside of the abdominal cavity, these were generally cooked and served with rice or sweet potatoes for a late breakfast, at about 10 a.m.

While the men smoked the ribs by suspending them over a wood fire, and rendered down the fat and skin for lard and *gratons* (large pieces of crackling), the women mixed the pig's blood with fat, onions and parsley, and funnelled the mixture into the cleaned intestines to make *boudin* (black pudding). Some of the minced meat would also be reserved for sausages.

Other cuts of meat would be salted for long keeping, the head made into a brawn or cooked on the spot, while traditionally the whole, unsplit spine or 'queen bone', which had morsels of choice meat still attached, would be braised for lunch or dinner. (This cut has disappeared because the modern commercial butcher who provides it would lose the high-priced, sought-after centre loin chops and roasts.) By the time the day's work was over, all parts of the pig would have been used except for the trotters and bones. Even the bladder would be blown up into a ball and given to the children for play.

A rather superior cut of the beast, however, goes into this stew:

Porc au Cresson
(pork with watercress)

1 kg (2 lb) boned leg of pork, cubed
3 large onions, finely chopped
oil
8 small tomatoes, blanched and peeled
60 ml (2 fl oz or ¼ cup) white wine
6 cloves garlic, crushed
3 cm (1 in) piece ginger, finely chopped
salt and pepper
pinch of saffron threads (optional)
1 bunch watercress, washed and large stalks removed

Sauté the pork cubes and onion in a little oil, then add the tomatoes and wine. Cover the pot and simmer until cooked according to taste (a Réunionnais cook would leave it for 40 minutes, but this results in pork with a dry texture; while not traditional, I prefer to leave the meat until only just cooked through – about 10 minutes – assuming, of course, that the pork was tender to begin with.)

Meanwhile, pour a dash of boiling water over the saffron in a mortar and grind until dissolved. Chop the watercress.

About 5 minutes before the end of cooking, add garlic, ginger and saffron. Season to taste with salt and pepper and mix in the watercress. Replace the lid, cook gently for another 5 minutes, then serve.

SERVES 4.

Oddly, the consumption of pork was adopted by Hindu Indian immigrants, despite an old custom which regarded the meat as impure, and yet the ban on beef is still observed, even by Christianized Indians. Beef, in any case, is mostly imported and expensive and little regarded, unlike goat, which is also costly, but prized. Lamb is virtually unknown. But chicken occupies centre stage: chicken curry is the classic Sunday treat, while in rural areas, a chicken would be killed if a visitor were to appear unexpectedly for dinner. If the guest were especially distinguished, duck would be served.

On festive occasions, such as baptisms and weddings, a turkey or even a goose would be roasted whole and served during the first part of the banquet, with such typically French accompaniments as a lettuce or watercress salad, fresh bread or macaroni with grated cheese. Regardless of the meat used for the roast, it would be ideally served with a light golden brown surface described as *rose*. Despite the pinkish connotations of the word, however, *rose* here means well done. The Réunionnais have a deep-seated aversion to pink or even slightly bloody meat, equating 'raw' with 'corrupt' – perhaps understandable in a climate where raw meat is quickly spoiled.

Then, for the second part of the banquet, Creole curries of pork and chicken appear on the table, with rice and beans, spicy goat and fiery hot *rougails*, all of which will be sampled for the sake of decorum. Guests traditionally finish off with *café-pays*, the sweet strong coffee laced with *rhum arrangé* – rum macerated with vanilla beans, or perhaps peach stones, tea leaves or lychees. Only after the meal do the sweets come out – marzipan, preserved papaya and crystallized grapefruit and so on.

Certain dishes are associated with particular events. On New Year's Day, for example, a pâté en croûte is served at the beginning of the meal with a glass of anisette. An old Creole custom calls for the man of the house to throw a small piece of this pâté outside, on to the soil. As in other cultures, a wedding table has as its centrepiece three genoese cakes of decreasing size, decorated with white icing and sugared almonds.

Despite being surrounded by the sea, the Réunionnais traditionally eat very little fresh fish, preferring salt cod. This is curried, made into croquettes, or simply grilled as a whole piece and served with warmed rice for breakfast. Of fresh fish, the grouper-like macabi (*Epinephelus merra*) is the most esteemed variety, but octopus is also popular. Capuchins and parrotfish are also sought after, the latter often stuffed with preserved chillies, Chinese style. Conger eels are largely used for bait; to many islanders all eels, whether saltwater or freshwater, bear rather too close an association to serpents. More expensive deep-sea fish are the preserve of the well-to-do, and are generally curried. For special occasions they are decorated in alternate bands of white, yellow and green, made by finely chopping the whites and yolks of hard-boiled eggs and the green parts of spring onions.

The greatest delicacy of all fish, however, are bichiques, nowadays quite rare. These are the tiny, almost transparent young of the *Gobiides* family, fished at river mouths at the beginning of the hot season, and sold still flapping in the baskets of market stall-holders.

Little freshwater crustaceans known as chevrettes are another disappearing delicacy, due to the practice of poaching them from the rivers. They would be hawked from house to house, sold by the cup and wrapped in a leaf related to the bramble family.

As for the staple foods, the Réunionnais gave up daily consumption of bread very early in their history. As Commandant Firelin noted in 1692, wheat did not last from one year to the next because of weevils. Besides, grinding the grains into flour was very tiresome with the small brass mills they had as their only tools. Maize, with its softer kernel, took over, and remained the staple until the 1960s, either ground into flour for cakes known as *lamsing*, or breads, or coarsely ground into rice-sized pieces known as 'maize rice' and eaten with curries. This grinding used to be done daily, on hand-cranked stone mills. Rice, which used to be reserved for Sundays and special occasions, has today taken over as the staple food, even though nearly all of it must be imported.

The importance of rice is seen in popular expressions which have grown up around it. 'He is earning his rice', they say of a man who works, or 'he is angry with the rice', for one who is dead. To a Réunionnais, the metropolitan habit of cooking rice as milk puddings is sacrilege, since it trivializes its primary function in the main course of the meal.

The adoption of rice facilitated a more Asian approach to cooking on Réunion. It is difficult to say exactly when the population began to assume a taste for Indian condiments such as chilli, ginger and turmeric, but it may well have begun in the beginning of the eighteenth century, when Europeans of Portuguese, Dutch, English or French origin in India began to marry Indian women and adopt the customs of the country. Since there was a shipping line between India and Réunion by then, it follows that a number of these merchants and sailors set up with their Indian wives on the island.

Furthermore, there was a significant number of Indian slaves on Réunion at this time. Père Barassin estimated that in 1709 Indians made up 23 per cent of the slave population. While this had declined to seven per cent by 1735 (due to the opposition of Indian princes to the trade), their culinary influence remained strong because, unlike the burly Africans who were sent to work in the fields, the Indians tended to be house servants. The style of cooking of these house servants would have adapted well to the foodstuffs available, while the spiciness of their cuisine served to awaken palates enervated in the tropical heat.

Nevertheless, it was a spicy cuisine muffled to some extent by French restraint. The number of spices in any one dish was, and still is, small by Asian standards: often only turmeric is used, alongside the classic Provençal trio of thyme, garlic and onion. Réunionnais pâté en croûte, for example, retains the archaic French name of *godiveau*, yet the ground pork and chicken mixture is seasoned Indian-style, with turmeric, sugar and salt.

French influence also explains why 'curry' is a somewhat toned down dish in Réunion. Usually it will not even contain chilli, the spicing being relatively simple. Turmeric, onions, garlic, salt, pepper, thyme, and sometimes the leaf of the allspice bush go into curries of meat and poultry, while fish and crustacean curries incorporate plenty of tomato and a little grated fresh ginger. This *cari* is cooked by all Réunion people regardless of race – Indian, Chinese, African or European. When the turmeric is replaced with red wine, the dish becomes a *civet*.

Cari de Porc aux Chouchoux
(pork and chayote curry)

750 g (1½ lb) pork, cubed
3 tablespoons oil
3 onions, chopped
4 cloves garlic, chopped
salt and pepper to taste
½ teaspoon ground turmeric

3 tomatoes, peeled and chopped
2 sprigs of thyme
2 chayotes (approx. 750 g (1½ lb)),
    peeled and cubed
3 tablespoons chopped parsley

In a heavy-bottomed pot, brown the cubed pork in the oil, then stir in the onion, garlic, salt, pepper and turmeric. Cover the pot and lower the heat, leave for several minutes, then add the tomatoes, thyme and a cup of water. Leave another 10 minutes, covered, on a low heat, then add the chayote pieces, and a further ½ cup of water. Cook for a further 10 minutes (a Réunionnais cook would allow longer). Serve sprinkled with parsley.

SERVES 4.

Variation: substitute chicken or beef for the pork.

Accompanying the curry is a side dish known as *rougail*. From a base of tomato, chilli, onion and garlic with seasonings, a *rougail* can be made with a huge variety of vegetables – avocado, aubergines, chayotes, bitter melons, tamarillos, preserved lemons, green mangoes. As with a curry, it can become a substantial dish when shrimps, smoked herrings, salt pork sausages or salt cod are used, so the distinction between the two can sometimes be vague. However, where the curry omits chilli, the rougail makes a feature of it. Its basic function as a side dish or condiment is further underlined by the fact that, unlike curry, the pieces are minced very small.

French speakers will often tell you the word *rougail* is an amalgamation of *rouge* and *ail*, that is, red (tomatoes) and garlic. In fact, it is descended from the Tamil dish *ouroukaille* which signifies a preserve of green fruit. Nevertheless, tomato – or rather, a particularly sweet variety known as the *pomme d'amour* – is the most commonly used base for a *rougail* (see plate 8).

Rougail de Tomate
(tomato rougail)

3 tomatoes, finely minced
1 small onion, finely chopped
2 small red or green chillies, finely
  chopped

1 tablespoon chopped parsley
2–3 tablespoons sunflower oil
salt and pepper

Mix together all ingredients and season to taste with salt and pepper.

Rougail Bringelles
(aubergine rougail)

1 large or 2 small aubergines
5 small green chillies (more or less
  according to taste)
salt
1 clove garlic

2–3 cm (1 in) piece ginger root
2 tablespoons oil
1 tablespoon wine vinegar
1 large onion, finely diced

Make a slit down the side of the aubergine and grill on all sides until the skin is thoroughly blackened and the flesh is soft and cooked. Drain off any bitter juice that may come out of the aubergine during cooking, then using a spoon, carefully scrape the flesh from the blackened skin (which is then discarded). Either purée the flesh in a food processor with the remaining ingredients, or to prepare the dish traditionally, mash the aubergine with a fork and add to the chillies, salt, garlic and ginger root which have been pounded in a mortar, then mix in the oil, vinegar and onion.

The third basic component of the everyday meal is *brèdes*, a dish of green leaves chopped and braised (either with water or stock or just with its own juices) and flavoured with onion, garlic and sometimes ginger or a piece of meat or fish.

The name brèdes descends from the classical Greek and Latin *bliton* and *blitum*, meaning a green leaf suitable for boiling. Although the word had survived in French as *blette*, the French Creoles derived the name *brèdes* from the Portuguese variant, *bredo*, used by early Portuguese mariners to describe any new edible green leaf they encountered and cooked during their travels around the Indian Ocean and Africa.

In Réunion, brèdes balances the heavy starch component of the routine evening meal. Its base might be chayote, vine leafshoot, or pumpkin leaves, cabbage, sow thistle, taro leaf or spinach. The pot is covered so that the dish is steamed. If the vegetables are allowed to cook in their own juices and remain fairly thick in consistency, the brèdes might also be called étouffé, whereas if more water is added, the dish becomes a brèdes bouillon.

Brèdes is also found in the French West Indies, having acquired its name by the same route. So too, did South Africa's famous Cape Malay dish, *bredie*. However, bredie long ago evolved into a dish of spiced mutton ribs, the greens today serving only as an adjunct.

Brèdes Chou de Chine
(Chinese cabbage brèdes)

This recipe calls for the common solid, barrel-shaped Chinese cabbage *(Brassica pekinensis)*, with broad-ribbed stalks and pale crinkled leaves.

1 Chinese cabbage, about 500 g (1 lb)	1 thumb-sized piece ginger, finely chopped
3 tablespoons oil	4 cloves garlic, chopped
1 medium onion, chopped	salt and pepper

Wash the cabbage, retaining only the leaves and the tender stalks. Shred finely. In a pot, heat the oil and lightly brown the onion. Add the ginger and garlic, season with a little salt and pepper, and cover the pot. Leave on a medium heat for 6–7 minutes, then serve immediately.

A great many of Réunion's vegetables are nineteenth-century introductions from India and America. Chayote, which is to be found growing, triffid-like, in almost every domestic courtyard in Réunion, was introduced from Rio de Janeiro in 1834. Okra came from the French West Indies in 1880, while both the tomato and the potato were introduced in 1775 (the latter even before Parmentier popularized it in France). Other popular vegetables include cucumbers, cabbages, aubergines, pumpkins and lettuce. Some vegetables, such as artichokes and cauliflower, are not widely eaten on account of their high price; carrots and beetroot have only a specialized use in Russian salad, while others are associated mainly with Chinese cooking, such as mung beansprouts, bamboo shoots, Chinese cabbage and coriander leaf.

Fruit forms an important part of the Réunion diet, consumed mostly between meals. Creole fruit salad, for example, is served in the middle of the afternoon rather than at the conclusion of a meal, and consists of mango and pineapple cut into small pieces and marinated for two hours in a lot of sugar, a little vinegar, and a hint of salt and crushed green chilli. Alternatively, ripe guavas are used as the base ingredient.

Fruit is still widely grown on the island, even if the ravages of cyclones and parasites, not to mention changing fashions, have taken their toll on traditional orchards. Many of Réunion's fruit trees were introduced from elsewhere in France's empire. From the French West Indies came the sweetsop *(Annona squamosa)* in the late eighteenth century, the giant grenadilla *(Passiflora quadrangularis)* in 1880. The breadfruit, no longer held in high esteem, was introduced from Tahiti in 1770, while the ambarella or Tahitian quince *(Spondias dulcis)* was introduced to Mauritius in 1768 by Bougainville or Comerson, and to Réunion a little later. The avocado, originally from Brazil but introduced via Mauritius in 1789, grows ever more popular.

Since the Second World War, increasing population and urbanization, as well as raised living standards, have seen an increasing amount of imported fruits from South Africa and Israel, along with other foodstuffs both perishable and frozen, air-freighted in from abroad. Old-fashioned groceries have given way to self-service supermarkets, equipped with freezers and cooling cabinets, introducing to a younger generation such foods as yoghurt and cheese, which their parents had not habitually eaten. French-style bakeries and pâtisseries are also a feature of modern Réunion. Until the 1960s, bread had been considered a delicacy, almost as a cake, bought on Sundays in the form of lightly sugared buns from Chinese stores. Known as *macatia* and today virtually unknown, they were eaten with chocolate or a cheese known as *tête de mort* (death's-head).

And yet, despite the proliferation of choice, there has been no fundamental modification of the diet. Certainly, increased wealth means that gas and electric stoves have replaced wood fires and the petrol stoves, still common in the 1970s, which were used in outbuildings or in courtyards beneath a shelter of thatched banana leaves. Refrigerators have removed the need for finely meshed food safes, hung by a chain from a ceiling beam, to keep food away from cats and mosquitoes. Cooks today might grate coconut with a store-bought grater, rather than improvise with a sardine tin pierced with holes as previous generations might have done. Yet still the same dishes are prepared.

This has much to do with a feeling of nationalism that has swept Réunion, a conscious searching for cultural roots which places a fresh value on traditional cuisine. Even tourism has been regarded as having a positive influence, particularly at the level of the homestay, where the guest dines with the family on their own terms. And regardless of the social or economic circumstances of that family, whether they live in a mansion or a cabin, the dishes on their table are the same – rice, grains, *rougail* and *brèdes*.

MAURITIUS

If one were to set about creating a futuristic epicurean utopia on a far-away tropical island, the starting point might well be the three Ur-cuisines – French, Indian and Chinese. Happily, the island already exists – Mauritius – where these cuisines both co-exist and mingle, enriched further by influences from nearby Africa and the odd lingering trace of colonial British.

Unpopulated even after the Portuguese discovered it in 1510, Mauritius was first settled in 1598, by the Dutch. They abandoned the island again a little over a century later, driven out by plagues of rats and cyclones, having razed the ebony forests, hacked down a respectable portion of the island's palm trees to eat their crunchy tender hearts, and joylessly munched to extinction the dodo. When they weren't abusing the bird for being a flightless simpleton *(doudo)* they were calling it *walghvogel* – nauseous bird with the tough unpalatable flesh. They did, however, leave two important food legacies – the Javanese spotted deer and the sugar cane. Sugar plantations today cover 90 per cent of Mauritius' land and thus play the largest role in the island's economy.

The French, who arrived in 1715, strengthened the export sugar industry in the latter half of the century, opened sugar mills and began to produce arrack and rum.

For their domestic use, they grew rice, millet and maize, and vegetables such as cucumbers, courgettes, pumpkins and sweet potatoes. On the hillsides, coffee plantations were established, and an unusual method of roasting the beans evolved, whereby sugar was added near the end of the process. The bean and sugar mixture was then pounded with dense guava-wood pestles in giant mortars made of jackfruit wood.

The deer-hunting season, from June to August, has traditionally thrown French gourmets into high gear, especially as the Javanese is a variant of the gastronomically highly favoured red deer. Traditionally, French high society has maintained grand hunting lodges on Mauritius, their timbered walls lined with trophy heads of the most impressively antlered males. A young tender deer is typically fried as steaks and served at grand dinners with a peppery, concentrated reduction of red wine and strong beef stock, boiled again with the deer bones, a little vinegar and tomato purée. Older beasts are more likely to be cut up into dice and stewed long and slow, perhaps as a mild curry-powder curry.

The avocado tree, a late eighteenth-century introduction from Brazil, thrived on the island and the delicacy of the fruit instantly appealed to the French, who still mash and mix it with chicken stock for a chilled soup, and combine it with gelatine and cream to make a mousse.

Similarly, palm hearts, at least those that survived the Dutch, quickly attained luxury status among the French, the scarcity fuelling rave reviews from those whose elevated social status was partly defined by their being able to afford to eat them. The early French also distilled liquor from the sap of the tree. Fortunately, Mauritians today cultivate stands of palms especially for the table.

The French community typically slices palm heart very thinly and eats it raw with vinaigrette, cooks it with prawns and béarnaise sauce, or turns it into a soufflé. Naturally it is expensive, since the whole tree must be sacrificed to get at the tubular heart which lies at the core of the palm just below the spot where the leaves begin to splay out.

The French penchant for seafood was fully gratified on Mauritius, even if some of their ways of preparing it began to take on Asian flavours:

Huîtres Pimentées
(chilli oysters)

24 oysters in the shell
2 stalks fresh or frozen lemongrass, bruised
4 kaffir lime leaves, bruised

3 spring onions, sliced
1 small red chilli, finely chopped
salt

Place the oysters in a large pot with 750 ml (1 ¼ pts or 3 cups) of water, the lemongrass and kaffir lime leaves, bring to the boil and boil until the oyster shells open. Remove the oysters, tug out the beards, and place each on its base shell.

Boil the cooking liquid with the lid off, until it has reduced its volume by half, then strain and add the spring onions and chilli. Season with salt if necessary, then drizzle over the oysters.

Freed from the strictures of classical cuisine, the French on Mauritius also cook the rock or spiny lobster with pineapple, a concept which gained only fleeting acceptance in metropolitan France during the era of nouvelle cuisine.

Langouste à l'Ananas
(rock lobster with pineapple)

2 kg (4–5 lb) rock lobsters	12 shallots, chopped
1 large pineapple	4 cloves garlic, crushed
4 tablespoons butter	500 ml (scant 1 pt or 2 cups) dry
6 tablespoons oil	white wine
4 medium onions, sliced	250ml (1 cup) double cream

Remove the tail meat from the lobsters and cut into medallions (use the bodies for making stock). Peel and cut the pineapple into small pieces. Place half the pineapple in a food processor, grind to a pulp and strain off the juice, squeezing against the strainer to extract every last drop (or process in a juicer).

Heat the butter and oil in a large frying pan, sauté the lobster meat briefly until the flesh whitens, then remove and set aside. Sauté the onion, shallots and garlic until the onions are transparent, return the lobster to the pan along with the pineapple pieces, pineapple juice and white wine, and simmer for 5 minutes. Just before serving, stir in the cream. Serve with a rice pilau.
    SERVES 4.

As plantation owners, the French enjoyed a privileged life which allowed them to import a great many luxuries from home, such as truffles, goose and gruyère cheese – with the prime example being set by a famous early governor, Mahé de Labourdonnais, a gourmet who nevertheless condemned the island's African slaves to a perpetually dull diet by introducing the cassava plant, which soon became their staple.

French wine, today subject to crippling import duty, flowed more freely in the nineteenth century. At plantation weddings it would be served to hundreds of guests seated at long tables laid with silver and white linen, under the shade of palm trees – the Salle Verte, as it was called. As in neighbouring Réunion, the crusted pâté known as *godiveau* would be served, with truffled mayonnaise and artichokes over heart of palm and prawns, with roast suckling pigs and pastries to follow, the whole affair orchestrated by the famous nineteenth-century firm of caterers, Flore Mauricienne.

Interestingly, Flore Mauricienne did not regard it as beneath its dignity to provide blistering Indian curries and pickles at these occasions, even serving mulligatawny soup at the official banquet in Port Louis for the Duke of Edinburgh on his visit in 1870. As another nineteenth-century visitor to Mauritius remarked of the French residents: 'they chew nutmeg and chillies as if they were sweets, and their pale features will hardly pink in the inferno of these condiments.' Curries and *rougails* were by then commonplace at the everyday dinner tables of the French.

When the English invaded and wrested sovereignty of Mauritius in 1810, they allowed the French to retain their language, religion, Napoleonic Code legal system and cane plantations. Consequently, French culture remained and, even today, the residents of French ancestry wield influence far out of proportion to their numbers – about 10,000 (just 1 per cent of the population). Certainly this has much to do with their wealth, derived from ownership of sugar mills and other big businesses, but it also manifests itself on a cultural level. *Pain maison* (so called because it was once home-delivered by mobile bakers), a crusty round bun with a slash down the middle for ease of breaking, is today as much a feature of everyday life in Mauritius as the products of the pâtisserie, where you'll find gâteau coco and napolitains, bright red fondant-coated biscuits which have dropped the fresh almond paste and royal icing of their Franco-Italian ancestors.

By contrast, the British who ruled until independence in 1968, had only a passing influence – though this has often been understated. In line with the French attitude of amused condescension towards English cookery, Philippe Lenoir and Raymond de Ravel state in *L'Ile Maurice à Table,* that the island 'hardly suffers from British culinary traditions, despite a presence of one and a half centuries!'. Yet their own book contains a recipe for palm hearts *a l'Anglaise* (cooked with bacon and milk) and a British influence does persist, albeit via India: two common flavouring ingredients in the Mauritian pantry – Worcestershire sauce and curry powder – are both famous products of the Raj. Curry powder enters into that British-Indian mélange, mulligatawny soup, along with a number of Anglo-Indian style curries also popular on the island.

As its multilingual name suggests, Dry Curry de Boeuf has drifted far from its Indian origins, with the curry powder and raisins of the English works canteen curry, as well as French touches like thyme, croûtons and a little rum to marinate the raisins before cooking.

Dry Curry de Boeuf

1 kg (2 lb) beef, cut into 2–3 cm
  (1 in) cubes
6 tablespoons oil
2 large onions, cut in thick rings
2 tablespoons curry powder
1 sprig thyme
large handful croûtons

3 tablespoons raisins soaked in
  rum
3 tablespoons salted roast peanuts
2 tablespoons grated coconut
  threads, fresh or desiccated
2 tablespoons chopped parsley

Sauté the onion rings in the oil until cooked through and slightly coloured. Drain on absorbent paper and keep to one side.

In the remaining oil, sauté the beef cubes in the oil until brown. Add the curry powder and mix through, then pour over 250 ml (9 fl oz or 1 cup) of water and add the thyme. Season to taste with salt and pepper, and simmer until the beef is tender. If using a tough cut of beef, cover the pot and allow 1½–2 hours, then remove lid and cook briskly until the moisture nearly all evaporates. If using a tender cut, leave the lid off and evaporate the water during cooking. The beef will be done once the liquid has evaporated.

Meanwhile fry cubes of bread in oil to make the croûtons and chop the parsley. To serve, discard the thyme sprig (from which the leaves will have fallen off by now) pile up the curry, then cover with alternate rings of coconut, raisins, peanuts and parsley.

SERVES 6.

The Indians who began arriving in the early nineteenth century came not only from the impoverished state of Bihar in the north, but also from the towns and villages around Bombay and Madras. Subsequent migrations have come from elsewhere in Tamil Nadu and in neighbouring Karnataka, contributing to the strong south Indian influence on the cooking of Mauritius. Equally, however, there are a great many non-Tamil Hindus, and some 180,000 mainly Urdu-speaking Muslims, many of them descended from traders from western India.

The most fundamental change wrought by the Indians was the greatly increased consumption of rice, which came to replace cassava root as a staple food. Other basic Indian foodstuffs to gain a foothold were ghee as a cooking medium, and dried pulses, particularly the yellow split pea referred to as dholl or dal.

Rasson

With the addition of ginger, aniseed and the ubiquitous taro leaf, the fiery, thin South Indian consommé known as *rasam* takes on a fresh Mauritian identity as *rasson*. Its use as a digestive or tonic in India has been extended in Mauritius as a cure for hangovers, which, ironically, some early versions may have helped to cause – at advanced stages of parties held on the feast day of Saint Anne, patron saint of the southern Chamarel parish, *rasson* was served laced with rum!

125 g (4½ oz) dal (yellow split peas)
salt
250 g (8 oz) *brèdes songes* (taro leaves) or spinach
2 tablespoons tamarind pulp
2 tablespoons oil
3 cloves garlic, crushed
½ teaspoon ground black pepper
1 teaspoon small aniseed, ground

2 tablespoons crushed root ginger
1 onion, chopped
4 whole dried chillies, crushed
6 curry leaves
2 teaspoons turmeric powder
2 whole cloves
1 tablespoon chopped fresh coriander leaves
1 tablespoon chopped fresh parsley

Boil the yellow split peas until soft and creamy, then season to taste with salt. Liquidize in a blender/food processor or pass through a sieve. Set aside. Boil or steam the taro leaves (or spinach) until cooked, chop finely and set aside. Soak tamarind pulp in half a cup of hot water for 5 minutes, massage the pulp and strain out the seeds and pith. Set aside.

In a pot, heat oil and sauté garlic, black pepper, aniseed, ginger, then add onion and chillies and sauté until the onion is lightly coloured. Add the yellow split peas along with 1.5 litres (2½ pts or 6 cups) of water, the curry leaves, strained tamarind juice, turmeric and cloves. Cook for 20 minutes. Prior to serving, add the cooked taro leaves, coriander and parsley.

SERVES 6.

One of the most important dishes brought to Mauritius, Réunion and Madagascar by migrant Indian workers was *achards* – a mixture of sun-dried vegetables, lightly pickled in oil and vinegar with spices and aromatics. The name is derived from the Persian *atchar*, suggesting the recipe came to India with the Mogul invaders. Pickles still play a small part in Persian cuisine, while Indian preserved pickles, especially the modern commercial brands, are world-famous.

Achards are found all over the former French empire – in New Caledonia, and in the Creole cookery of the French West Indies and French Guiana. In mildly different forms, and with only a slight variation in the spelling of the name – *acar* – the dish is likewise entrenched in the former Portuguese enclaves of Macau and Malacca, from where the recipe has spread into the mainstream cuisines of Malaysia, Singapore and Indonesia, usually with the addition of typically South East Asian aromatics such as lemongrass, galangale, candle nuts and shrimp paste.

Achards travelled so widely in the days of sail because their long keeping qualities made them ideal shipboard fare; the first known reference, to 'achar or Indian fruits preserved in salt', is in the 1658 memoirs of a traveller on a Portuguese ship, le Sieur de la Boullaye Le Goutz.

Perhaps as a concession to the tastes of their French colonial masters, the Indo-Mascarene version is fairly mild, both in terms of spicing and the length of pickling. In this recipe I have taken up the excellent Malaysian idea of adding a little sugar.

Mixed Vegetable Achard

2 large carrots, cut into sticks about 5 x ½cm (2 x ¼ in)

¼ large cauliflower, sliced thinly

¼ large cabbage, sliced into 5 mm (¼ in) strips

500 g (1lb or 5 cups) sliced green beans, fresh or frozen

250 ml (9 fl oz or 1 cup) oil

5 red chillies, split lengthways

8 cloves garlic, crushed

2 tablespoons ginger root, crushed

2 tablespoons turmeric root, crushed, or turmeric powder

1 teaspoon whole peppercorns

1 teaspoon mustard seeds

125 ml (4 fl oz or ½ cup) white wine vinegar

1 tablespoon sugar

1½ teaspoons salt

Ideally, the vegetables should be left out in the hot tropical sun for a day, but in temperate climates, they are best oven-dried: set the oven as low as it will go, turn on the fan if you have one, and spread the cut vegetables over three trays, or preferably racks. (If using oven racks, place over smaller cake racks to prevent the vegetables falling through the gaps.) Push the door to, but jam it slightly open with the handle of a wooden spoon (in order to allow air to circulate and steam to escape).

Leave for about an hour, or until the vegetables are somewhat shrivelled. If you are using trays rather than racks, you will need to stir and turn them occasionally.

Heat 4 tablespoons of the oil in a large saucepan or wok, then add the chillies, garlic, ginger, turmeric, peppercorns and mustard seeds. Stir-fry for 30 seconds, then add the remaining oil. Bring back to the boil, then add the vegetables, vinegar, sugar and salt.

Stir-fry for only a minute, then leave to cool. Transfer to a large bowl or jar, and allow to marinate, covered, in the fridge for 24 hours before serving as an entrée or side dish.

Note: if you can't be bothered with the oven-drying business, you can simply blanch the vegetables for a minute in boiling water, dry them, then proceed as above. The results are satisfactory, but you miss out on the crunchy texture which is half the delight of the authentic recipe.

In both the Mascarene islands and the French West Indies, achards are also made with tropical produce such as palm hearts, bitter melons, unripe mangoes and jackfruit, and quartered limes (see plate 9).

To some extent, the 158 years of British rule in Mauritius had a debasing effect, in that Raj-style curry powder sometimes came to replace the spice masala of old. Yet concepts unknown in India also came into being, such as mixing chicken with the prized local freshwater prawns known as camarons:

Curry de Poulet et de Camarons
(chicken and prawn curry)

1 chicken, about 1 kg (2 lb)	2 medium onions, finely chopped
500 g (1 lb) camarons (substitute prawns or shrimps)	5 *pommes d'amour* (substitute ordinary tomatoes)
2 tablespoons oil	1 teaspoon salt
3 tablespoons butter	¼ teaspoon sugar

3 cloves garlic, crushed	2 teaspoons turmeric powder[1]
2 teaspoons fresh ginger root, crushed	5 curry leaves, sliced finely
1 tablespoon curry powder	3 tablespoons roughly chopped fresh coriander leaves

Cut the chicken into 5cm pieces, preferably using a sharp Chinese cleaver so you can cut through the bones.

Peel three-quarters of the prawns, leaving the remainder intact.

Heat the oil and butter together in a heavy casserole dish, add the chicken pieces and brown on all sides. Remove and set aside. Add the onion and sauté until slightly browned.

Meanwhile, cover the tomatoes with boiling water, leave for several minutes, peel and then chop roughly.

Add the chopped tomato to the pot, stir over a high heat for about 5 minutes until the moisture evaporates. Stir in the garlic, ginger, curry powder, turmeric and curry leaves. Add the chicken pieces and simmer for 25 minutes. About 10 minutes before the end of cooking, add the unshelled prawns. About 5 minutes before the end, stir in the shelled prawns. Adjust seasoning if necessary.

To serve, pick out the unshelled prawns and arrange on top of each serving. Sprinkle with coriander. Serve with rice, *brèdes* (see page 59-60) and chutney.

SERVES 4.

Descended both from the French and from African slaves who came in brigs from Mozambique and Madagascar, the Creoles are in the minority in Mauritius. In view of this, it is perhaps not surprising that their cuisine should have been influenced by the Indian majority. While these savoury snacks, for example, have a Creole name – Creole being the *lingua franca* – they are unmistakably Indian in inspiration.

Gateaux Piments

On Réunion, these savoury snacks are called, with typically Creole penchant for changing the original meaning of French words, *bonbons piment* – when the little balls are anything but a bonbon or sweet. They are sold in the street by stall-holders, who would usually spurn the use of egg as a convenient binding agent.

300 g (10 oz) dal (yellow split peas)	3 shallots, finely chopped
	2 cloves garlic

2 small fresh green chillies
2 teaspoons ground caraway or
  cumin
½ teaspoon turmeric powder
pinch of bicarbonate of soda

1 egg, lightly beaten
2 tablespoons chopped coriander
leaves
salt and pepper
oil for deep frying

Wash the split peas and soak in plenty of cold water for 6 hours. Drain well and set aside.

Drop shallots, garlic, chillies, caraway seed, turmeric and bicarbonate into a running food processor, followed by the egg and finally the split peas (traditionally this is done with a flat rock and a cylindrical stone known as a baba). Add the coriander leaves and briefly mix in, using the pulse button. Form into small balls, indenting each one to allow better penetration of the hot oil.

Heat oil in a wok and deep-fry until golden, remove with a slotted spoon and drain on absorbent paper. Eat while still hot.

Makes 25–30 balls.

A distinct Indian flavour also runs through the spicy Creole pickled fish dish known as *vindaye*. Despite claims that it owes its linguistic origins to *vin d'ail* – garlic wine – the presence of vinegar suggests that the word is more likely a corruption of *vinde auly* or *vinde aulx*, the ancestor of the Anglo-Indian vindaloo – a spicy vinegar-based pickle found both in Portuguese Goa and in Madras, used mainly for pork but also occasionally for fish.

Vindaye of Fish

4 cloves garlic, peeled
1 thumb or knob fresh ginger,
  peeled
1 tablespoon mustard seeds,
  crushed
250 ml (9 fl oz or 1 cup) white wine
  or cider vinegar
4 fillets firm-fleshed fish

salt
6 tablespoons oil
1 medium onion, chopped
10 shallots or baby onions, sliced
3 green chillies, de-seeded and
  halved
2 teaspoons turmeric powder
3 sprigs of fresh thyme

In a running food processor, drop in the garlic cloves, ginger and mustard seeds. With the motor still running, add just enough of the vinegar – a few tablespoons – to coax the mixture into a paste. Alternatively, chop and crush ingredients by hand.

Dry the fish fillets and salt them. Heat 3 tablespoons oil in a frying pan, fry the fish on both sides until just cooked through (don't over-cook). Remove and set aside. Add remaining oil to the pan, fry onion and shallots until transparent. Add remaining vinegar and other ingredients to the pan and simmer for 3 minutes.

Place some of this pickling mixture in a dish, lay over the fish and cover with remaining mixture. Cover and leave in the fridge to improve its flavour. Eat cold with rice and pickles.

SERVES 4.

Whereas a *rougail* in Réunion refers to a raw preparation, usually of tomatoes, onion, chillies and parsley, on Mauritius this is known as 'tomato chutney'. A *rougail* as prepared on Mauritius takes on a new meaning as a cooked dish.

Mauritian-style Rougail

3 large tomatoes
3 cloves garlic
1 thumb or knob fresh ginger
1 red chilli
2 tablespoons oil

1 large onion, finely chopped
1 tablespoon tomato paste
1 sprig of fresh thyme, de-stemmed
   and chopped
1 large sprig of parsley, chopped

Either blanch, peel and chop the tomatoes, and pound garlic, ginger and chilli, or place each of these ingredients in a running food processor and grind to a paste.

Heat the oil in a wok, add the onion and cook until lightly coloured. Add the tomato, garlic, ginger and chilli paste and stir for 10 seconds, then add tomato paste and thyme. Stir, cover and cook for 5 minutes, covered. Just before serving stir in the parsley.

Serve with fried fish or meat.

Beef Rougail

750 g (1½ lb) topside beef, thinly
   sliced
oil
2 large onions, sliced
2 tablespoons freshly grated ginger
3 cloves garlic, chopped
2–3 chillies, chopped

2 tablespoons chopped parsley
2 teaspoons chopped fresh thyme
8 medium tomatoes, blanched,
   peeled and quartered
3 spring onions, finely sliced
1 tablespoon fresh coriander,
   chopped

In a pan or wok, briefly sauté the beef in oil over a high heat until browned on both sides, then remove with a slotted spoon and set aside. Lower the heat and in the remaining oil, sauté the onion until transparent and soft. Add the ginger, garlic, chillies, chopped parsley, fresh thyme and tomatoes. Cover and cook for 8–10 minutes. Return the beef to the pan and reheat, along with the spring onions and half the fresh coriander. Sprinkle with the remaining fresh coriander before serving.

Variation: omit the beef and you have a versatile Creole sauce, suitable for steak, fried fish, roast meat, grilled blood sausage and most barbecued foods.

Various culinary curiosities are associated with the Creoles. Monkeys, for example, are hunted and curried, as is the tenrec. With the aid of trained dogs, the furry hedgehog-like tenrec is hunted at the beginning of winter, when it is at its fattest. Males are said to have more flavour than females. Due to the strong smell of the meat, it is usually marinated beforehand with wine and a spice masala.

For the determined forager, the larvae of the yellow wasp *(Polistes herbraus)* are considered a prize. Having located a wasp nest in a tree or among sugar canes, the adult wasps are smoked out with the aid of burning rags or twigs tied to the end of a pole. With a sharp smack, the nest is brought to the ground, and after any wasp stings have been attended to, the nest is held over a charcoal fire and then knocked with the palm of the hand to coax out the larvae, which are gathered on a plate. Fried with onions until crisp, the larvae are dressed with chillies and lemon or vinegar, and eaten with rice and vegetables.

Although in many cases their ancestors arrived in the nineteenth century as indentured labourers following the abolition of slavery, the Chinese on Mauritius today are mainly involved in commerce, and the contents of typical grocery, from soya sauce to dried mushrooms, have all made inroads into the local cuisine. Chinese restaurants help to maintain the integrity of Chinese cooking in Mauritius, yet even the Chinese have not remained impervious to other culinary worlds. Tamarind, chillies, coconut cream, pineapples and peanuts have been known to appear on Chinese tables, sometimes in rather peculiar forms. One Chinese-Mauritian specialty, for example, is a soup made with roast peanuts, sugar, sesame seeds and watered-down cream, and their chicken in coconut sauce makes use of such un-Chinese spices as cardamom and coriander seeds. Even British traditions have left their mark: when traditional sweetened rice wine is not available, Chinese-Mauritian cooks readily substitute port.

Beef with Oyster Sauce

750 g (1½ lb) lean tender beef, cut
   into thin strips
3 tablespoons oyster sauce
2 tablespoons sweet rice wine or
   port
1 tablespoon soya sauce

2 tablespoons oil
juice of 1 lime or lemon
pinch of sugar
3 cloves garlic, crushed
3 tablespoons fresh chopped
   coriander leaves

Give each strip of beef a few bashes with a mallet or rolling pin, in order to flatten. Mix remaining ingredients except the coriander and marinate the beef in this for at least 20 minutes, preferably 2 hours.

Heat some oil in a wok or frying pan and sauté the beef very quickly over a high heat, until just cooked. Add any leftover marinade at the end of cooking. Sprinkle over chopped fresh coriander and serve with plain rice.

SERVES 4.

THE SEYCHELLES

As in Mauritius, French culinary influence in the Seychelles has proven remarkably tenacious, given that French rule lasted only forty years. On the other hand, few culinary traces are left of the British, who took over in 1811 and stayed for over 160 years. Undoubtedly the French influence had much to do with the intermarriage between former African slaves and descendants of the original French settlers, the *vieux blancs* or *blancs rouilles*. While their ancestors may have possessed large estates, over time these became greatly fragmented by French succession law, under which an estate of a deceased is divided equally among all heirs. Illiterate and impoverished, these *vieux blancs* were not averse to marrying or mating with Africans or mulattos, with the result that the French patois known as Kreol (Creole) is today the *lingua franca*.

A number of Creole wedding customs, now moribund, can be ascribed to French tradition, such as the *serenade* or procession of the bridal party to the wedding feast, headed by a band of musicians, the 'romances' or songs sung at the reception, the formal speeches in French (which used to be recorded in old copy-books) and the *levée de chambre*, or visit paid by the parents to the bride and groom on the day following the wedding to establish the bride's purity (which was invariably found to be unassailable). A cake similar to wedding cake would then be cut and shared, to the explosions of fireworks, to proclaim the news to the neighbourhood.

Seychellois cuisine closely conforms to the Creole pattern found elsewhere in the islands of the Indian Ocean. Staple foods are rice and *gros manger* – tubers such as cassava and sweet potato, breadfruit and plantains (especially the variety known as St Jacques). Beef and poultry are eaten only by the wealthy, and while pigs are kept as a form of investment by nearly every rural family, pork is associated only with weddings and feasts. Eggs, bread and milk are also scarcely eaten on the grounds of cost.

What does sustain the population is a stupendous amount of fish: with an annual per capita consumption of over 80 kg (around 175 lb), the Seychellois are among the greatest fish eaters in the world. While commercial fishing is today largely in the hands of large international companies, there is a fifty-strong island-based fleet, and a major cannery in Victoria, the capital. The most commonly caught fish is mackerel, and a stout silvery fish known as the karang. Favoured species include cordonnier, parrotfish, grouper (vielle), jack fish and, rather surprisingly, shark and becune, a type of barracuda. For barbecuing, nothing surpasses the tasty red snapper (bourgeois), however.

Poisson Grillé à la Seychelloise
(grilled fish Seychelles-style)

This is traditionally served with grilled breadfruit, for which baked or boiled potato may be substituted.

1 red snapper or other large firm fish, about 2.5 kg (4–5 lb)
6 cloves garlic, chopped
1 thumb-sized knob fresh ginger, chopped
2 spring onions, chopped

3 tablespoons tomato ketchup
3 tablespoons soya sauce
2 tablespoons oil
juice of 1 lime or lemon
1 tablespoon sugar
1 teaspoon salt

Clean, scale and gut the fish. Make deep diagonal slashes every 3 cm (1 in) or so along its length, on both sides.

Mix together all remaining ingredients. Fill each gash with a little of the mixture. Pour over any remaining marinade and leave for 2 hours in the refrigerator. Turn once or twice.

Grill or barbecue the fish for about 15 minutes per side, basting frequently with leftover marinade.

SERVES 4.

The rather coarse flesh of the shark is ideally suited to this filling for cassava pancakes. In the absence of cassava, the pancakes can be made from ordinary flour, or substitute any type of shop-bought flat bread, such as pitta bread, chappatis or tortillas. The *bilimbi* referred to here is closely related to the acidic carambola, or starfruit. It resembles a gherkin in flavour and is put to similar savoury uses, for rice, fish and meat.

Chatni de Requin
(shark chutney)

750 g (1½ lb) shark flesh, cubed
4 tablespoons oil
4 cloves garlic, chopped
2 shallots, chopped
1 thumb or knob ginger root, finely
  chopped

1 *bilimbi* (substitute 1 gherkin),
  chopped
1 teaspoon turmeric
juice of 2 limes or 1 lemon
salt
1 tablespoon chopped chives

Boil the shark for 10 minutes, drain well, pressing out all moisture, and remove any traces of cartilage.

Heat oil in a pan and sauté garlic, shallots, ginger, *bilimbi* (or gherkin). Sprinkle over turmeric and mix through. Cook a few minutes longer. Remove and add shark along with the lime juice and chives. With a fork, mix everything together and thoroughly mash the shark flesh into fine shreds. Add salt to taste and use as a filling for pancakes or flat breads. A variation on this recipe calls for dried shark.

Seafood delicacies include crayfish, crab and the freshwater shrimp or camaron. From the beaches, a fine-tasting clam known as tec-tec is collected and fried open in butter, then made into a simple soup with water, chillies and lime juice. In the shallow lagoons, octopus is speared and cooked with coconut cream and cinnamon, a spice formerly of major commercial importance.

Ourite au Lait de Coco
(octopus cooked in coconut cream)

1 kg (2 lb) octopus
4 tablespoons oil
2 onions, finely sliced
4 cloves garlic, chopped
1 thumb-sized knob fresh ginger,
   chopped

2 teaspoons turmeric powder
¼ teaspoon ground cinnamon
500 ml (scant 1 pt or 2 cups)
   coconut cream, tinned or fresh
salt and pepper

Place the octopus on a flat surface and beat thoroughly with a mallet or pestle for at least 20 minutes. Wash and place in a pot. Cover with water, add a little salt and a dash of vinegar, and boil the octopus until tender. This will take anything from 30 minutes to several hours, according to the age of the octopus. Drain and cut the octopus into 1 cm (½ in) pieces.

Heat the oil in a large casserole dish, fry the onion until transparent, then add octopus, garlic, ginger, turmeric and cinnamon. Mix well, then stir in the coconut cream. Cook over a low heat for 20–25 minutes, season to taste with salt and pepper. Serve with Creole rice.
SERVES 6.

Riz à la Creole
(Creole rice)

Creole rice, as Western hotel chefs understand it, is a mixture of fried onions, mushrooms, green peas, peppers and tomatoes, folded into cooked rice with a little saffron or turmeric for colour. Such a recipe, however, is not in common usage among Creole cooks, either in the Indian Ocean or the Caribbean. The nearest approximation might be this Seychellois dish, except that it is served cold.

500 g (1 lb or 2 cups) rice
2 medium onions, chopped
60 ml (2 fl oz or ¼ cup) oil
2 teaspoons turmeric powder
250 g (8 oz) salted fish
1 red pepper, sliced
1 green pepper, sliced
250 g (8 oz) octopus

150 g (5 oz) shelled clams
200 g (7 oz) green runner beans
250 ml (9 fl oz or 1 cup) oil
125 ml (4 fl oz or ½ cup) vinegar or
   lemon juice
salt and pepper
2 tomatoes, quartered
2 tablespoons chopped parsley

Place the rice in a fine sieve and massage it with your fingers under a cold tap, until the water running off turns from milky to clear.

In a saucepan, fry the onions in the oil until they turn transparent, then add the rice along with 750 ml (1¼ pts or 3 cups) of hot tap water, the turmeric and ½ teaspoon salt. Bring to the boil, cover tightly and boil gently until all the water is absorbed. Turn off the heat and keep the rice covered until cooled. Fluff it up with a fork.

Gently boil the fish for 5 minutes, remove any bones and shred the flesh.

Boil and slice the octopus as in the preceding recipe. Steam the clams until tender.

String the beans if necessary, steam for 6 minutes, plunge immediately into cold water to retain their colour. When cool, cut into batons.

Make a vinaigrette by mixing the oil and vinegar (or lemon juice) and adding salt and pepper to taste.

Mix together rice, fish, pepper, octopus, clams, beans and vinaigrette. Heap up on a serving platter and decorate with quartered tomatoes and parsley. Serve cold.

In former times, the meat of both the giant tortoise and the green turtle were major delicacies, but both were hunted mercilessly, the former to extinction, the latter nearly so. Unlike Mauritius and Réunion, the tenrec is not hunted, but the fruit bat (chauve souris) is still shot at night. It is turned into curries for, despite being a rodent, it is a clean eater, living solely on fruit. Tern eggs are gathered, as are fouquets – the young of the sooty shearwater.

Bananas, of which some twenty-five types grow in the Seychelles, are sometimes picked green and combined with fish and coconut cream for a dish known as kat-kat. Mangoes, papayas, fruits de cythère (golden apples) custard apples, passionfruit, guavas and pineapples are eaten in abundance, compensating for the relative shortfall in green vegetables of the island cuisine. As on other Indian Ocean islands, palmiste from the apical bud of the coconut palm and of the wild palmiste palm, provide the basis for Salade du Millionaire. Everyday dishes comprise brèdes of both wild and cultivated green vegetables, and chatnis of green fruits.

Tourism is steadily raising the standard of restaurant cuisine, and the Seychelles Hotel and Tourism Training School at Bel Ombre turns out chefs for about thirty hotels and thirty-five guest houses.

MADAGASCAR

Unlike other Indian Ocean islands whose societies were shaped by immigration during the French colonial era, the kingdom of Madagascar had evolved a complex culture over a thousand years before French annexation in 1896. This included an austere but well-defined cuisine, based on coagulated and often unsalted rice three times a days, supplemented with fatty, virtually unseasoned meat stews. These meals, as the traveller David Curl rather unkindly put it, comprise 'skin and rice, gristle and rice, fat and rice, and bones and rice' – meaning, respectively, chicken, beef, pork and fish!

The standard dishes are livened up with the great triumvirate common to the region: *achards*, *rougail* and *brèdes*. Indeed, it is believed that *brèdes* – green leafy vegetables cooked in water with onions, garlic and tomato – may have originated in Madagascar.

The great national dish, *romazava*, a meat and vegetable stew spiced with ginger, can either comprise beef from the common zebu, or hump-backed cow, or a mixture of meats, in which case they are added in order of their necessary cooking times. The garlic, ginger and green leaves are added just before serving, the idea being that everything arrives at the table perfectly cooked.

Romazava

500 g (1 lb) blade or chuck steak, cubed
2 tablespoons peanut oil
2 medium onions, diced
salt and pepper
500 g (1 lb) lean pork, cubed
1 kg (2 lb) fresh tomatoes, skinned and chopped

500 g (1 lb) chicken, skinned and jointed
8 cloves garlic, chopped
thumb or knob fresh ginger, grated
500 g (1 lb) spinach, minus stalks, large leaves torn
2 tablespoons tomato paste (optional)

Sauté the beef in the oil until lightly browned, remove with a slotted spoon, then add the onion and sauté until transparent, adding more oil if necessary. Return the meat to the pot with enough water to barely cover. Season to taste with salt and pepper. Bring to the boil, covered, then reduce heat and simmer gently for one hour.

Add the pork and tomatoes, simmer for a further 30 minutes, then add the chicken and simmer for 30 minutes longer, stirring occasionally to avoid sticking. (The casserole can also be cooked in a 160°C (325°F/Gas 3) oven.)

About 10 minutes before the end of cooking, add the garlic and ginger. About 5 minutes before serving, add the spinach. Stir the spinach gently into the stew, allowing it to wilt. If the stew is too liquid, it can be thickened with tomato paste. Serve the romazava while the spinach is still green.

SERVES 6.

The influence of French colonialism is seen mainly in hotels and superior restaurants, which usually list their menus in French, and offer seafood delicacies which, despite being fished in the waters around Madagascar, are beyond the pockets of most of the inhabitants.

Salade de Crustacés
(crustacean salad)

The French vinaigrette in this recipe is also used to dress cooked octopus.

1 large crab	1 small onion, finely chopped
1 rock lobster	2 teaspoons fresh ginger, finely
1 kg (2 lb) prawns	chopped
juice of 2 lemons	1 head lettuce
125 ml (4 fl oz or ½ cup) oil	3 tomatoes, quartered
¼ teaspoon salt	6 olives

In a pot of boiling salted water, boil the crab, lobster and prawns in succession. Remove the meat from the crabs. Slice the rock lobster tail and remove the meat from the larger legs. Peel the prawns.

In a small bowl, whisk together lemon juice, oil and salt, then add onion and ginger.

Arrange lettuce leaves over a platter. Toss the seafood in the dressing, then arrange over the lettuce and garnish with tomatoes and olives. Offer remaining dressing separately in a sauce boat, jug or bowl.

SERVES 6.

As in most former French tropical colonies, bananas flambéed in rum is a common dessert – so much that a promiscuous male is popularly known as a *banane flambé*. While the Malagasy diner needed no encouragement from the French to eat frogs' legs, under Gallic influence they began to lightly flour them and fry them in oil with garlic and parsley. A wild fowl known as the acoho found great favour among the French. 'Its flesh, at least that of the female,' wrote de Noter in *La Bonne Cuisine aux Colonies*, 'is excellent, and resembles the wild duck of Europe. It is cooked lightly in various ways, all resembling our familiar culinary formulas.'

A great many other traditional food items, such as cicadas, weevils and rotten fish, were always beyond the pale for the French administrators, who did, however, manage to have bakeries established. Today, it is possible to buy baguettes and pain au chocolat in the major towns and there is even a small wine industry in the highlands. Domaine Côtes d'Isandra and Domaine Côtes de Famoriana, both near the hill town of Fianarantsoa, are the two largest producers.

COMOROS AND MAYOTTE

North-west of Madagascar lie a group of remote islands, three of which form the Federal Islamic Republic of the Comoros, and a fourth, Mayotte, which retains its colonial status as a *collectivité territoriale* of France. Always a backwater, it was said back in 1870 by the *proceureur imperial* Gevrey at Pondicherry: 'A European would be able, without inconvenience, to spend three years on Mayotte if his temperament is choleric, six years if he is cheerful and ten years if he is sluggish.'

As in Madagascar, the first settlers of the Comoros were probably of Malay-Polynesian origin, blended with later waves of Africans, Arabs and Persians, and more recently, Indo-Pakistanis. The cuisine reflects all these cultures, with a strong overlay of France. The old colonial *rhum arrangé* (rum marinated with vanilla beans, spices and brown sugar), for example, is consumed at Comoran festivals, along with vast quantities of coconut toddy, despite the inhabitants having converted to Islam as long ago as AD 642.

To be sure, pork is forbidden and pigs are banished from domestic backyards, yet there is ample goat, mutton, zebu and, above all, chicken:

Poulet au Coco
(chicken with coconut cream)

Coconut cream is central to Comoran cuisine, lending flavour not only to chicken, but also to fish, rice and various vegetables such as cassava leaves, aubergines and peas. As elsewhere on the French-speaking islands of the Indian Ocean, a dish such as this might be accompanied by plain white rice and a tomato *rougail* (see page 59), and preceded by mixed vegetable *achards* (see page 68).

1 chicken, skinned, boned and cut into pieces	1 teaspoon turmeric powder
2 large red onions, sliced	¾ teaspoon salt
2 tablespoons oil	ground black pepper
1 tablespoon butter	300 ml (10 fl oz) tinned coconut cream
1 teaspoon cumin, ground	4 tomatoes, blanched and peeled
1 teaspoon cinnamon, ground	

In a large pot, sauté the onion in oil and butter until translucent. Add the chicken, sauté until it turns white, then add cumin, cinnamon, turmeric, salt and a few grinds of black pepper. Stir until the yellow colour has dispersed through the dish, then add the coconut cream and the tomatoes. Simmer gently, uncovered, for 25–30 minutes. Serve with rice.

SERVES 4.

Fish abound in the tropical waters surrounding the Comoros, especially around Mayotte, which has 140 kms (88 miles) of coral barrier reef enclosing the largest lagoon in the world. Resembling a vast aquarium, it is heavily stocked with tuna, barracudas and groupers, all of which are speared with a large harpoon called a *foene*. Smaller fish such as anchovies and sardines are caught communally, with fine nets. Hand nets are also used for freshwater shrimps and for mangrove crabs.

Seafood, along with locally produced spices (vanilla beans, cardamoms, coriander, black pepper, cloves, nutmegs and cinnamon), are to been seen at Mayotte's market in the main town, Mamoudzou. Built in 1986, it also provides impressive arrays of vegetables such as yams, aubergines, taro and manioc, and a local pea known as ambrevade, as well as abundant fruits: rambutans, lychees, pineapples, guavas and mangoes. Around the fringes of the market and in the town itself, even in some of the offices of the administration, are to be seen food hawkers, an increasingly rare sight nowadays in former French colonies. These *marchands ambulants* sell varieties of *grignotage* (literally 'crispness') – kebabs, hard-boiled eggs, crusty breads and pastries.

INDIA

With its Hôtel de Ville, and a tricolour flag fluttering over the French Consulate-General, not to mention the red kepis and belts worn by the local police, the city of Pondicherry is an enduring pocket of French culture on the Indian subcontinent. Its streets of restored colonial villas gleam with fresh whitewash, and polished brass plates mark the entrances to gardens ablaze with bougainvillea.

Formerly known as the White Town, Pondicherry, in the southern state of Tamil Nadu, was founded in 1674 and rebuilt by Jean Law in 1756–77. Separated by a canal from the Tamil quarter (which in less culturally sensitive times was known as the Black Town), this was the capital of French settlements in India right up until 1 September 1954. Together with the former French enclaves of Karaikal (also in Tamil Nadu) Mahé (12 kms/7 miles north of Calicut in modern Kerala, and founded as a trading post in 1721) and Yanam (in Andhra Pradesh) it today forms the Union Territory of Pondicherry.

Its heyday was during a period of flourishing trade in the early eighteenth century, until war broke out with the British in the 1740s. Its bazaar, nicknamed 'the pagoda' by the French, bustled with fruit and grain merchants and sellers of spices and betel leaf, leather tanners and weavers. Cloth dyers were everywhere, producing Pondicherry's main export commodity – raw cotton dyed blue – staining the already dirty streets with streams of indigo. Shop after shop selling fresh provisions, ropes and sails underlined Pondicherry's importance to ships' captains as a stop-over on the trade route further east, while gambling dens and brothels catered to the less savoury needs of their crews.

The men of the French and Tamil communities had regular dealings on a professional basis and occasionally dined together, but almost never did their families socialize, the Tamil women retaining their traditional reticence while their French counterparts did their best to maintain the illusion of Parisian high society, entertaining guests in their best frilly dresses and gravity-defying hairstyles. Nevertheless, the French did not practise racism to nearly the degree of the British in India, and showed noticeably greater enthusiasm about attending the major Hindu festivals such as Pongal and Dipavali, with their garlands of flowers, dancing girls and processions of chariots. More importantly, there was a great deal of intermarriage. The great eighteenth-century governor of Pondicherry, Joseph Dupleix, himself married a

Creole from Chandernagore (another small French enclave in Bengal), while his friend and colleague Jacques Vincens had married a woman of Portuguese and Tamil ancestry. By 1790, there were said to be only two French families in Pondicherry of pure blood, of whom the sons of one had married local Indian women.

Not surprisingly, this intermarriage caused the French to adopt Indian customs, and during the eighteenth century young men fresh from France were shocked to find women offering them powdered betel nuts from their own silver confit boxes. Since the social consequences of refusing such an offer would have been worse than being forced to taste a strange substance that turned one's lips red, they accepted, and before long had adopted the habit themselves.

French cuisine also underwent a spicy metamorphosis, resulting in a small collection of unique hybrid dishes which survive in Pondicherry to this day. Pork-based sausages such as *saucisse* and *boudin* are noticeably spicier than their French counterparts, for example, while there is also a distinct spicy edge to the minced beef base which is used either for meatballs *(boulettes)* or to fill hollowed-out tomatoes *(tomates farcies)*. In the hands of Tamil cooks, lamb noisettes came to be fashioned from chump chops and loosely termed roulades. Such a bland description gave little warning of the hot and spicy filling of this cross-cultural dish. Served at grand festive occasions, it must have sent the sensitive palates of visiting French dignitaries into interesting contortions:

Panchanaga Seekarane
(Pondicherry lamb roulades)

8 boned lamb chump chops, sliced thinly (5 mm or ¼ in thick)
1 clove garlic, finely chopped
1 thumb-sized knob fresh ginger, finely chopped
1 small onion, finely chopped
2–3 green chillies, finely chopped
2 tablespoons coriander leaves, chopped
1 tablespoon raisins
1 tablespoon slivered almonds
2 medium onions, quartered
2 tablespoons ghee
2 teaspoons white poppy seeds, ground
½ teaspoon turmeric powder
1 teaspoon garam masala
2 teaspoons coriander seed, ground
2 teaspoons ground cumin
½ teaspoon salt
2 tablespoons plain yoghurt

Mix together garlic, half the ginger, onion, chillies, coriander leaves, raisins, and slivered almonds. Spread a little mixture along the inside of each chop, roll each up tightly into a round roulade and secure with small skewers or cocktail sticks (alternatively, bind with light string).

Drop the two quartered onions into a running food processor, along with the rest of the fresh ginger, and grind to a paste.

Heat the ghee in a large pan and fry the onion and ginger paste until cooked through, then stir in 3 tablespoons of water, poppy seeds, turmeric, garam masala, coriander, cumin, salt and yoghurt. Place the lamb noisettes into the pan, turning them over to cover with the mixture, and settling each well into the mixture. Cover and cook gently over a medium-low heat for 20 minutes. Add a little more water during cooking if necessary.

SERVES 4.

Jambon, which is pork cooked in beer and then smoked, tastes rather like the *boucanage* of the French islands of the Indian Ocean and the Caribbean. Pâtés in various forms were popular from the earliest days in Pondicherry (Yvonne Gaebele, in her *Vie de Johanna Begum*, mentions a picnic attended by Madame Dupleix where the duck paste was particularly appreciated), a common modern form being made from steaming a spiced paste of pork liver, liberally doused with cognac.

A French diner would find nothing unusual about the roast fillet of beef served in Pondicherry, or the slow cooked ragoût of beef and mixed vegetables. The local fish croquettes, rolled in breadcrumbs and baked, would also be familiar, as would the following recipe, in content if not in name.

Poisson Capitaine

1 kg (2 lb) fresh fish fillets, suitable
for steaming
8 large cloves garlic, minced finely
1 egg

pinch of salt
250 ml (9 fl oz or 1 cup) light oil
1 tablespoon lime or lemon juice

Smear the fish fillets with garlic paste and steam in a covered pan for about 10 minutes, or until cooked through.

Meanwhile make a mayonnaise: in a food processor fixed with the metal blade, mix the egg and salt, then with the motor still running, dribble in the oil in a thin but steady stream. Once about half the oil has been amalgamated, you can speed up the pouring process slightly. When the mayonnaise has thickened, add the lime juice and serve a generous dollop over each portion of fish.

SERVES 4–6.

Pondicherry is one of the very few places in India where French breads such as baguettes and croissants are made and sold, and the desserts there also retain a French flavour, with creations such as gâteau mocha, a sponge cake layered with coffee and rum-laced whipped cream. Crème caramel as served in Pondicherry may well have inspired the ubiquitous caramel custard of British India, though a variation flavoured with nutmeg, known as *flanc*, in turn suggests a Portuguese influence.

The French planted vineyards in Pondicherry, and while conditions were too hot for the production of noble wine, they did manage to produce large quantities of grapes for the table. These were a source of both delight and irritation to the British at Madras, for the French would not budge from their astronomical asking price of a rupee per bunch.

The French may not have been the first to plant grapes in India, they did introduce several important varieties of bean – the broad bean *(Vicia faba)*, known in India as the French bean, and the haricot or navy bean *(Phaseolus vulgaris)*, a large botanical family which includes the popular red kidney bean or *rajmah*. The French were the first to grow these at Karaikanal, Mahé and Pondicherry, from where their popularity rapidly spread throughout India during the early twentieth century. The Tamils of Pondicherry absorbed all these, and in addition took to the small variety of green bean known the world over as French beans. Inspired by the ready availability of fresh milk in Pondicherry, they tweaked a traditional Tamil coconut cream gravy into an East-West dressing for the beans:

Green Beans Pondicherry-style

2 tablespoons ghee
½ teaspoon cumin seeds, bruised
  with a pestle
1 small onion, halved and finely
  sliced
1 teaspoon coriander seed, ground
small pinch of cayenne pepper

3 tablespoons yoghurt
125 ml (4 fl oz or ½ cup) milk
¼ teaspoon turmeric powder
pinch of salt
250 g (8 oz) fresh runner beans,
  cut into batons

Heat the ghee in pan and fry the cumin seeds lightly for about a minute, then add the onion along with the coriander and cayenne. Fry until the onion is cooked through and transparent. Whisk the yoghurt into the milk and add to the pan. Stir in the turmeric powder, season to taste with salt. Bring just to the boil, reduce heat immediately, add beans, and cover. Simmer for 6–8 minutes until green and still crunchy, or for 15 minutes until olive-coloured and soft, according to how modern or how Tamilian you wish the dish to be.

As in British India, mulligatawny was a common festive dish. Here is a recipe from the poet Stephane Mallarmé, published in 1874 under the pseudonym of Marasquin in the French women's magazine *Dernière Mode*. Its title suggests it be served for Christmas Eve supper. Despite the attribution at the recipe's end, Mallarmé assures us it is from one 'Zizy, a half-caste from Surat':

Moulongtani pour un Réveillon

Fry an onion in butter with curry and saffron. Add a chicken, cut in pieces, after having fried it very lightly. Pour over the milk yielded by a grated coconut which you have pounded in a mortar and to which you have added some hot water. Let it simmer and serve with riz à la Créole.

Signed: Olympe, Négresse.

3 French Canada

QUEBEC

Cowering beneath a little fishing boat hauled ashore, then turned over in the snow as a makeshift shelter from a blizzard, the cook tends to be concerned less for culinary refinement than a full stomach.

Until well into the twentieth century, this sort of predicament would not have been unusual for French Canadians, since most were occupied with fishing, farming and lumbering, pitted against the harsh northern environment. It is hardly surprising, then, that the traditional cuisine of Quebec and of the long-settled French-speaking communities in the Maritime Provinces is not, in general, greatly complex. The number of ingredients is kept to a minimum, and if in the past the intake of calories was huge, the work demanded it.

The pattern for later French cooking in America was set by the *voyageurs*, the seventeenth-century fur traders who went out into the wilderness among the Indians. Describing a typical repast, one trader wrote:

> The tin kettle in which they cooked their food would hold eight or ten gallons. It was hung over the fire, nearly full of water, then nine quarts of peas – one quart per man, the daily allowance – were put in; and when they were well bursted, two or three pounds of pork, cut into strips, for seasoning, were added, and all allowed to boil or simmer until daylight, when the cook added four biscuits, broken up, to the mess, and invited all hands to breakfast. The swelling of the peas and biscuit had now filled the kettle to the brim, so thick that a stick would stand upright in it . . . The men now squatted in a circle, the kettle in their midst, and each one plying his wooden spoon or ladle from the kettle to mouth, with almost electric speed, soon filled every cavity.

Quoted by Evan Jones, in *American Heritage Cookbook*, New York, 1961.

In time, onions, garlic, bay leaves and other seasonings were added to the *voyageurs'* stew, and the pork might be replaced by pemmican.

As originally prepared by the Cree and other Indian tribes, pemmican comprised the meat of buffalo, deer, elk or sometimes bear, cut into thin slices, sun-dried, pounded, and then formed into cakes with melted fat and berries. The *voyageurs* simplified the process, merely drying strips of meat in the sun or over fires. It was the ideal convenience food, since it kept indefinitely, and if necessary could be gnawed on in its dry state as well as being soaked in water before stewing.

From the Amerindians also came a method of cooking hare, reminiscent of the Polynesian earth oven (see page 170). A hole would be dug in sand, then lined with rocks. A fire would be made in the hole, and when it had heated the rocks, a skinned and gutted hare would be wrapped in fir branches and placed in the earth oven, covered with loamy soil, to bake for about three hours.

During the early days, when the forests were being cleared for farmland, the Quebecois settlers had huge recourse to the game which abounded, both furred and feathered. Yet even after the crops had been sown and the pigs had been reared, hunting continued to exert a strong attraction for *habitants* (smallholder farmers) of French Canada. They could not quite believe their luck. Back in France, hunting had always been the preserve of the aristocracy and the wealthy. Hunting estates were privately owned, membership of hunting associations restricted, hunting licences costly. While farming placed increased demands on their time, the *habitants* could easily justify a Sunday afternoon hunt on the grounds of the game they inevitably brought back, which eased the necessity to cull their growing herds.

Buffalo, being virtually indistinguishable from beefsteak, was understandably popular, and there was also an ingrained taste for venison. All parts of the elk were used, the heart being stuffed with a herbed breadcrumb farce, the tongue boiled, pressed and jellied like ox tongue, the snout fried with onions. Wild duck, too, was a familiar taste from France, though a fishy taint often had to be ameliorated with prior blanching in boiling water. Hare was a common item in the cooking pot, often joined there by a partridge, or perhaps some elk.

The Quebecois penchant for mixing game meats is evident in *cipaille*, their famous multi-layered pie with as many variants on the spelling – *ci-pâte*, *cipâte*, *cipâtre*, *chipaille*, *sipaille*, *six-pâtes*, *six-pailles* – as ingredients. *Cipaille*, it seems, may be made with an elaborate assortment of elk, roebuck, partridge and hare, or a mixture of game with domestic meats such as beef and pork, or a single variety of fish such as salmon or herring. There is even *cipâte aux yeux bleus*, a dessert pie made with blueberries.

It has been conjectured that *cipaille* is merely a French corruption of the English 'sea-pie', that notorious hash of left-over meat and vegetables recycled under the cover of pastry. However, the variant *cipâte* implies a crust – in fact five or six layers of crust *(cinq/six pâtes)* which, in the old days at least, may have been literally true. Traditional *cipailles* had at least two, if not several, layers of pastry interleaved with fillings of game, poultry, pork and vegetables. And as if the extra layers of pastry did not render the dish sufficiently heavy, pieces of chopped, salted lard were frequently thrown in for good measure. Truly a dish for lads who had spent the day chopping wood or fighting bears.

A Canadian author, Sondra Gotlieb, describes big-game bear as 'the worst-tasting wild meat', though young bear is apparently somewhat more edible, similar in flavour to pork. Perhaps this explains why Quebecois recipes for roast bear call for strident seasonings such as mustard and summer savory. As for porcupines, musk-rats and fish ducks, Mrs Gotlieb advises they are only good to eat when you are lost in the woods and starving, or drunk.

On the other hand, beaver tail is sufficiently mild in flavour to be simply fried in butter with onions, salt and pepper, while the host of squirrel recipes in Quebecois cookery books suggests this familiar rodent may also be a treat. Yet despite being commonly seen among the trees of suburbia, squirrel has yet to replace chicken as the *pièce de résistance* at Sunday afternoon barbecues in Canada.

Another wild food, maple syrup, did catch on, however. Indeed, in the eyes of the rest of the world, maple syrup is synonymous with Canada – souffléd, moussed, baked and otherwise worked into every official VIP Canadian dinner from Paris to Perth. While this may irritate Canadians who live in areas where the sugar maple is not common, it does fairly represent Quebec, whose 10,000 producers account for 80 per cent of the world's supply.

Maple sap had always been collected by the Amerindians and drunk as a beverage, although their primitive method of dropping hot stones into earthenware containers did not allow them to reduce the sap to the consistency of the syrup we know today. Some say the Amerindians taught the French colonists the technique of tapping the sap, others claim it was independently devised by Dr Michel Sarrazin, a military surgeon who arrived in Quebec in 1685.

In any case, the Amerindian technique, of piercing the tree with a tomahawk and then inserting a small piece of wood or bark, was very similar to that used by the French, who devised a wooden spout, or spile, to draw off the sap which was then collected in a small receptacle underneath. A round tip on the spile, invented at the beginning of the twentieth century, eliminated the need for a brace and bit to pierce the bark, hence reducing the damage to the tree. Then in the 1970s producers devised a network of plastic tubing which linked a group of trees to a central sugarhouse (where the sap is collected), which meant that workers no longer had to run from tree to tree in snowshoes, collecting the little tin pails of sap.

The sap is then boiled down for syrup, or reduced still further for maple 'butter', the consistency of smooth peanut butter, or dried completely into the old-fashioned blocks of maple sugar which must be grated before use. A more recent innovation is a softer maple sugar, the texture of brown sugar.

Roughly speaking, the lighter the maple syrup, the better the quality; experts are able to discern the difference between unblended syrups from various regions, and each May the Quebec Provincial and International Maple Contest awards the top producer the title of Grand Maître Sucrier. The event takes place in Plessisville, the oldest city of the Boisfrancs area (founded 1835), and coincides with the Festival de l'Erable de Plessisville – three days of parades, cooking sessions, dinners and fireworks held annually since 1959.

Whole cookbooks have been written to list the various cakes, puddings, muffins, scones, crêpes, blinis, tarts, gratins, charlottes and ice creams using maple sugar or syrup. To a Frenchman, if not to an American, some Quebecois uses of maple syrup may seem bizarre, but there is a long established tradition for sweet-savoury dishes such as eggs cooked in boiling maple syrup, hams glazed in maple syrup and maple syrup as a moistener for pork and beans. A traditional Quebecois lumberjack lunch comprises ham steaks which are grilled with a mixture of maple syrup, mustard powder and cider vinegar. This recipe is from the heart of maple country – the Mauricie-Boisfrancs area in the centre of Quebec.

Crème à l'Erable
(maple syrup cream)

300 ml (½ pt or 1¼ cups) maple syrup
2 eggs, separated
pinch of salt

50 g (2 oz or ½ cup) plain flour
450 ml (¾ pt or 1¾ cups) milk
2 tablespoons butter

Reserve about 3–4 tablespoons of the maple syrup and mix the rest with the egg yolks and salt. Gradually add the flour and beat until the mixture is smooth.

Heat the milk. In a double boiler, or in a bowl placed over a saucepan of boiling water, gradually add the milk to the maple syrup mixture, beating continuously until it thickens.

Remove from the heat, beat in the butter, and return to the heat, cooking and stirring for another 2–3 minutes. Allow to cool a little.

Whisk the egg whites until stiff, adding the remaining 50ml of maple syrup little by little. Fold the cooked and cooled maple syrup mixture through the stiffened egg whites, ladle into individual serving dishes, and refrigerate.

SERVES 6.

Given that France lost Quebec to British North America as long ago as 1763, it is not surprising that the culinary influences of the conquerors are everywhere to be seen. Worcestershire sauce occurs time and again in the recipes of Quebec, *daubales* (doughballs) enter their soups and stews, while *les muffins* and *marmalade anglais* clearly reveal their origins. *Le crapaud dans son trou* is none other than toad in the hole, while such is the antiquity of *Plum-pudding des Loyalistes,* brought over the border by eighteenth-century British refugees after the American War of Independence, that it is now considered part of the Quebecois repertoire. The greater emphasis on cool-climate vegetables such as turnips, and the prevalence of molasses (Quebec consumes eighty times more molasses than the rest of Canada) also reflect an English style. It must also be remembered that the founder of Quebec, Jacques Cartier, along with most of his men, was from Brittany, whose ancient roots are intertwined with the Celts of Britain, not with any stock of France. A love of mutton, potatoes and pancakes is shared by Bretons, Britons and Quebecois alike. The preponderance of beans in Quebecois cuisine, either by themselves or with mutton or pork, is also part of this Breton legacy.

Dumplings are also integral to the cuisine of Brittany's neighbour, Normandy, the other ancestral homeland of Quebec. These, along with other rustic dishes such as *potage habitant*, the savoury meat pie known as *tourtière* and the meatball stew called *ragoût de boulettes*, are adaptations of old Norman cuisine to ingredients found in Canada over 350 years ago.

Potage Habitant
(pea soup)

500 g (1 lb) yellow split peas
1 kg (2 lb) smoked ham hock or
    500 g (1 lb) salt pork
1 large onion, chopped
2 carrots, chopped

handful celery leaves, chopped
1 tablespoon chopped parsley
1 tablespoon chopped fresh
    summer or winter savory

Pick through the peas and discard any discoloured pieces. Place in a large pot and soak overnight in about 3 litres (5 pts) of water. Add remaining ingredients, bring to the boil quickly and skim. Cover, reduce the heat and cook for 2–3 hours until the peas are soft and creamy, stirring from time to time and scraping the bottom of the pot in order to prevent the soup sticking.

If using a ham hock, remove before serving and when cool enough to handle, strip off and discard the skin, fat and bone. Cut the meat into small cubes and return to the pot. Season with pepper and add salt only if needed (probably the pork will have rendered it quite salty enough) before serving.

Around Beauceville and in eastern parts of Quebec, a little barley is commonly added.

SERVES 6–8.

While *tourtières* of mixed domestic meats (beef, pork) and game (hare, partridge, duck) are not unknown, pork *tourtière* is the classic pie served on Christmas Eve, reflecting the high status of the pig in French Canadian cuisine.

Tourtière

600 g (1¼–1½ lb) minced pork
1 small onion, finely chopped
salt and pepper
½ teaspoon dried savory or sage

¼ teaspoon ground cloves
2 bay leaves
2 sheets pie pastry

Combine all ingredients (except pastry) in a pan, add 4 tablespoons of hot water and simmer over a low heat for 20 minutes.

Line a 23 cm (9 in) pie plate with pastry, pour in the meat and cover with the other sheet of pastry. Brush with egg wash if desired.

Bake at 190°C (375°F/Gas 5) for 25–30 minutes, or until the pastry is nicely browned and cooked.

SERVES 4.

Variation: in the Quebec City area, about 250 g (8 oz) mashed potato is mixed into the meat after it is cooked.

Ragoût de Boulettes
(meatball stew)

1 kg (2 lb) minced pork	1 egg
1 small onion, finely chopped	flour for dredging
3 cloves garlic, crushed	4 tablespoons lard or oil
½ teaspoon ground cinnamon	2 litres (3½ pts or 8 cups) broth or
¼ teaspoon ground ginger	water
¼ teaspoon ground cloves	50 g (2 oz or ½ cup) flour, browned
salt and pepper	(see below)

Place minced pork, onion, garlic, cinnamon, ginger, cloves, salt and pepper in a bowl. Make a well in the minced meat, crack in the egg and beat it lightly with a fork. Mix all ingredients well, then form into meatballs and roll them in flour.

Heat the lard or oil in a large pot, fry the meatballs until browned on all sides. Remove the meatballs, drain off the fat, then return the meatballs to the pot with the broth or water. Cover and simmer for 20 minutes until the meat is cooked, then thicken the liquid with the browned flour mixed to a paste with a little water.

Note: Flour can be browned on an oven tray in the oven set at 200°C (400°F/Gas 6). Stir with a spatula, often, to prevent lumps and to obtain an even colour. Store excess in a tin. Alternatively, the ragoût might be thickened with a little cornflour mixed to a paste with water.

(The presence of cinnamon, ginger and cloves in the recipe, incidentally, shows the extent to which Quebecois cuisine remains almost a gastronomic time capsule of ancient France. Nowadays, the French only use cinnamon in such homely puddings as apple compôte and rice pudding, having gradually dropped spices from meat dishes after the Middle Ages.)

Part and parcel of every rural holding in Quebec was the fruit and vegetable potager, complete with potting shed. There would be a table full of seedlings growing in tins, their bottoms pierced with holes and partially filled with potsherds for drainage, resting on saucers in order not to spoil the surface of the table when the seedlings were watered.

Laid out in rows marked with sticks and lines of scrap wool, the more delicate plants were staked with individual sticks, over which were placed, on nights when frosts threatened to strike, large paper bags saved from grocery purchases at the village general store. (People would even book these bags from the storekeeper in advance, or buy a few extra potatoes or turnips in order to ensure they were given one each visit).

Once harvested, the staple root vegetables – potatoes, turnips and carrots – would be stored in the *caveau*, a small cellar dug in a cool, dry, well-ventilated place not too far from the house (in order to remain accessible throughout the winter). These root vegetables were conserved in dry sand, while herbs, onions and cabbages were hung from ceiling beams. In particularly cold areas, cabbages were uprooted but left in the fields over the winter, to be brought in and thawed as needed. Beans and maize would be sun-dried and then stored in the loft, ready to be turned into solid stews with lard and molasses.

Quebec still has an annual glut of strawberries in July, and each year old ladies and little girls may be seen offering them for sale beside the road on the Ile d'Orléans near Quebec City, wearing the traditional headdress and costume of the Berry area. In the past, the surplus used to be made into jam. Since the advent of the freezer, however, French Canadians have discovered that by washing the strawberries and rolling them in caster sugar while still damp, then freezing them laid out on trays, the strawberries retain something of their texture once thawed – provided they are eaten quickly.

In contrast to the sturdy rustic cooking of the *habitants*, the seigneurial class, or the middle and upper classes of urban Canada, have always enjoyed a classical bourgeois French cuisine which is indistinguishable from France itself. As cooked in Montreal and Quebec City, dishes such as *coq au vin* and *boeuf bourguignon* are remarkable for their use of wine, an ingredient which, due to rigid government import controls on alcohol, was always beyond the pockets of most rural dwellers, who had to make do with their own rather dubious *vins maison* fermented from carrots, rhubarb, blueberries, dandelions and the like.

In the past, most restaurants in Montreal and Quebec City served classical French cooking rather than that of Quebec, although in the 1970s this began to change with the rise of Quebec nationalism, and today a handful of restaurants such as Aux Anciens Canadiens (housed in a 1677 stone cottage), specialize solely in *habitant* cuisine, with items such as cabbage soup, *darne de saumon en cidre* and maple sugar cake. The cheese boards of such restaurants are able to boast some cheeses of notable lineage. Oka, Quebec's most famous cheese, was developed by Trappist monks in Oka, and is similar in taste to the classical Port Salut of France – although it lost much of its character after the 1930s, when the federal government began to enforce a ban on the making of unpasteurized cheese. Another order of monks, the Benedictines in St-Benoît, invented a strongly seasoned, almost peppery blue cheese called Ermite, while the earliest and longest continuously made cheese has been Fromage Ile d'Orléans, made on the island by successive generations of the Aubertin family, beginning in 1679.

ST PIERRE AND MIQUELON

Nestled off the southern coast of Newfoundland are two tiny islands, St Pierre and Miquelon, which remain colonial possessions of France.

First claimed by Jacques Cartier in 1536, subsequently annexed by the British and returned to France in 1816, today the islands are Collectivités Territoriales and, as such, are only slightly lower in political status than the Départements d'Outre-Mer – the French West Indies, French Guiana and Réunion.

Cold, windswept, dominated by rocky hills, the islands do not lend themselves to large-scale agriculture, and the inhabitants have always supported themselves by fishing. The original settlers were Bretons, who were later joined by Normans and Basques. Coming from parts of France where fishing is second nature, these pioneers adapted themselves to the environment rather more easily than later arrivals from Poitou, Touraine and Charente – all people of the land and forest.

Until the beginning of the nineteenth century, the inhabitants benefited from the *rations du roi,* consisting of flour, lard, butter and oil, to which was added brown sugar and molasses imported from the French West Indies. These dry provisions, together with fish, game and a preponderance of potatoes, set the tone for the subsequent diet of the islands. As might be expected of a people engaged in heavy labour in the face of an adverse climate, their cuisine is equally heavy: plenty of slow-cooked ragoûts, fricassees, soups with dumplings and countless dishes which begin with a roux.

It was a frugal existence where nothing was wasted: during the fishing season, from May to September, all the unsaleable parts of the cod – the cheeks, tongues, hearts and livers – would be carefully collected, salted and kept in kegs along the walls of their tiny shingleboard cabins. In the past, stomach of cod stuffed with cod liver provided a dubious delicacy, and nor were the islanders averse to the fishy flavour of seagull. Even the bland-tasting starch of fern roots was extracted in times of need.

Throughout the long winter, families were confined to their cabins, typically very small. There were three rooms – a bedroom for the parents and another shared by the children, and a main room dominated by a cast iron stove set in bricks, with a flue of riveted sheet iron. Besides being used for cooking, the stove provided the heating and warmed the sand with which to fill sodden boots. There would be a few wooden chairs, perhaps a wooden rocking chair for an elderly family member, benches and a wooden table laid with an oilskin cloth. Behind the door would be hung fishing and hunting clothes and a gun, while along the walls there would be sideboards and cupboards, together with kegs of provisions such as apples and sugar. Jars of jam lined the shelves, and apart from a crucifix, the sole object of decoration might be a whatnot containing a few trinkets. Two small, multi-paned windows admitted a meagre amount of light, supplemented by a petrol lamp.

Come the spring, cabbages, carrots, onions and especially potatoes could be planted in the family garden. A common joke among the islanders concerns the mother who would boast that with a skylark and ten kilos of potatoes, she could feed a family of thirteen.

On Miquelon, cattle, sheep and even horses were kept for their meat, while in former times game also alleviated the monotony of the fish diet. Rabbits, and especially game birds such as bustards, wild geese, duck and snipe, are still shot today, and in the spring, ortolans provide a delicacy now forbidden by law in metropolitan France. However, the snow partridges which pass over the islands in winter are now left in peace, since the species is threatened with extinction. Indeed, wildlife in general has declined significantly on the islands, to the advantage of rats and fieldmice, introduced from shipwrecks. There are, however, still stocks of lobsters and crabs around the coasts, along with shellfish such as mussels, cockles and periwinkles, while in the late summer there is communal picking of wild berries, such as bilberries and whortleberries, all of which help to enliven an essentially spartan cuisine.

ACADIA

Although the Acadians of the Maritimes Provinces on Canada's Atlantic seaboard are French-speaking, they feel themselves somewhat removed in cultural background from Quebec. True, their ancestors came from similar, if not the same regions of France – from Normandy, Brittany and the neighbouring Poitou, from Santonge and the Atlantic fishing port of La Rochelle. Yet many traditional dishes of the Acadians are unknown to the Quebecois, having arisen as a response to their forbidding coastal terrain – and their distinctly troubled history.

It all began pleasantly enough in the spring of 1604, when a group of merchants sailed up the Bay of Fundy and selected a site for a settlement on the north bank of the Annapolis River in what is today Nova Scotia. The new colony was named Acadia. Others followed from France; dwellings were constructed, gardens planted, a trout pond established, a mill-wheel built for their grain. To allay the boredom of long winter evenings, the gentlemen established 'The Order of Good Times'. Each day in turn, one was responsible for the food and entertainment. The good times rolled, then abruptly ground to a halt when a raiding party from Virginia sacked and burned the buildings.

Worse was to follow. In 1713 France was forced to cede Acadia to the British, who insisted all Acadians sign an oath of loyalty in order to remain in the country. Most refused. Finally, after decades of bitterness, in 1755 the British expelled the Acadians from their homes, burned their villages, tore families apart and dispersed most of them among various British colonies further south, from Maryland to Georgia. Some went to the French West Indies, some to France, a great many to Louisiana.

Some Acadians made the mistake of trickling back to their old homeland after 1763, only to discover to their immense disappointment that in their absence New Englanders had swiftly occupied their farms, situated on the best land of Nova Scotia. The Acadians now had no option but to resettle the poorer areas of Nova Scotia, as well as the nearby Prince Edward Island, the Magdalen Islands and the shores of New Brunswick.

While the Acadians had some success in draining and diking the marshy soils, their repertoire of vegetables was severely restricted: potatoes were the staple, with grains (wheat, barley, oats, buckwheat) for bread and pancakes. When Diéreville wrote of the Acadian 'love' of turnips and cabbage in his *Relation du voyage du Port-Royal de l'Acadie ou de la Nouvelle-France* in 1708, he was probably referring more to a marriage of convenience than a heart-felt passion, since preservation practices of the time permitted the keeping of little else. Cabbages, he noted, were simply picked and left upside down in the field, where they froze of their own accord and were brought in to be thawed as required. Peas, corn and beans were dried in the attic, while potatoes, turnips and onions were kept in the basement or a special outhouse. These vegetables represented the sum total of the average Acadian potager until carrots, lettuce, tomatoes, beets and sweetcorn were introduced early in the twentieth century – although the vitamin intake was boosted by gathering wild plants such as marsh samphire and goosetongue greens, along with wild berries such as blueberries, partridgeberries and cranberries. Often the berries were made into jams in order to preserve them (a necessity in the case of the bakeapple, which resembles a large yellow raspberry but which is too tart and seedy to be pleasant raw). However, since sugar was a luxury, cheaper methods of preservation had to be devised: cranberries could be kept in their natural state or in cold water, while blueberries and apples could be sun-dried in well-lit attics. The apple was virtually the only fruit tree which would grow.

At times the villagers were so poor that a single bone might be passed around several families for the making of soup, the first family merely suspending the bone above the cauldron on the fire, so the fat and nutrients could drip down into the pot once the bone was heated. This was called *Soupe à l'ombre*, Shadow Soup. Another practice was to leave a pot of mixed vegetable soup on the woodstove while the family went to Mass on a Sunday. Such soup, which formed a complete meal, was often called, besides Sunday soup, *Soupe à n'importe quoi*, Soup with Just About Anything. Verily, we are not discussing haute cuisine.

Pigs provided the bulk of the meat, slaughtered during Advent at *les boucheries*, communal butchery-come-charcuterie sessions where the unspeakable parts of the animal were transformed into black puddings and brawns. Unlike similar *boucherie* sessions in sweltering French colonies such as Réunion and Louisiana, however, there was no pressure to preserve the larger cuts of meat by smoking or salting, since they only had to be placed in barrels and buried in the snow to freeze. Salt pork was made by choice rather than by necessity.

Cows were milked and oxen were used for haulage, only slaughtered at the end of their working lives. Sheep were raised for their wool but despised as meat, since Acadians complained the latter had the taste of the former.

The Acadians persisted with such traditional farming but eventually it proved too great a struggle. In time, those who had been forced to resettle into the poorer agricultural areas of the Maritimes after the expulsion were forced to shift their primary attention to hunting and fishing. There were rabbits and porcupines, duck, Canada goose and teal to be shot, and, in lean times, small birds such as skylarks, pigeons and blackbirds to be trapped. Above all, there were fish.

Until the 1960s cod was found in immense quantities along the Acadian coast. The fish were salted and laid out on screens, taking advantage of sun and the crisp, dry, ice-cold winds to cure the salt cod into stiff white boards, known simply as *morue*.

Every fishing village workforce was organized for the task: *le piqueur* cut open the stomach, *le décolleur* cleaned the fish and cut off the head, and *l'habilleur* removed the backbone. After spending several days in salt barrels, the fish were washed, drained and then dried on large screen tables called *galaires*. *Morue verte* ('green cod') was merely salted, without being dried, and kept for family consumption, as were all the odd parts of the fish – the tongues (said to taste like scallops), cheeks and sounds (glutinous bits from the back). On Prince Edward Island and in some parts of New Brunswick, the stomachs were stuffed with the cods' livers and boiled, as on the islands of St Pierre and Miquelon. Although a portion of the catch was kept for personal use, the bulk, once salted, was exported to Boston and the Caribbean, where it was formerly a mainstay in the diet of the French West Indies.

Herring, the other major catch, was either salted and dried, or smoked in the family *boucanière* – a little shack in the backyard, in which the salted herrings were hung over the smouldering sawdust of the spruce tree for weeks on end.

Considering that fish was part of almost every meal, and that the Acadians were sometimes dubbed 'fish-eaters', it might be assumed a rich repertoire of recipes would evolve – but it did not. There was, in fact, only one main recipe for fresh cod – simmering in water with salt, pepper and *herbes salées* (chopped shallots and chives or the green tops of spring onions preserved in rock salt, a common Acadian seasoning unknown in Quebec). For variation, potato might be boiled with the cod, while mackerel might be casseroled with onions and milk. For a 'treat', eel would be boiled with salt herbs and water, then made into a pie. As with other peoples possessing plain cuisines, the Acadians argued that first-rate ingredients need no masking with fancy sauces, which in the case of cod, had some justification. An Acadian, for example, would never dare serve day-old cod to guests, since a fellow Acadian would be able to discern the difference in flavour between day-old and fresh.

Lobster, until the establishment of a commercial industry in the early 1900s, was speared with a gaff at low tide. Until stocks declined and prices soared in the 1970s, lobster could be eaten more or less as and when the Acadians desired, which perhaps explains why it does not appear to have been greatly prized in Nova Scotia. Indeed, Helen Wilson, the daughter of a lobster fisherman, writes in her book *Tales From Barrett's Landing*: '. . . we ate lobster because we were poor. I remember that sometimes Mama put fresh boiled lobster in our school lunches and we always threw them away on our way to school. We were ashamed to let the other kids see them because they would know that we didn't have anything else to eat in the house.' This lends weight to sociologist Thorstein Veblen's scarcity theory of value, according to which objects increase in value in direct proportion to their perceived rarity, rather than intrinsic merit or interest.

Chicken is another case in point. In modern Western countries, industrialized farming has reduced this meat to the status of an everyday commodity, yet to the Acadians, as well as the Quebecois, chicken was once the ultimate luxury, virtually never killed and eaten until the *poulet* had matured into an elderly *poule*, her useful egg-laying years well behind her. As economic circumstances improved after the Second World War and chicken became common, the older generation maintained these 'blue chickens' were not as tasty as the hens of old.

Nowadays, hens are difficult to obtain, and chickens are commonly used for old Acadian specialities such as *fricot*. This soup of potatoes and meat or fish was traditionally considered party food, to the extent that a dinner invitation might be expressed as: '*Vous êtes invités au fricot!*' In the past, *fricots* were made of various game birds – duck, goose or pigeon, perhaps meadowlark or partridge. When fish formed the main ingredient, *fricot* was often called *tchaude* or *chaude*, a word which along with its New England counterpart, chowder, refers to the large cast iron pot, or *chaudière*, in which this hearty soup was cooked. The favourite *fricots*, however, were those cooked with beef, hare or chicken:

Fricot à la Poule
(chicken fricot)

1 large chicken, cut into pieces	1 tablespoon fresh summer or
2 tablespoons butter	winter savory, chopped
2 medium onions, diced	3 litres (5 pts) water
6 medium potatoes, peeled and	dumplings (recipe follows)
diced	salt and pepper

In a large pot, sauté the chicken in the butter until browned on all sides. Remove, then sauté the onion until it begins to brown. Add the potatoes, the summer savory and the water, then simmer for about 20 minutes. About 10 minutes before the end of cooking, add the dumplings and cook with the lid on the pot. Season to taste with salt and pepper.

SERVES 6.

Note: the dumplings can be omitted, in which case stir in 1 tablespoon flour while sautéing the onions.

Poutines
(dumplings)

100 g (4 oz or 1 cup) flour	½ teaspoon salt
1 teaspoon baking powder	125 ml (4 fl oz or ½ cup) water

Mix together flour, baking powder and salt in a bowl, then gradually mix in the water. With a teaspoon, break off pieces of the dough, form into balls, and drop into the soup.

Dumplings are an optional addition to a chicken *fricot*, but would invariably eke out a plain everyday *fricot* made with onions, potatoes, salted herbs and water, known jocularly as *fricot à la belette*, or 'weasel' *fricot* ('because the weasel went right on by'). At Christmas the dumplings are elaborated into *poutines rapées*, in which mashed and grated raw potato are combined and made into large balls with centres of fatty salt pork.

Another famous Acadian Christmas dish is a pie known variously as *pâte à la râpure, pâte râpé, chiard* or, in the English-speaking communities of Nova Scotia, rappie pie. It is a complicated dish which needs chicken, salt pork, pork fat, grated potatoes and onions to be authentic, but since salt pork is difficult to find and the result in any case tends to be rather too fatty for modern tastes, I present here a leaner reinvented version, using bacon:

Pâte à la Râpure
(rappie pie)

1 whole chicken, skinned and cut
   into quarters
3 onions, sliced
3 kg (6–7 lb) (about 12) potatoes,
   peeled

salt and pepper
250 g (8 oz) streaky bacon,
   chopped

Remove all fat from the chicken, place in a pot with the onion and barely cover with water. Simmer for 40 minutes, then strain off the broth and chop the chicken into smaller pieces. Boil the broth vigorously to reduce its quantity by half (this concentrates the flavour).

Grate the potatoes and squeeze through muslin to remove as much of their juice as possible. Sprinkle with salt and pepper. In a large ovenproof pot, sauté half the bacon to release its fat, then layer over half the potato. Moisten the potato with some of the chicken broth. Spread over a layer of chicken meat, then a second layer of potato. Pour over the remaining chicken broth and sprinkle the remaining bacon over the top. Cover and bake at 180°C (350°F/Gas 4) for 1½ hours.

SERVES 4 as a complete dinner, with steamed green vegetables or a salad.

A goose would be roasted on Christmas Day, and served along with hare stew, cakes and pastries. For the children, mothers would bake little biscuits shaped to represent the baby Jesus.

A white cake known as *galette des rois* eaten on Twelfth Night, 6 January, perpetuated an old French custom in that it contained a bean and pea (sometimes a black and a white button) symbolizing the king and queen, ready to be retrieved by two lucky people. This tradition was to find an even richer expression in Louisiana (see next chapter).

Easter Sunday may well have had sulphurous consequences for Acadian families, since they stockpiled eggs for a month in advance, then settled down on the day to eat the lot – boiled for breakfast, accompanied by ham or salt pork for lunch, made into omelettes and baked as flans with maple syrup for dinner.

A particular feature of Acadian weddings were the desserts. As a matter of pride, fifteen or twenty desserts, cakes and doughnuts would be put out for guests, with the centrepiece a rice and raisin pudding, symbolic of married life. There might also be home-made ice cream if the wedding were held in winter and ice was abundant, and delicious little apple- and cranberry-filled pastry balls known as *poutines à trou* – poutines with a hole. Such dishes gave a foretaste of the blossoming of Acadian cuisine in its new homeland of Louisiana. But only a soupçon of a foretaste, mind you, because if we are to be brutally honest, we must conclude that in its old form at least, Acadian cuisine seems more Scots Presbyterian than French Catholic in spirit: infinitely economical and sensible, certainly, but also just a wee mite grim.

4 Louisiana

THE CAJUNS

To see how fundamentally geography shapes a cuisine, you only need to compare the spartan, somewhat dour cooking of old Acadia in the icy wastes of Canada with the exuberant, hot and spicy cuisine that emerged when the exiled Acadians evolved into laid-back, fun-loving Cajuns amid the steamy heat of the bayous and backwoods of Louisiana.

Coming from the barren rocks and the blizzards of the north, the Acadians must have been amazed at the fecundity of the slightly creepy mossy overgrown swamps of the bayous, which immediately make you think of alligators and water snakes (with some justification!), yet are such a rich playground for hunters, fishermen and foodies, teeming as they are with edible wildlife: crawfish, a delicacy long appreciated by the French as *écrevisses*, along with fish and all manner of game, not to mention oysters, shrimp and crab.

Somewhere between 3,000 and 8,000 Acadians (historians disagree as to the exact figure) arrived in Louisiana between 1756 and 1805, most after the signing of the Treaty of Paris in 1763, which allowed all exiled Acadians then held in British colonies to regroup in Louisiana, at that time France's most important possession in the Americas.

Although they landed in New Orleans, the Acadians were not city folk, and immediately began spreading out into the hinterland, initially upriver in St James Parish. Later waves spread westward along the banks of Bayou Teche, to Bayou Lafourche just south-west of New Orleans, and along the thousands of inlets forming the vast Atchafalaya Basin. Today, Acadiana occupies roughly the southern third of the state of Louisiana, and while many of its inhabitants still prefer to be known as Acadians, over time the word got shortened to Cajun, coming to embody a caricature of the baseball-capped rustic, knocking back Wild Turkey and waltzing to black Creole zydeco music at a *fais-dodo*, or country dance.

Until the oil boom of the 1960s thrust Acadiana into the materialism of the twentieth century, providing instant riches for those whose land contained oil deposits, and work on the rigs for the others, the

Cajuns largely earned their living on small family farms. Having little money or formal education, or, indeed, ambition, they had to survive on what they could catch, trap or grow in their kitchen gardens, besides receiving a modest income from cash crops such as rice, beans, sugar cane or cotton. For their domestic requirements, they grew celery, onions and peppers, the so-called Holy Trinity of Cajun cuisine, along with tomatoes and parsley. Field gardens, containing several rows of each of the major staples, were drawn upon when guests and relatives arrived for dinner, which was frequently; Cajun hospitality is legendary.

In the early days, the Acadians carried on their old Canadian habits, flavouring their dishes with onion or shallot leaves preserved in salt, using molasses and maple syrup to season meat, and throwing the entire contents of their hunting bags together to make a *fricot*, always using a single giant black cast iron pot.

In many ways this pot, slung from a hook over the fire on the hearth of their cabin, its coating containing the ghost of many good meals past, provided a metaphor for the rough and ready nature of the cuisine, always noticeably more rustic, spicy and hearty than the refined, urbanized Creole cuisine of New Orleans. The components of Cajun main dishes were typically thrown together in this single iron pot, with the meat stewed in the soup. Some pots had legs and an indented lid designed to take glowing embers and thus provide top heat for baking cornbread. These were intended to be free-standing over an open fire at hunting camps.

The male-only hunting expedition remains very much alive in both urban and rural Louisiana today, and while the women may grizzle a little, it still provides so much obvious enjoyment and camaraderie for the men. True, they all disappear together for days if not weeks on end, but one really positive spin-off is that it reinforces their enthusiasm for cooking. Some Cajun men go so far as to say the cooking is as much of the experience as the actual hunt. It's certainly true that, unusually for the generations of males who grew up prior to feminism, Cajun men always placed a high priority on eating well and knowing how to cook, even if their skills have been geared more towards *charcuterie* and the smoking and barbecuing of meat and fish.

Anticipation of the hunting camp being half the enjoyment, there is always lengthy planning and preparation: the meticulous oiling and cleaning of shotguns, the packing of decoys, cooking gear and crockery emblazoned with flying ducks and hunting motifs – not to mention the cost of boat hire, licences, hunting rights to a particular piece of land, and of buying supplies of food, ammunition and liquor.

Since drinking and gambling are after-hunting distractions, it may be that the onions, peppers and celery are not chopped quite as finely as they might be for the *étouffée* but, never mind, the uneven chunks have their own charm as camp-style cooking, enjoyed all the more through being associated with a group of friends cooking together in the wilderness for the love of it. Nevertheless, any teenage boy going along on one of these trips with the older men for the first time had better know how to make a proper *étouffée*, for as part of his coming-of-age initiation he might well be asked to cook a meal for the whole group.

Even for a fifteen-year-old Cajun boy, who may have cooked his first fish when he was ten and his first duck gumbo when he was twelve, this amounts to a challenge, though he is certainly helped by the abundance of ingredients usually to be found in the camp larder. There might be wild duck, freshly caught oysters in the shell and a length of *andouille* sausage, for example, to stew together with some celery, onions, garlic, tomatoes and okra. A well-primed novice would also have been informed prior to setting out to the camp, that a meal is incomplete unless it contains at least four starches: typically, rice, potatoes, cornbread and sweet potatoes. To pass the test is to be welcomed into manhood; fail it, and you might never be asked to cook again!

It is circumstances such as these – a variety of game and seafood, but with only a single black pot in which to cook them – that gave rise to the most famous of all Cajun dishes, gumbo.

The natural successor to the *fricot*, gumbo is a soup, yet so thick and stew-like as to be served with rice. It may be thickened with okra pods or filé powder (never both) and a heavy roux, but modern versions are just as likely to omit all three of these.

Rather than view gumbo as a single recipe, it is best to think of it as a technique or category of dishes, arising out of Cajun thrift and the need to use up carcasses and spare the rubbish bin. Sometimes it appears the cook has simply emptied the contents of the bayou into a cauldron: shrimps, crawfish, crabs, oysters, terrapins and alligators. When the boys out in the marshes have been shooting straight during the breaks between restorative shots from the bourbon flask, there is also duck, guinea fowl, wild geese, wild turkey, deer, rabbit, plus the odd squirrel. Then of course there's chicken, ham, or if you prefer it, a little of the peppery smoked ham they call tasso. Such looseness would horrify the French and indeed just about anybody from the Old World, barring the Spanish.

Gumbo evolved during the eighteenth century, being well known and recognized by name in 1803, when twenty-four different gumbos (six or eight of them containing sea turtle) were served at a welcoming banquet held by the Spanish governor of Louisiana, when French envoy Pierre Clement de Laussat had been sent to prepare Louisiana for a French army of occupation.

About this time, gumbo appeared on the menu of the Café des Refugiés, New Orleans' first known restaurant. Doubtless the chef would have purchased supplies of filé powder from the French Market, conveniently located almost at the front door. Filé powder was brought there twice a week by the squaws of the indigenous Choktaws and Chickasaws, who had a cottage industry in gathering the young leaves of the sassafras tree, drying them, pounding them and passing them through a fine hair sieve. The powder was also sold as a tonic and a tea, though goodness knows who would drink it for the sake of its flavour, which is essentially non-existent. To keep the tourists happy, much of the filé powder sold in the historic French Quarter of New Orleans is now flavoured with a fair amount of thyme. Alas for the Chocktaws, who were 'resettled' in Oklahoma in 1803, filé powder production has long since passed into the hands of corporations.

Filé powder tends to be used in the more refined Creole cuisine of New Orleans, where there was not quite the same demand for, or access to game, and where gumbo is typically made with a light chicken or even vegetable stock. The Cajuns, on the other hand, consider filé far too insipid for their palates, preferring a hearty, smoky gumbo, dark with browned roux, spiced with tasso, and thickened with gluey okra. The name gumbo, in fact comes from a Portuguese corruption of *quin gombo*, which in turn is a corruption of *ki-ngomgo*, the indigenous word for okra in the Congo and Angola. The seeds were brought to the West Indies and thence to America by African slaves, smuggled, so the story goes, in their noses and hair.

Gombo z'herbes is a specifically African-American version of gumbo, derived from a soup of the Congo and a close relative of calalou (see page 29). The name is a Creole vernacular corruption of *gumbo*

1 Guadeloupe: Coconut seller,
Pointe-à-Pitre.

2 Martinique: Fish market,
Fort-de-France.

3 Guadeloupe: Selling the catch,
Pointe-à-Pitre.

4 Guadeloupe: Baguettes, Pointe-à-Pitre.

5 Martinique: Swordfish with Shrimp and Creole sauce, Hotel Diamant les Bains, Le Diamant. (p.12)

6 Martinique: Chef Jean Pierre St Aude making Court-bouillon Creole, Hôtel La Batelière, Fort-de-France. (p.13)

7 Martinique: Vivaneau (Caribbean red snapper) at the fish market, Fort-de-France.

8 Réunion: Tomato rougail. (p.59)

9 Mauritius: Mixed Vegetable Achard. (p.68)

10 New Orleans: French Market.

11 New Orleans: The Bistro at the Hôtel Maison de Ville. Louisiana Crawfish with a Spicy Aïoli and Vine Ripe Tomatoes. (p.136)

12 New Orleans: Broussard's Restaurant. Shrimp and Crabmeat Cheesecake Imperial with Roasted Red Pepper and Dill Cream. (p.139)

13 Vietnam: Coffee farmer sun-drying his crop, Central Highlands.

14 Vietnam: Catholic nunnery, Dalat.

15 Vietnam: French Colonial villa, Dalat.

16 Vietnam: Cabbage harvest, Dalat.

17 Tahiti: Mango seller, Papeete public market. (p.163)

18 Tahiti: Wild red mountain bananas, Papeete public market.

19 Tahiti: Raising of food from an earth oven, Maeva Beach. (p.170)

20 Marseilles: Produce stallholder in the North African quarter.

21 Marseilles: Fishmonger in the North African quarter.

22 Marseilles: Fishing boat leaving the port.

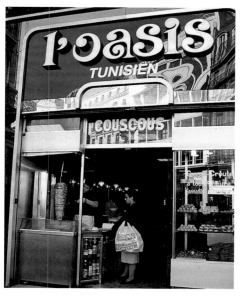

23 Marseilles: Tunisian restaurant on La Canebière.

24 Provence: Colonial spices at the Friday market, Arles.

aux herbes. It is a soup made only from green leaves and herbs, and because it is meatless, it is served in Catholic homes in New Orleans each Good Friday. According to Creole superstition, if you ate seven greens and met seven people during the day, you would have good luck in the year to come. Tradition also had it that for every green that was put into the gumbo, you would gain a new friend in the coming year.

I learned about gumbo in New Orleans from Etienne Dupépé Devlin, executive chef at his family-owned Hotel Provincial. Belying its Anglo name, the Provincial is a charming French-style hotel, with courtyards and annexes that ramble across an entire block in the French Quarter. The Dupépés emigrated from France and settled in New Orleans in the 1700s, though the father later returned to France, leaving behind his wife and his young son, who went on to found the American line.

Etienne grew up on a ranch, where African-American housekeepers cooked Creole-Cajun food handed down through six generations: fried chicken, smothered pork, beans and mustard greens stewed in bacon fat. 'Real healthy,' says Etienne with an ironic grin. He began cooking for family Thanksgivings – turkey with oyster 'dressing' (stuffing), sweet potato pie, turkey and pumpkin pie. 'But I didn't enjoy not knowing what I was doing', he says, and so he enrolled at the Culinary Institute of America, graduating in 1989.

Etienne Devlin's Gumbo

More properly, this should be called Miss Bella's gumbo, since the recipe was passed down to Etienne Devlin by an elderly woman ('the anchor of our family') who cooked for many years at the Hotel Provincial. At one stage, a 90-year-old, an 80-year-old and a 70-year-old all worked together in the kitchen. Miss Bella retired at the age of 92, and then only because she had to care for her 55-year-old son, who had suffered a stroke. 'Miss Bella, your life is over – not that you've got any left anyway – but it's over!' was Etienne's response when she announced this decision. ('We always used to talk to each other like this,' he explains).

The beauty of this recipe is its simplicity – no roux, and only one variety of seafood.

2 onions, diced
2 green peppers, diced

½ bunch (about 3) spring onions, chopped

1.5 kg (3 lb) okra, frozen or fresh

125 g (generous 4 oz) tomato
   purée

3 litres (5 pts) water

1 tablespoon mashed garlic

1 tablespoon garlic powder

2 good shakes of a Tabasco sauce
   bottle

salt to taste

750 g (1½ lb) shrimps, raw but
   peeled

½ bunch parsley, chopped

Over a high heat, sweat down the onions, green peppers and spring onions. Add the okra, and continue to cook the mixture over a high heat until the okra turns slimy. If the okra sticks to the bottom, don't panic, just scrape it off. 'That's flavour,' says Etienne.

Just before the okra begins to dissipate, add the tomato purée – 'for colour'. Add the water, garlic, garlic powder, Tabasco sauce and salt, bring to the boil and simmer for 1–1½ hours. 'You want to break up the okra a little – that's what thickens the gumbo,' says Etienne.

Add the shrimp, bring to the boil, cook only for 2–3 minutes. Add the parsley, and cool the gumbo without covering it. Don't eat it until the next day.
   SERVES 8.

Chicken and Okra Gumbo

1 small chicken, about 1.2 kg

1 tablespoon flour

6 tablespoons lard or oil

1 onion, finely chopped

1 green pepper, chopped

500 g (1 lb) okra, finely sliced

3 medium tomatos, chopped

Remove the fatty flaps from the rear of the chicken and discard. Cut the chicken into 8 pieces. Place in a plastic bag with the flour and shake well. Remove, shaking the excess flour off each chicken piece. Reserve this excess flour.

Heat half the lard or oil and fry the chicken pieces until browned. Remove and drain on absorbent paper. Add a tablespoon of flour to the lard or oil remaining in the pan (of which there should also be about a tablespoon). Stir over a low to medium heat until the mixture is pale nut brown. Set aside.

In a large pot (not black cast iron or the okra will be blackened) heat the rest of the lard or oil and sauté the onion and green pepper until softened. Add the okra and fry for several minutes longer, before adding the tomato and 1 litre (1¾ pts) of water. Simmer for an hour adding the chicken 20 minutes before the end. Serve with rice.
   SERVES 4.

The next recipe comes from my fellow New Zealander, Steve Logan, a chef and partner in one of Wellington's leading restaurants, Logan Brown. Logan formerly owned both a Cajun restaurant (Brer Fox) and a Creole restaurant (Laffite) in Wellington. To learn about gumbo, jambalaya and all that jazz, he made a pilgrimage to New Orleans in the late 1980s and sat at the feet of the master, Paul Prudhomme.

Ensconced for five days in Prudhomme's famous restaurant, K-Paul's Louisiana Kitchen, he watched with fascination as the portly Prudhomme drove around in his kitchen on a golf cart, followed by a woman with a clipboard and a phone. To see Prudhomme delicately chopping onions, he says, was an experience, since his fingers were the size of sausages. A passionate chef with a touch of volatility, Prudhomme pointed his finger at Logan and said: 'Don't you go back to New Zealand and say you worked here or were trained by me!', shouting, when Logan reacted with a nervous titter, 'Now you take me seriously, boy!'

Well, Logan never did make such a claim, but he had already learnt the art of the perfect gumbo and has used this recipe ever since. It is a classic gumbo, in that it uses the Cajun roux, made with oil rather than butter, and differing also from the French original in that it is cooked until dark brown.

Gumbo with Seafood, Smoked Sausage and Okra

Stock
Make 1.2 litres (2 pts) of good
    seafood stock using lobster
    heads, fish bones and clean
    vegetables

Roux
200 ml (7 fl oz) soy bean oil
75 g (3 oz or ¾ cup) flour

Vegetables
250 g (9 oz or 2 cups) onions, finely
    diced
75 g (3 oz or ¾ cup) celery, finely
    diced

1¼ cups green peppers, finely diced

Soup base
2 large cloves garlic, crushed
½ teaspoon cayenne pepper
½ teaspoon black pepper
½ teaspoon white pepper
½ teaspoon thyme leaves
2 teaspoons salt
2 bay leaves
400 g (14 oz) tin whole peeled
    tomatoes
1 tablespoon tomato paste

Other ingredients
A mixture of okra slices, smoked sausage, white fish, scallops, prawns, diced chicken, oysters etc. in proportions according to preference, totalling about 350 g (12 oz or 2 cups).
About 4–6 tablespoons hot cooked rice
spring onions and minced parsley to garnish

First make the roux. Carefully clean and dry a large, heavy-based pot and place on the stove. When hot, add the oil and heat until it starts to smoke. Carefully whisk in the flour one third at a time, always moving the roux to prevent burning. If it gets any black bits in it, throw it away and start again. (If this is the first roux you are making it may be wise to adhere to the traditional method, which is to begin by mixing the oil and flour together in a cold pan and cook on a low heat, which is safer but takes longer to produce the desirable dark red-brown colour.)

When the roux has gone a dark red-brown, turn off the heat and add half the diced vegetables while continuing to stir until the roux has stopped cooking. Set aside.

In a large pot, sweat the remaining vegetables, add the garlic and spices, and continue cooking for 2 minutes. Then pour in the stock. Crush the tomatoes in your hand and add, along with tomato paste.

When stock comes to the boil begin whisking in the roux a spoonful at a time, until the desired consistency is reached. Simmer for about 2 hours, regularly skimming off the oil. Add more stock if too thick. Check seasoning.

To finish, sauté okra slices, smoked sausage, white fish, scallops, prawns, diced chicken etc. Separate into bowls containing a generous tablespoon of hot rice. Add some raw oysters and pour some hot soup over everything.

Garnish with spring onions and minced parsley.
SERVES 4.

Writing about Louisiana cuisine is so frustrating because it all hinges so much on the unique richness and confluence of all this wild food. To know it, you really have to travel to Louisiana, where seafood forms the natural basis for the cuisine, and taste the shrimps, the crawfish and the scallop-sized lumps of crab meat yourself. Even if Louisiana could supply enough crawfish for the outside world in frozen form, for example, it would not be very satisfactory unless you were sure the crawfish were not more than two weeks old, otherwise the so-called fat (actually the liver and pancreas) in the head of the crawfish, considered by Cajuns to be the prized part for flavour and texture, would already have begun to taste rancid.

Because the crawfish is such a self-contained delicacy, the people of Louisiana have long been content to sit at a table with a pile on a newspaper, and shell, pick and eat their way through perhaps 15 lb at a time (this being the equivalent of a pound of pure meat). The same applies to crab.

The seafood boil is a well-established Cajun social event, where the men boil crawfish (cleaned of their mud beforehand) and crabs in outdoor cauldrons, often adding ears of corn, onions and potatoes, always flavouring the water with 'seafood boil' a commercial spice blend which typically contains mustard seeds, peppercorns, bay leaves, allspice, cloves, ginger and chilli.

The crab boil, the barbecue, the many public fairs and festivals celebrating crawfish, shrimp, catfish or frogs, and Acadiana's private dining clubs (whose members entertain the others once a year in their own homes) are all modern manifestations of Cajun conviviality. In the past, even work-related events turned into family gatherings, such as the shelling of peas and beans from the spring garden, seated under shade trees and accompanied by the exchange of jokes and gossip. More importantly, there was *la boucherie*.

As in other French colonies, the pig slaughter was a social event, although in Cajun country it was larger than usual, often involving a group of seven or ten families, each of which would take turns holding the *boucherie* at their farm, killing and processing up to five pigs at a time. These events took place most times of the year except summer, when the heat would have spoiled the meat before it could be processed. While the owner of the pigs would take most of the meat, everybody got a piece to take home, along with a can of lard.

Some of the pig was roasted or stewed for consumption on the day, with the unmentionable parts going into a big pot of soup, a *bouilli*, also for general consumption. The head and feet were kept to make *fromage de tête de cochon* – hogshead cheese, a porcine form of brawn. As in French Canada, the French West Indies and the islands of the Indian Ocean, the blood was collected and made into *boudin noir*. However, in Louisiana, *boudin noir* always took second place to *boudin blanc*, a sausage made from pork, liver and kidney, eked out with rice and onions, and flavoured with chilli. Finally, after the fat had been rendered down to make lard, the pork rinds would be cut into dice and fried as *gratons*, or crackling.

Today, with freezers and refrigerators in the homes, and large community meat lockers in country areas, the raison d'être for the *boucheries* has largely disappeared, along with the events themselves. However, they still occur, rather like a giant barbecue, with events such as the Louisiana Boudin Festival helping to keep the tradition alive.

The first Acadians learnt to grow corn from Native Americans, and to dry and grind the corn kernels into cornmeal. From the little Indian corn cake called *appone*, baked by covering with hot ashes, came cornpone, at its most basic level made simply with cornmeal and hot water, Indian-style. Later, cornpone incorporated lard and, eventually, milk, eggs and baking soda. From cornpone, it was a short step to corn bread.

Corn Bread

170 g (6 oz or 1½ cups) fine yellow cornmeal
100 g (4 oz or 1 cup) flour
1 teaspoon salt
3 teaspoons baking powder
½ teaspoon chilli powder
225 g (8 oz or 2 cups) freshly stripped or tinned whole kernel corn

215 g (7 oz or 1 cup) sweetened condensed milk
3 eggs, beaten well
60 ml (2 fl oz or ¼ cup) oil
110 g (4 oz or 1 cup) grated tasty cheddar cheese

Mix together cornmeal, flour, salt and baking powder. Add chilli powder, corn, condensed milk and beaten eggs. Mix well.

Heat the oil in a large heavy cast iron frying pan with a heatproof handle. Tilt the pan to completely coat the bottom and sides. Tip the excess oil into the batter and mix in. Pour half the batter into the frying pan, sprinkle over half the grated cheese, then spread over the batter and sprinkle the remaining cheese over the top. Bake at 140°C (275°F/Gas 1) for 45–50 minutes. Cut into generous wedges. Best eaten while still warm.

The Native Americans are also credited as the source of this recipe, which began as a means of storing corn for the winter in jars.

Maque Choux

12 ears fresh corn
50 g (2 oz or ¼ cup) butter
1 large onion, finely chopped
2 large green peppers, finely
  chopped
2 cloves garlic, chopped

4 large tomatoes, chopped
1 teaspoon salt
1 teaspoon ground black pepper
125–250 ml (4–9 fl oz or ½–1 cup)
  milk

Husk the corn. Place the corn cobs in a large bowl to catch the juices. Strip the kernels from the cob with a sharp knife, not cutting all the way into the core with the first stroke (in order to avoid getting whole kernels). Once stripped, extract any further 'milk' from the husks by scraping them with your knife. Set aside.

Melt butter and sauté onion and green peppers until they soften and the onion turns translucent. Add the garlic, tomatoes, salt and ground pepper, and the corn.

Cook, covered, on a low heat for 20 minutes, stirring from time to time and scraping the bottom of the pot. If the mixture begins to dry out, add the milk. Eventually the mixture should reduce to the consistency of a thick porridge.

SERVES 8.

Since the 1920s rice, and to a lesser extent wheat bread, have gradually supplanted corn and cornmeal as the foundation of the Cajun diet. A century after the British attempted – and failed – to grow rice in Virginia, it was introduced to the swamplands of Louisiana in 1718 by the grandly named Company of the West. It really took off after 1884, when mechanization rendered cultivation viable in the broad prairies of the Southwest. Today Louisiana is America's largest producer.

Dirty Rice

The 'dirty' aspect of this Cajun dish derives from the scattered pieces of chicken or pork liver which discolour the pristine whiteness of the rice. The recipe may be old, but the name is not: formerly, the dish was better known among Cajuns as rice dressing.

3 tablespoons oil
1 small onion, finely diced
1 small red pepper, finely diced
1 small green pepper, finely diced

3 cloves garlic, crushed
4–5 chicken livers, chopped
½ teaspoon sugar
¾ teaspoon dried thyme

¼ teaspoon ground allspice

¼ teaspoon ground mace

¼ teaspoon cayenne pepper

¾ teaspoon paprika

125 ml (4 fl oz or ½ cup) water or chicken stock

600g (1 lb 5 oz or 3 cups) cooked rice

Heat the oil in a large frying pan and sauté the onion and peppers until softened, which will take about 5 minutes. Add the garlic and chicken livers and stir-fry for 2 minutes.

Add sugar, thyme, allspice, mace, cayenne pepper and paprika, stir-fry for 30 seconds, then add stock or water. Mix in the rice and stir to heat through.

SERVES 4.

THE CREOLES

The urban refinement of New Orleans. While it admits the odd influence here and there from Spanish and Italian immigrants, Native Americans and African slaves, the foundations of Creole cuisine are unquestionably French.

So too, are the origins of Louisiana itself. Claimed for France by Cavalier de la Salle in 1682, it was a young but distinguished French Canadian, Baptiste Le Moyne, Sieur de Bienville, who ordered the clearing of forests and canes for the foundation of New Orleans in 1718. Appointed Royal Governor in 1722, one of Bienville's first challenges was to meet a delegation of fifty angry women pounding their frying pans with metal spoons and demanding he do something about their dreary diet of cornmeal mush. Bienville referred the women to his cook, a certain Madame Langlois, who restored calm by passing on the benefit of her cooking experience among the Choktaw Indians: the techniques of making corn bread, how to use powdered sassafras (filé powder) and how to best prepare the region's abundant seafood, fish and game.

The Ursuline nuns who arrived in 1727 to care for the sick and educate the young also learned from the Indians the use of cornmeal, and it was they who first concocted the delicately seasoned fried cakes they called *croquettes de maïs*, today better known as hush puppies. Their other great contribution to New Orleans cuisine was a form of confectionery: they adapted a recipe for almond *praline* from Orléans, France, substituting the locally plentiful pecans for the unavailable almonds. A herb garden planted for their hospital also had spin-offs for their kitchens, in the form of bay, marjoram, dill and oregano. Chervil was used to make vinegar, and coriander as a pastry flavouring.

A young Ursuline nun from Rouen, Marie-Madeleine Hachard, otherwise known as Sister Saint-Stanislaus, wrote a number of letters to her father soon after her arrival in 1727/8, which give an insight into the diet of the early inhabitants:

> Hunting, which begins in October, lasts all winter and is done at ten leagues from the city. Wild oxen are caught in large numbers . . . We pay three cents a pound for that meat and the same price for venison, which is better than the beef and mutton which you eat at Rouen . . . In fact, we live on wild beef, deer, geese and wild turkeys, hare, hens, ducks, teals, pheasants, partridges, quails and other fowl and game of different kinds. Wild ducks are very cheap . . . we buy few of them for we do not want to indulge in dainties. In a word, it is a delightful country all winter, and in summer, fish are very common and very good . . . The fish are prodigious in size and very delicious . . . There are none like them in France . . . We accustom ourselves wonderfully well to the wild foods of this country . . . and we are better off than we expected to be.

She also wrote of the magnificence of the local dress, of how everybody wore velvets and damask, despite such materials being three times what they cost in France.

When the Marquis of Vaudreuil became governor of Louisiana in 1743, he set up a miniature court, called Le Petit Versailles, with his high-born officers in uniforms of gold braid. This set the tone for much of the glittering New Orleans high life which was to follow, with parades, balls and banquets catered for by classically trained chefs brought out from France.

Meanwhile, French aristocrats, having been granted vast estates out in the Louisiana countryside by the king of France, began to establish their fortunes, first in indigo and tobacco, later in sugar, rice and cotton. From 1750 to 1760 the first great plantation mansions were built, stocked with French furniture and family silver.

These vast plantations were of course built on the labour of African slaves. Interestingly however, the slaves on the large estates fared better than those who ended up on the farms of poor whites, who themselves subsisted rather miserably. For both master and slave the daily diet was built around pork and maize, usually in the form of corn bread, served warm for breakfast, sometimes with salt pork crumbed in cornmeal and fried, along with potatoes and sweet potatoes. Sometimes, if the men had been out trapping or fishing the night before, there might also be fish, rabbit, opossum or racoon. Perhaps there might also be a dish made from the offal and entrails of a pig – crumbs, as it were, from the master's table. In such circumstances, soul food was born.

Lunch was brought in baskets out to the field, again comprising potatoes or sweet potatoes roasted in the embers of a fire, galettes of cornmeal, fried onions and pumpkin. For master and slave alike, dinner usually comprised the cold left-overs from lunch. If for no other reason than to serve the self-interest of the slave-owners in maintaining a healthy and efficient work-force, slaves were usually well fed, and despite persistent problems with bodily parasites, cases of vitamin deficiency and malnutrition were relatively rare.

For four to six days around Christmas, the slaves were allowed a holiday, and often the plantation owners would take it in turns to host a large Christmas dinner for the slaves from their own and neighbouring estates. Tables would be set up out in the open, and besides the usual pork and cornmeal products, there would be jams, compôtes and tarts. Sometimes a whole cow was roasted on a spit, and often there were roast turkeys, ducks and chickens. Invariably there would be singing and music, from the banjo and violin, and if the slave was lucky, he or she might receive a gift from the slave-owner, such as a sack of maize, a cooking utensil or a coloured neckerchief.

No sooner was this agricultural economy established, however, than Louisiana suffered a political upheaval: in 1762, facing defeat in the Seven Years War, Louis XV of France handed over Louisiana to his Bourbon cousin, Charles III of Spain, rather than cede the treasured colony to England. The action was also partly inspired by Louisiana's failure as a speculative venture.

Although the French colonists initially revolted (unsuccessfully) against Spanish authority, the thirty-eight years of Spanish rule in Louisiana proved remarkably benign. The Spanish intermarried with the upper reaches of French society (thus stabilizing the social and political atmosphere) and allowed the French to retain their language and customs. They gave this society its name, Criollo, meaning 'a native'. Transformed by the French into Creole, it originally referred only to those born in Louisiana, either of French or mixed Spanish and French ancestry. In time however, as in the French West Indies, 'Creole' also came to refer to people of mixed European and African ancestry, and to aspects of the culture such as cookery and music.

The most visible legacy of the Spanish period is seen in the architecture of the French Quarter in New Orleans – in the heavily walled brick buildings with wrought-iron railings, patios and courtyards, built after two great fires in 1788 and 1794 destroyed the French city of wooden cottages and houses.

However, there were Spanish culinary influences too. The taste for olive oil and chocolate became widespread, as did coffee, especially after the introduction of the Cuban-Spanish drip coffee pot, called the *greca*, which in Cajun-Creole parlance became known as the *grègue*. The Spanish pork sausage, *chorizo*, became rendered into *tchourisses* in the Creole dialect spoken by Africans, before settling into the *chaurices* as they are known in Louisiana today: sausages of pork or beef flavoured with cayenne (which gives them a red tint), garlic, thyme and allspice.

The barbecue, while never as popular in Louisiana as elsewhere in the American south, also dates from the Spanish occupation. Oranges became commonplace, as did aubergines (known to the Cajuns as *brème*, a corruption of the Spanish *berenjena*) while sugar cane, introduced by the Spanish from what is today the Dominican Republic, began to interest some planters. The Cajun taste for spices may also date from this era. Perhaps the most famous Spanish introductions, however, were two rice dishes: jambalaya, and red beans and rice.

Red 'n' Rice – red beans and rice – is still regarded with huge affection in New Orleans. Upon its introduction in the late eighteenth century the city's inhabitants initially first referred to the dish as *Moros y Cristianos* – Moors and Christians – a name borrowed from Cuba and still applied there to a closely related dish of black beans and rice. For all its homely simplicity – it amounts to little more than red kidney beans stewed with a ham bone and vegetables, then served with rice – the dish is found on the menus of scores of cafés around the city, and in a few plush hotels too.

'We used to cook it for our employees each Monday, but now we find our customers in the Rib Room asking for it,' says Raymond Toups, executive chef at the Omni Royal Orleans Hotel. This Monday custom is rigidly adhered to in New Orleans, with many restaurants offering the dish on that day only. 'If there is a major baseball game screening on television on a Monday night, you can bet 90 per cent of the bars and cafés here will be offering red beans and rice,' says Toups.

So why Monday in particular? The usual explanation is that Monday used to be wash day in New Orleans, so housewives had no time to cook, preferring to leave a pot of beans simmering away for hours on the stove, to look after itself.

'How true that legend is, I don't know – there's no way to trace its accuracy,' says Gene Bourg, food historian and erstwhile restaurant critic for the city's *Times-Picayune* newspaper. But he does point out that Sunday dinners were traditionally elaborate in New Orleans, so there might well have been the urge to serve something simple the next day. Furthermore, baked ham was a common Sunday luxury, so a nice meaty ham bone would often be left over for Monday.

It is also necessary to remember that 'wash day' was not just a matter of flicking on a washing machine. It was an arduous, all-day affair, involving soaking, scrubbing on a washboard, then further dipping in water with bluing or starch, and from time to time boiling up white shirts and sheets to restore their colour. So the 'cook's day off' story probably does contain a kernel of truth.

Louisiana is too hot to grow kidney beans successfully, though drying and packing them has been a local industry since 1923, and the red bean has become something of a leitmotiv for New Orleans. The *Times-Picayune*, for example, awards beans rather than stars for its restaurant ratings, and in a subtle adaptation of French tradition, the woman who finds the gold kidney bean is nominated Queen of the annual Twelfth Night Revellers Carnival Ball.

Everybody has their own way of cooking red beans and rice, and everybody else's is wrong – which is another way of saying there is a great deal of latitude in the ingredients list. Hot and spicy sausage is a common addition, but this is not necessary if you use a ham bone or bacon hock.

Red Beans and Rice

500 g (1 lb) red kidney beans
4 tablespoons butter
1 onion, chopped
1 carrot, chopped
2 sticks celery, chopped

1 meaty ham bone or bacon hock
3 tablespoons tomato paste
  (optional)
3 bay leaves
2 cloves garlic

10 cm (4 in) piece of pepperoni or   salt and pepper
    other spicy sausage, sliced
    (optional)

Soak the beans for 3–4 hours (you can get away without soaking, but you have to cook the beans for 1–2 hours longer). Drain the beans, place in a pot, and cover by about 5 cm (2 in) of water. Boil gently for at least 2 hours, stirring occasionally to avoid sticking, until the beans are soft and mushy. You may have to add more water during cooking.

After the first hour, melt the butter in a frying pan and sauté the onion, carrot and celery until tender. Add to the beans along with the ham bone or bacon hock, tomato paste (if using) and bay leaves. About 10 minutes before the end of cooking, add the garlic and spicy sausage (if using). Add a little hot water if the mixture seems too dry. Season with pepper to taste at the end of cooking; if you have used a bacon hock, it will almost certainly not need extra salt. The beans should be partially broken up, and have a creamy consistency.

Just before serving, remove the bone. Cut off and chop any meat, then stir it back into the beans. Leave in the bay leaves – good luck is supposed to fall upon whoever finds them in their portion. Serve with plain boiled rice. SERVES 6.

Note: this is even better made a day ahead and reheated, and it also freezes well.

The last words belong to Louis Armstrong, who signed off his letters: Red Beans and Ricely Yours.

Add to Louisiana rice the ham or bacon of the hog (which historically was favoured over cattle and sheep in the south because of its ability to root up the undergrowth and live off wild vines, nuts and berries) plus the abundance of seafood, and you have the makings of a jambalaya.

While jambalaya may owe something to joloff rice (see page 233), a dish brought to Louisiana by slaves from Senegal, its more obvious ancestor is the Spanish paella. A jambalaya tends to be less cluttered with ingredients than a paella (and more attractive for that reason if made from delicately flavoured seafood) and unlike the paella, is not coloured yellow with saffron.

The name jambalaya is thought to be derived from *jambon*, the name for ham in French and, almost, in Spanish, to which was added *a-la-ya*, an African expletive which denotes either acclaim or scorn.

Jambalaya

Stock
1 chicken (an old boiling fowl),
   skinned
1 large onion, roughly chopped
1 stick celery, roughly chopped
bunch of celery leaves and tops
1 carrot, roughly chopped

Jambalaya
125 g (4½ oz) bacon
a little oil
1 large onion, finely diced

2 green or red peppers, diced
250 g (8 oz) short-grain rice
400 g (14 oz) tin whole tomatoes in
   tomato juice
5 cloves garlic, chopped
½ teaspoon dried thyme
1 teaspoon salt
dash of chilli sauce
3 bay leaves
400 g (14 oz) mixed seafood
   (choice of prawns, shrimp,
   crawfish, crab meat or lobster)

Place the stock ingredients in a pot, cover with water, bring to the boil, skim off the scum. Reduce the heat and simmer, covered, for at least an hour, preferably three or four. Strain off the stock (the chicken meat can now be fed to your cat) and measure. If there is more than 300 ml (½ pt), reduce it down to 300 ml (½ pt) by boiling, uncovered.

To make the jambalaya, cut the fat from the bacon. Chop it finely, and fry over medium heat in a heavy pot smeared with a little oil, until the fat has been rendered down. Add the onion and peppers, along with the lean bacon meat, also chopped finely. Fry for 6–8 minutes.

Add the rice and stir until the grains are coated with oil, then pour in the stock. Add the tomatoes and their juice, the garlic, thyme, salt, chilli sauce and bay leaves. Bring to the boil, cover and simmer for 20 minutes. About 5 minutes before the end of cooking, fold in the seafood.

Serve either directly from the pot or pile high on a heated platter.
SERVES 4.

Jambalaya of Fowls and Rice

Cut up and stew a fowl; when half done, add a cup of raw rice, a slice of ham minced, and pepper and salt; let all cook together until the rice swells and absorbs all the gravy of the stewed chicken, but it must not be allowed to get hard or dry. Serve in a deep dish. Southern children are very fond of this; it is said to be an Indian dish, and very wholesome as well as palatable; it can be made of many things.

La Cuisine Créole, Lafcadio Hearn, 1885.

During the French Revolution many aristocrats found asylum by moving to Louisiana, escaping the guillotine which was the fate of Louis XVI and his queen Marie Antoinette. Despite the news of his death being greeted by some in New Orleans by the singing of 'La Marseillaise' and the shouting of revolutionary slogans, the Spanish governor and his troops kept order. Indeed, the Spanish government itself extended the invitation to the aristocrats to move to Louisiana.

In what many hoped would be a temporary arrangement, these aristocrats settled both in New Orleans and on Bayou Teche, where they established the colony of St Martinsville. They brought not only their taste for fine dining, but their chefs. Kitchen brigades were set up, gigantic roasting spits were built, and béchamel and other sauces introduced into the Creole repertoire.

Many of the now jobless chefs to the former aristocracy also moved independently to New Orleans after the revolution, where they established coffee houses, precursors to the cafés and restaurants of today.

New Orleans' first known restaurant, the Café des Refugiés, was begun at the turn of the eighteenth and nineteenth centuries, by and for refugees from the slave uprising in what is now Haiti. Among these Haitian newcomers were descendants of prominent French families such as that of the bird artist John James Audubon, and they contributed much to the intellectual life of New Orleans.

In addition, African cooks arrived from Haiti with their French employers. Already familiar with the fish and seafood which New Orleans had to offer, these Haitian cooks also introduced the skills of drying and smoking fish, making desserts from bananas, and juicing fruits to make planter's cocktails. It was also thanks to them that the Creoles of Louisiana became familiar with chayotes (christophines, or mirlitons, as they became known), vanilla, avocados and rum.

All these elements had coalesced into Creole society by 1803, when Spain ceded Louisiana back to the French, who in turn promptly sold the state to the Americans under the Louisiana Purchase.

Although the Creoles resented becoming *Américains*, the period from 1800 to 1860 proved to be the most prosperous in their history. The fortunes being made in the rural cotton, sugar and rice plantations had huge benefits for the commercial life of New Orleans, in the form of banks, brokerage firms and export houses. Haughtily refusing to take off their coats and sit behind desks, the Creoles conducted most of their business informally, in coffee houses and bars, or 'exchanges' as they were called.

A plantation owner, headed for New Orleans to arrange the sale of his cotton, would board a Mississippi steamboat, taking a first-class cabin for himself. The other classes reflected the prevailing hierarchy: second class would be occupied by children and their white governesses, along with officers of the steamship company; third class was for poor whites, fourth for white servants, and fifth for blacks, whether free men or slaves. The food, which in first class was nearly as good as on land, would be served in the dining room adjacent to the bar and the smoking room.

Some Creoles were descendants of both the French and the Spanish aristocracy, with ancient coats of arms and vast land holdings. The family tree meant everything, and their social gradations were as intricate as the Hindu caste system: descending in order beneath the Creoles, were Chacks, Chacas, Catchoupines, Chacalatas (considered rustic yokels), Bambaras and Bitacaux (both labouring classes); at the bottom of the heap were the Cachumas, who had African ancestry.

For those with names like de Marigny, de Mandeville, Villerès and Livaudais, life in the French Quarter was an incessant round of soireés, held in their dining rooms beneath brilliant chandeliers, where guests would sit on gilded chairs around a table spread with richly embroidered cloth, and eat *daube froide, vol-au-vents* and *petits fours* laid out on Limoge porcelain and English silver. Fine old burgundies and bordeaux would be served in glasses of delicate crystal. During the hot summer months a slave, often the son of the cook, would stand to one side, pulling the rope which operated the overhead fan known as the *punkah* – an import from British India.

More importantly, there were grand public occasions – the nights at the French Opera House, the races, the banquets and the balls. In 1838 the city saw its first Mardi Gras parade, with clowns and knights on horseback, and queens riding decorated carriages. Originally an excuse for gustatory excess before the onset of Lent, Mardi Gras today combines the best of both worlds – an occasion for feasting without the subsequent fasting.

Out in the kitchen, the preparation of the food for all this feasting and festivity was almost exclusively left to African cooks, some of whom might stay with the same family for a lifetime, finally being buried in the family tomb at St Louis Cemetery. Having been denied the skills of literacy, these cooks had little use for the American cookbooks which began to emerge in the first half of the nineteenth century (such as Catherine Beecher's *Domestic Receipt Book* of 1846), relying instead upon recipes handed on by word of mouth from friends or members of the employer's family.

On the plantations, the cookhouse was generally a separate building, situated some distance behind the main house, in order to minimize the fire risk as well as odours and noise. The cookhouse, which on larger plantations might include a separate smokehouse and dairy, was dominated by a single large fireplace, in front of which would be spits for roasting meat. All about were the mortars and pestles, ladles, skimmers, fish kettles, pots and cauldrons necessary for large-scale entertaining, while from the rafters hung whole hams and bunches of dried herbs.

The planter's day generally began early with coffee and biscuits, served in his bedroom. After returning from an inspection of his fields at around 9 a.m., *déjeuner* would be served – egg and bacon or ham, cornmeal muffins or 'corndodgers', perhaps also fish, shrimps or veal. On account of its toughness, meat was usually boiled before roasting. After the main course, jams and preserves would be laid out, the meal finishing with fresh fruit. In the early days, wine might be drunk at this hour, although under English influence towards the end of the eighteenth century, tea became more common.

Lunch, or *dîner* as it was called, was served late – between 2 p.m. and 3 p.m., following the Spanish custom. The most lavish meal of the day, it comprised soups, crustaceans, fish, meat, vegetables, tarts and desserts. Often one or two slaves had the daily task of supplying game for the master's table.

By contrast, dinner, or *souper*, was usually much lighter, usually comprising cold left-overs, perhaps with freshly made corn bread, and perhaps eaten informally, from a tray set out on the verandah.

This way of life ended abruptly with the American Civil War. At first, food supplies were not affected, but with the men gone off to war, most slaves fled. The sugar plantations were abandoned and women took over the roles of market gardeners, hunters, housekeepers and eventually nurses for the infirmaries which were set up for wounded soldiers in the plantation mansion houses.

Supplies of sugar dried up, and so too did coffee, the roasted seeds of the persimmon, the melon and the okra providing fairly unconvincing substitutes. Beer was also made from persimmons, as it had been in previous centuries by the Native Americans, while teas were concocted from holly leaves and sassafras root. The quality of the pork got steadily worse, until it too, became unavailable and all that was left were chicken and game. As pressure on natural resources increased, the wild turkey was driven almost to extinction and duck populations were severely reduced. Small game, however, remained in large numbers.

In the wake of the defeat of the Confederate South, the Creoles were ruined. Ironically, the African slaves, on whose behalf the war had been fought, found themselves even worse off than before. With the plantations in tatters, banks and brokerage houses in New Orleans went bankrupt. As much as the Creoles might continue to control the social life of New Orleans, the Americans were now clearly in the ascendancy, both in financial and in political life.

In the mid-nineteenth century, other immigrants began to assert their culinary influence. The Irish, driven from their homeland by the potato famine, brought their love of the potato and cabbage with them, turning them into boxty and colcannon. A traditional dish known as *cruibins* struck a note among the city's African Americans, being very similar to their pig's feet stew. In the late nineteenth century Germans established New Orleans as a major brewing centre and opened restaurants, introducing the city to potato dumplings, apple *streusel* and a variety of sausages, such as *blutwurst*, *leberwurst* and *braunschweiger*.

A wave of Sicilians in the early twentieth century arrived in such numbers that they were not absorbed into the French culture of New Orleans as earlier Italians had been. In 1919 the city's first Italian restaurant, Turci's Italian Garden, opened on Decatur Street, offering tagaliatelle, ravioli, cavatoni, veal cutlets *alla milanese*, as well as risotto – a dish which was not seen again on New Orleans restaurant menus until the 1980s. Italian market gardeners supplied the city with the so-called Creole tomatoes – not a specific variety but full of sun-ripened flavour, grown in the fertile soil of the Mississippi delta.

In 1900 Salvatore Lupo, proprietor of the Central Grocery in Decatur Street, established a custom of giving Italian farmers a piece of round bread, known in Sicily as a *muffuletta*, along with little bowls of olive salad, salami and cheese. Balancing these ingredients awkwardly on their knees, there were a number of spillages before Lupo had the idea of putting the ingredients *inside* the bread. Thus the muffuletta sandwich was born. Today, it typically contains marinated olives, mortadella, ham and mozzarella, although, this being America, all sorts of unusual ingredients, including soft-shelled crabs, may now be included.

Croatians from the Dalmation coast in the former Yugoslavia, who had been avid shellfish gatherers since Roman times, settled happily in Louisiana and began working the oyster beds as early as the 1840s. Their descendants continued to dominate the oyster industry until the 1950s, and even today names like Mandich, Uglesich, Cvitanovich and Vuskovich still operate some of New Orleans' best known seafood restaurants and oyster houses. At oyster bars such as the Acme in the French Quarter, customers stand at a marble bar with an ice cold glass of beer and concoct their own sauce from an array of seasonings (horseradish, tabasco sauce, tomato ketchup, oil) while oyster shuckers steadily extract oysters from their shells – on average 5700 a day.

Perhaps the greatest tribute to the Creole cooking of New Orleans is its durability. As food fashions come and go, the French Quarter's grand old restaurants carry on as they always have – in some cases for more than a century. Indeed, the oldest of them all – Antoine's – also has the distinction of being the oldest restaurant in America. Founded in 1840, its menu is interesting for archaeological reasons. Having changed little since 1880, the bill of fare affords a rare insight into what was eaten in New Orleans in the nineteenth century. Written entirely in French, it lists all the dishes which have become by-words for Creole cuisine, such as oysters rockefeller, Creole gumbo and Creole bouillabaisse.

Bouillabaisse

New Orleans in the spring time – just when the orchards were flushing over with peach-blossoms, and the sweet herbs came to flavour the juleps – seemed to me the city of the world where you can eat and drink the most and suffer the least. At Bordeaux itself, claret is not better to drink than at New Orleans . . . Claret is, somehow, good in that gifted place at dinner, at supper, and at breakfast in the morning . . . At that comfortable tavern on Pontchartrain we had a bouillabaisse than which a better was never eaten at Marseilles: and not the least headache in the morning, I give you my word; on the contrary, you only wake with a sweet, refreshing thirst for claret and water.

William Makepeace Thackeray, *The Roundabout Papers*, 1856.

While modern versions of Creole bouillabaisse spill forth with luxuries such as shrimps, oysters, crabs and crawfish, the bouillabaisse eaten by Thackeray at Boudro's Restaurant would have been a more restrained affair, consisting of only two species of fish, red snapper and redfish. Furthermore, the original New Orleans Creole bouillabaisse was a dish of marinated, pre-cooked fish with sauce, rather than the fish cooked in broth of the more familiar Marseilles version.

Creole Bouillabaisse

1 large fish head and carcass
1 onion
1 carrot
1 stick celery
3 bay leaves
1 kg (2 lb) fish fillets, preferably of more than one species
salt and pepper
2 teaspoons fresh thyme, finely chopped
2 bay leaves, very finely chopped
1 tablespoon parsley, finely chopped

2 cloves garlic, finely chopped
½ teaspoon ground allspice, very fine
3 tablespoons olive oil
1 large onion, finely chopped
125 ml (4 fl oz or ½ cup) sherry
250 ml (9 fl oz or 1 cup) tomato pulp
juice of ½ lemon
pinch of saffron
buttered French bread

Place the fish head and carcass in a large pot, add the onion, carrot, celery and bay leaves, and barely cover with water. Bring to the boil and boil for 20 minutes. Strain off the stock, discard the solid matter, return to the pot, and boil until reduced to about 500ml (a scant pt).

Meanwhile, rub the fish fillets with salt, pepper, thyme, bay leaves, parsley, garlic and allspice.

In a very large pot, large enough to take all the fish at once without overlapping, fry the onion in the olive oil until transparent, then add the fish and gently fry (or 'smother', as the Creoles would say) the fish, with the lid on the pot, about 5 minutes per side. Add the sherry, tomato pulp and lemon juice to the reduced stock, and bring to the boil to evaporate the alcohol from the sherry.

To serve, place a piece of buttered French bread in each bowl, and over it place a piece of cooked fish. Ladle over the reduced broth and sprinkle with saffron (either whole strands, or ground to a paste with a little of the sauce in a pestle and mortar).

SERVES 4.

Antoine's founder, Antoine Alciatore, was a wool merchant's son. He had apparently cooked in a restaurant in his native Marseilles, where, the story goes, he received praise from the statesman Tallyrand for his beefsteak. Reaching New Orleans at the age of twenty-seven, however, he discovered that despite the many public ballrooms and large hotels in the French Quarter, the restaurant as such did not exist. Apart from one or two of the larger hotels, the only institutions serving meals were saloons and boarding houses. Alciatore followed suit and opened a boarding house, but as the fame of his cuisine grew, he moved to grander premises, eventually settling in its present location at 713 St Louis Street.

Antoine's had its heyday during the 1880s, under the ownership of Aliciatore's son Jules. Noticing that the *escargots bourguignonne* – snails in a thick purée of greens – were not selling well, Jules ordered that the snails be substituted with oysters in the half-shell. Somebody remarked that the new dish would be rich enough to satisfy a Rockefeller, and oysters rockefeller was born. To this day, the restaurant has refused to divulge the recipe, but it hardly requires the intellect of an Einstein or the palate of an Escoffier to discern that oysters rockefeller comprises oysters grilled beneath a thick buttery purée of spinach (along with a little spring onion, celery, parsley and perhaps lettuce) flavoured with Pernod or some such anisette, Worcestershire sauce, chilli and perhaps a soupçon of anchovy.

Just as Antoine's was about to reach its zenith, another restaurant opened at the opposite end of the scale, in a squalid back street building at 160 Dryades, on 2 March 1879. This was The Hard Times, offering all dishes for five cents, and 'everything half the price of the markets.'

The Hard Times was the bizarre brainchild of the writer-journalist Lafcadio Hearn, author of *La Cuisine Créole*, the original Creole cookbook, who led a miserably poor life in New Orleans. Hearn believed that money could be made in New Orleans out of the poor, but he was never given the time to test his theory, for just twenty days later, his business partner decamped with what little cash they had, along with the cook; whereupon Hearn returned to the work he did best – writing newspaper columns and books.

One step up from The Hard Times were the solid bourgeois meals offered at Madame Bégué's, by the madame herself, a German who had married a French restaurant-bar owner. Known especially for her hearty breakfasts, she began to challenge the supremacy of Antoine's.

Even more traditional than Antoine's, and also still in existence today, is Galatoire's, which opened its doors in 1905. Famous as the restaurant which refuses to take reservations, its pavement queues are one of the lunchtime sights of the French Quarter. The old Southern gentry haughtily stand in line, champing at the bit, while over the road a ragged hobo might be sitting on the pavement swigging his eye-opener. Inside, much of the attraction lies in the brass coat hooks, the mirrors and the waiters in 1950s dinner suits whose chatty familiarity borders upon condescension, although admittedly the fantastic food does help. One of the house specialities is shrimp served with a Creole interpretation of rémoulade.

Sauce Rémoulade

The classical French prototype of this flavoured mayonnaise contains capers and anchovy (and assuredly no celery or chilli!). In addition to shrimps, rémoulade may be served over pan-fried fish or with cold meat.

1 clove garlic	2 tablespoons chopped gherkin
1 egg	2 tablespoons chopped parsley
250 ml (9 fl oz or 1 cup) light olive oil	1 tablespoon mild Dijon-style mustard
salt	½ chilli, finely chopped
3 tablespoons tarragon vinegar or lemon juice	ground black pepper
	1 stick celery, finely chopped

Drop the peeled garlic clove into a running food processor. Turn off and add the whole egg. Turn on again and wait until the egg is beaten, then begin to pour in the oil, in a very slow but steady stream. At first, the stream should be needle thin, but after half the oil has been added and the mayonnaise shows signs of thickening, the rest can be added in a thicker stream. Finally, pour in the vinegar or lemon juice. Once the mayonnaise is made, turn off the machine. Add the remaining ingredients and use the pulse button of the food processor to fold them in.

Typical of classical New Orleans restaurant cooking is this rich and complex dish wrought from simple ingredients:

Pan-fried Fish with Maître d'Hôtel Sauce

1 whole fish about 1 kg (2 lb), scaled and gutted	1 tablespoon flour
1 onion, roughly chopped	juice of ½ lemon
1 carrot, roughly chopped	1 egg yolk
1 tablespoon butter	2 tablespoons chopped parsley
	salt

Skin and fillet the fish. Make a fish stock: place the head and carcass in a medium-sized pot, add onion and carrot, pour over water to barely cover. Cover with a lid and bring to the boil, reduce the heat a little and simmer, uncovered, for 20 minutes. Strain, and if there is more than about 500 ml (1 pt), return the stock to the pot and boil to reduce.

Melt the butter in a saucepan, stir in the flour and simmer gently for several minutes. Add the fish stock and lemon juice, bring to the boil, stirring, and simmer for 8–10 minutes.

Meanwhile, place the fish fillets in a plastic bag with flour, shake to coat them, then fry on both sides, allowing about 4 minutes per side.

When the fish is nearly ready, remove the saucepan of sauce from the heat and stir in the egg yolk, beating with a whisk or a fork, until the mixture is slightly thickened. Stir in the chopped parsley, add salt to taste, and pour over the cooked fish fillets.

Co-existing with the grand restaurants built on the French model are a great many small neighbourhood restaurants and cafés, often owned by African-Americans. These cafés were the mainstay of New Orleans throughout the dark years of the Great Depression and the Second World War. Often oriented more towards the lunchtime trade, they offered – and still offer – the humbler staples of the Creole repertoire: red beans and rice, jambalaya, corn bread, fried chicken. Dooky Chase, opened in 1941 and today operated by Leah Chase, daughter-in-law of the original owners, is a good example. Another is Dunbar's, serving classic gumbo, crawfish étouffée, and peppers stuffed with rice, pork and shrimp.

In the 1950s an old Irish New Orleans family, the Brennans, emerged as innovators, soon gaining international fame for their restaurant, Brennan's, by offering creations such as Crêpes Fitzgerald, filled with cream cheese and sour cream and drizzled with crushed strawberries flambéed in kirsch. Bananas Foster, their invention named after the owner of a local awning company, has today been enshrined as the most famous dessert in the Creole repertoire. Essentially it comprises cinnamon-flavoured bananas flambéed with dark rum and banana liqueur, served with a scoop of vanilla ice cream.

Emboldened by the success of Brennan's, the Ponchartrain Hotel's Caribbean Room also began pushing the boundaries with their variation on Sole Véronique – a dish so out of fashion since the 1960s that it today qualifies as retro chic.

Trout Fillets Véronique

Sole Véronique is, of course, from the classical French repertoire. As the use of trout in this spicy Creole version indicates, the technique can be adapted to a wide variety of fish, the only requirement being that the flesh is sufficiently firm to withstand poaching.

1 kg (2 lb) trout fillets or other firm fleshed fish

500 ml (scant 1 pt or 2 cups) off-dry white wine, e.g. riesling

4 whole dried allspice berries, bruised with a pestle

4 peppercorns, bruised with a pestle

6 whole cloves, bruised with a pestle

2 bay leaves, whole
grapes to garnish

Hollandaise sauce
4 egg yolks
250 g (8 oz) butter
2 tablespoons white wine vinegar

First make the hollandaise: have the four egg yolks sitting in a food processor or blender. Use a very small saucepan, preferably of cast iron (to retain the heat off the stove) and with a lip for ease of pouring. Heat the butter until very hot – boiling and bubbling.

When the butter is coming to the boil, turn on the food processor and start the egg yolks beating. Wait until the butter is bubbling furiously but not smoking (although with practice, you can let the protein begin to brown without burning).

Hold the still-bubbling and boiling butter over the feed tube of the processor (or the central hole in a blender). Start pouring in an even dribble, about the thickness of string, and continue pouring in an even stream until the pan is empty.

By gradually adding the piping-hot butter, you cook the egg yolk just sufficiently. Keep the motor running while you heat the white wine vinegar in the same pan you used for the butter. When boiling, dribble this slowly into the moving sauce in the same way.

The result should be a very respectable chef's hollandaise, velvety without being too thick, coating the back of a spoon. Set this aside, but every so often give it a short whizz with the pulse button – I have known hollandaise to spontaneously 'split' (curdle), just sitting on a bench after cooking.

So far, I've never suffered a failure by this method, which I wish I had known when I was a chef, freaking out with whisks over double-boilers in restaurant kitchens – and still having the hollandaise split now and then.

Prepare the grapes. In a posh New Orleans restaurant, these would be plunged into boiling water, left a minute, then each grape would be meticulously peeled before being sliced lengthways and any pips removed. For a homely version, the grape skins can be left on (especially if they are thin).

Now for the fish: set two frying pans on the stove and pour half the wine into each. Divide the bruised spices and the bay leaves between each pan. Place the fish fillets in both pans, add hot water to the wine – just enough to barely cover them.

Have plates ready in a cool oven.

Poach the fillets, covered, for 6 minutes without allowing the liquid to boil. With a fish slice, carefully transfer the fish to the plates warming in the oven (they will be underdone, but the heat of the oven will finish the cooking.)

Pour the poaching liquid through a sieve into a bowl, to catch the spent spices. Discard these, then return the poaching liquid to the pans and boil over the highest heat, evaporating furiously, until the volume of the liquid has been reduced by half.

Turn on the food processor once more, and add up to 125 ml (4 fl oz or around ½ cup) of this to the hollandaise (use more or less depending on how thin or thick it is).

Heat the grapes in the microwave for about 30 seconds.

To assemble, pour the sauce over and around the fish fillets, then sprinkle the grapes over everything.

The New Orleans culinary scene's biggest shake-up of all occurred during the 1980s. Nowadays, 'Cajun' blackened fish has descended to cliché status on international restaurant menus, while supermarkets stock a plethora of 'Cajun' spice mixes manufactured as far afield as Australia and New Zealand. These items are no more native to the bayous and backwoods of Louisiana than jalapeño muffins, complicated cream sauces, meat 'debris' or fettucine. That the rest of the world now identifies such contemporary dishes with Cajun cooking is due to the extraordinary talent for publicity of just one chef, Paul Prudhomme. Having opened his second café, K-Paul's Louisiana Kitchen, to instant critical acclaim in 1979, the big man went on to wow America – and the world – with a series of cookbooks and television appearances throughout the 1980s.

Whether intentionally or not, Prudhomme has convinced everybody that his own refined and highly eclectic creations are part of his Cajun heritage. Yet, as we have seen, authentic Cajun cooking is anything but sophisticated. Cajun blood sausage and stuffed pig's stomach may have a certain rough, hearty rustic charm but, traditionally at least, they were hardly considered suitable dishes for New Orleans restaurants. Indeed, before K-Paul's Kitchen, the only other Cajun restaurant in New Orleans had been the Bon Ton Café on Magazine Street, opened by Al and Alzina Pierce of Lafourche Parish in the 1960s, and still in operation today.

It may come as a surprise to the tourists who still queue down Chartres Street to eat at K-Paul's Louisiana Kitchen, that blackened redfish is not Prudhomme's creation at all. According to Ella Brennan, co-owner of the Commander's Palace, the dish originated when Prudhomme was chef there in the 1970s. One afternoon she was sitting in her office between services, and posed a question to Prudhomme: 'If we were out fishing and I caught a fish – a firm-fleshed fish – how would you cook it on the spot?' Prudhomme suggested they go down to the kitchen. There, the restaurant's German sous-chef, Gerhardt Brill, was asked the same question. 'I'd do this,' Brill replied, and proceeded to rub a redfish with spices and flash-fry it on both sides in a smoking hot black iron frying pan. Meanwhile, Paul Prudhomme was standing alongside – watching. But blackened redfish aside, it has to be said that Prudhomme almost single-handedly reinvented Louisiana cooking with his own undeniable exuberance and creativity, bringing in outside influence and loosening up a cuisine frozen by tradition.

Until Prudhomme came along, it was joked that New Orleans had become a city with 500 restaurants – and only five recipes. By the early 1980s, it was increasingly obvious that it was simply not enough, any more, for a restaurant to produce a passable gumbo, jambalaya, trout meunière, étouffée and rémoulade, and still expect to thrive.

New Orleans was not immune from the huge changes which were beginning to sweep through the entire Western world at that time, and freed by Prudhomme's example, a new wave of chefs began mixing and matching the famous native ingredients of Louisiana with those brought from further afield, notably California and New England. The Grill Room at the Windsor Court Hotel had the audacity to fly in fresh oysters from the Pacific Northwest, said to have more flavour than those produced in the warmer waters around New Orleans. Prudhomme's prize protégé, Frank Brigtsen, opened Brigtsen's in Carrollton and took the classic oysters rockefeller one step further by turning it into a cream soup which, if anything, is an improvement on the original. While a taste for spaghetti with meat sauce and lasagne had been spread by the Italian community of New Orleans, the city joined the international craze for fresh pasta in the 1980s, and the equally fresh sauces which accompanied it.

During the early 1990s, in the bog area of east New Orleans, an immigrant Vietnamese green market sprang up, selling hitherto unknown fresh herbs such as Thai basil, lemongrass and coriander. On the west bank of the Mississippi a Vietnamese supermarket opened, while a Vietnamese restaurant, Kim Sun, began turning local seafood into salt-baked shrimps and salt-baked crabs. Later came the Lemongrass Café, also operated by a Vietnamese chef, but one who was merging traditional country style cooking with complex Western-style sauces. Inevitably, such Asian influences began to spread the other way, into Cajun-Creole kitchens. At Mike's on the Avenue, Mike Fennelly is grilling local oysters with Korean barbecue sauce, and putting Louisiana spices into black bean soup.

Despite Prudhomme's departure, Commander's Palace continues to be a breeding ground of innovation, as has another launching pad for many an ambitious chef, the Bistro at the Maison de Ville. Perhaps New Orleans' most charming boutique hotel, the Maison de Ville was built in 1880, but across the courtyard are four former slave quarters believed to be constructed fifty years earlier, with cast iron fountain and bricks original to the location. If so, then these buildings, along with the Ursuline Convent, are the oldest in New Orleans. Tennessee Williams completed *A Streetcar Named Desire* in room nine, while in a cottage which forms an annexe of the hotel, John James Audubon painted a portion of his *Birds of America* series in 1821.

One of the new generations of talent to be nurtured by the Maison de Ville is Dominique Macquet, an energetic young chef from Mauritius. Born into a French family which lived on the Indian Ocean island for five generations, Macquet personifies the linkage between the Creole food found there, in the Caribbean and New Orleans. Yet his style is even more global than that, reflecting his wanderings, first as a 16-year-old apprentice chef to South Africa, later to Japan, England, Thailand and California. Traditional Creole cooking, to Macquet's taste, is too heavy and spicy: 'I want to have flavours which play with your palate and develop gradually in your mouth – a tinge of chilli first, then ginger and cilantro – not just a blast of straight chilli which dies down.'

In 1997, Maquet launched his own restaurant, Dominique's, and on the menu are several of Macquet's most famous signature dishes, carried over from the Maison de Ville.

Louisiana Crawfish with a Spicy Aïoli and Vine Ripe Tomatoes

125 g (4–5 oz) green part of leek
1 red pepper, chopped
500 g (1 lb) crawfish tails
   (substitute king prawns)
2 sticks celery, diced
1 large gherkin, diced
1 medium red onion, sliced

1 teaspoon chilli powder
1 teaspoon granulated garlic
   powder
½ tablespoon celery root
3 tablespoons home-made
   mayonnaise

Sauté the leeks until slightly burnt, add the red pepper and the crawfish tails. Let cool and blend all the other ingredients with the mayonnaise. Serve with sliced tomatoes and slices of garlic French bread, drizzled with pesto if you wish (see plate 11).
   SERVES 8.

Goat Cheese Wrapped in Filo with a Sweet Onion Thyme Fricassee

10 white onions
300 g (10 oz) goat's cheese
500 ml (scant 1 pt or 2 cups)
   balsamic vinegar

250 ml (9 fl oz or 1 cup) honey
2 teaspoons thyme, chopped
12 sheets filo pastry
50 g (2 oz) clarified butter

The day before, slice onions and cook on a low heat for 4 hours in their natural juice.

Cut the goat's cheese into six portions. Over a low heat, cook the onions another 2 hours or until like a compôte. Add half the balsamic vinegar and half the honey. Reduce and let cool down. Add chopped thyme.

Lay 4 sheets of filo pastry on top of each other, brushing each layer with clarified butter. Cut pastry in half. Repeat three times to give you six portions of 4-ply pastry. Place a segment of goat's cheese in the middle of each pastry portion. Add 1 large spoon of onion fricassee and wrap it like a beggar's purse. Bake in the oven at 200°C (400°F/Gas 6) for 5–6 minutes and sprinkle with the rest of the honey dissolved into the remaining balsamic vinegar. Garnish with mâche lettuce.

SERVES 6.

Meanwhile, some revered institutions in the French Quarter are also trying to bring their food into the new millennium – but without giving up the dishes which made them famous. A good example is Broussard's, where pesto, chicken satay, tuna carpaccio and salmon gravadlax are beginning to sneak in alongside the shrimp rémoulades and the bread puddings with whisky sauce.

Broussard's began life in 1920, when Joseph Broussard, a Louisiana Creole who had been trained as a chef in Paris, opened a restaurant in Conti Street, in what had been his wife's childhood home. A small man with a fiery temperament, he was such a task master that if a dish did not meet his expectations, he would hurl it out the kitchen door, at the feet of startled pedestrians. If diners complained about his food, he tore up the bill and threw them out of his restaurant. Another of his eccentricities was a fixation with Napoleon Bonaparte. Whenever a Napoleon brandy was ordered, there was a standing order that the waiters must converge around a statue of Napoleon in the courtyard, and sing 'La Marsellaise'.

The current proprietors, Gunther and Evelyn Preuss, combine the same exacting standards with rather more urbanity and charm. The New Orleans-born chef, Harvey Loumiet, comes from a heavily food-oriented family, where both his grandmothers spoke an old-fashioned dialect of French. Although he did not begin cooking professionally until the age of thirty-five, he made up for lost time by cooking at some of the best kitchens of New Orleans – Sazerac, Willy Coln's Chalet in Gretna and for five years at the prestigious Windsor Court Hotel. He even cooks at home on his days off, for family and friends. 'People say I'm crazy, but cooking for me is a hobby as well as a passion. This business has to be a love, it can't just be a job – if it is, you're never going to be as good.'

Some traditional Creole items on Broussard's menu, such as the *daube glacé* (cold jellied beef) he remembers from his childhood, and he daren't remove it from Broussard's menu. He has begun, however, to exercise his own creativity with dishes such as Crabmeat Broussard's.

Crabmeat Broussard's

8 jumbo prawns, peeled
1 tablespoon butter
2 tablespoons olive oil
1 small onion, diced
2 preserved artichoke hearts,
　chopped
1 clove garlic, crushed
30 g (1 oz or ¼ cup) flour
4 tablespoons white wine

500 ml (scant 1 pt or 2 cups)
　chicken stock
250 ml (9 fl oz or 1 cup) single
　cream
75 g (3 oz) brie
large handful breadcrumbs
1 tablespoon whole thyme leaves
3 tablespoons olive oil
350 g (12 oz) lump crabmeat

Preheat oven to 200°C (400°F/Gas 6).

Make a cut into each shrimp or prawn down the back and spread out like a butterfly. In a large frying pan, melt butter and lightly sauté the shrimps. Set aside to cool. In a heavy saucepan, heat olive oil. Sauté onion, artichoke and garlic over a medium heat until the onion becomes limp. Sprinkle in the flour and mix well. Pour in wine and stock, stirring well, then reduce heat and simmer for 3 minutes. Add cream and simmer for another 5 minutes. Remove from the heat and let stand for 2–3 minutes.

Take the brie, scrape off the white skin and cut into little pieces. Add brie to cream sauce and stir until all cheese is melted and mixed well. Let cool. Mix the breadcrumbs with thyme and olive oil, and set aside.

After cheese mixture has cooled, gently fold in the crabmeat. Take eight small ramekins or ovenproof dishes. In each dish place one shrimp in the centre, so it stands. If this proves too tricky, make the butterfly cut deeper. Spoon the crabmeat mixture around the shrimp and sprinkle with the breadcrumb mixture.

Place dishes on a pan and place in the pre-heated oven until hot and bubbly.

SERVES 8.

Shrimp and Crabmeat Cheesecake Imperial with Roasted Red Pepper and Dill Cream

500 g (1 lb or 2 cups) mayonnaise
500 g (1 lb or 2 cups) sour cream
60 ml (2 fl oz or ¼ cup) freshly
squeezed lemon juice
125 g (4½ oz or ½ cup) Dijon mustard
4 tablespoons chopped fresh dill
2 teaspoons dried tarragon leaves,
soaked in white wine for an hour
and drained
2 teaspoons minced roasted garlic
1 bunch chopped spring onions
2 teaspoons paprika
350 g (12 oz) cooked shrimp,
peeled, deveined and chopped
125 ml (4 fl oz or ½ cup) plus
2 tablespoons cider vinegar

80 g (3 oz or ½ cup) granulated
unflavoured gelatine
120 g (4½ oz) backfin lump
crabmeat
Roasted red pepper and dill cream
(see below)

Pecan mixture
2 tablespoons butter
250 g (8 oz) pecan pieces
½ teaspoon salt
pinch of cayenne pepper
1 teaspoon Worcestershire sauce

In a large mixing bowl, combine the mayonnaise and sour cream with the freshly squeezed lemon juice, Dijon mustard, dill, drained tarragon leaves, garlic, onions and paprika. Mix well until all ingredients are well incorporated, then fold in the chopped shrimps.

In a small sauté pan, combine the cider vinegar and gelatine, place over a moderate heat, and stir constantly until the gelatine granules are completely dissolved. Add the gelatine and vinegar mixture slowly to the other ingredients and mix well as you go.

Now, quickly but gently, fold the lump crabmeat into the mixture. Be sure that it is well distributed but don't work it so much that you break up the lumps.

Pour the mixture into a 20 cm (8 in) springform pan, cover with plastic wrap and refrigerate overnight.

To make the pecan mixture, melt the butter in a sauté pan and add the pecan pieces, salt, cayenne pepper and Worcestershire sauce. Sauté for 2–3 minutes until the pecan pieces are nicely browned, but not overly so. Cool the pecan mixture and roughly chop. Don't refrigerate before pressing into the sides of the cake.

To complete the assembly of the cake, remove it from the springform pan and place it on a plate. Spread the roasted red pepper and dill cream evenly over the top. Garnish the sides of the cake with the pecan mixture, pressing it into an even layer around the sides (see plate 12).

Makes 15 servings.

Roasted Red Pepper and Dill Cream

400 g (14 oz) can whole red pimentos, drained	225 g (8 oz) cream cheese
	1 teaspoon salt
125 g (4 oz or ½ cup) double cream	2 tablespoons fresh dill

In a blender, combine the red pimentos with the cream, cream cheese and salt. Blend into an homogenous mixture. Transfer the mixture to a container, fold in the fresh dill, cover and refrigerate overnight. Makes enough topping for one cake.

That recipe surely makes one thing clear: however much New Orleans chefs incorporate new concepts such as puréed red peppers, they will never eschew 300 years of rich Creole culinary tradition. Health nazis may rule the roost in California, but in New Orleans they are not keen on lean and mean. In all probability, seafood from the bayou will forever be smothered in egg and butter liaisons, and the bourbon soufflés whipped up with mounds of sugar and basins of cream. How could things be otherwise, in a city which hosts annual bingefests like the Mardi Gras and the gay parade known as Southern Decadence, where it is not unusual for participants to spend US$1000 on a costume?

In New Orleans, hedonism rules. Every night – literally – is party night, as all along Bourbon Street, closed to traffic, tourists swarm from one bar to another or simply stand out in the middle of the crowded street, drinking from 'go-cups' – styrofoam cups of beer which, by local ordinance, can be legally consumed in public. Because the hotels and restaurants are so geared to fulfilling what visitors expect of Creole food, the health food movement has never had much of an impact on New Orleans.

'This is where America comes to let everything hang out,' explains local food historian Gene Bourg. 'People come here not to look for healthy food but for food based on fat and spices – despite the tropical climate.' The continuing popularity of New Orleans food, he says, is due to its flavour. 'I travel often, but I often find the food very bland elsewhere in the United States. Go even 100 miles north of New Orleans, and you are immediately back into the realm of the generic American TV dinner.'

His comments are verified by chef Raymond Toups: 'My customers say they want light and healthy dishes, but when we put them on the menu, nobody actually orders them.'

And who could blame them, when the alternative could be shrimps in a deliciously creamy, buttery sauce, a dish known as Shrimp Grand Isle. This is one of Toups' signature dishes and one of the best things I tasted in New Orleans. The flavour of the sauce is rich, yet there are no pungent herbs and spices to overshadow the star of the show – the shrimps. Grand Isle is a barrier island near New Orleans, enclosing the largest marsh in the United States. It is extraordinarily rich in fish and seafood: crabs and shrimps hatch, then hide in the marsh areas to grow – and to provide food for the fish which station themselves by the tufts of grass and wait for the crustaceans to emerge.

Shrimp Grand Isle

36 extra-large shrimps or prawns
5 eggs
salt and ground black pepper
1 tablespoon chopped parsley
1 tablespoon minced garlic
250 g (8 oz or 2 cups) flour
250 ml (9 fl oz or 1 cup) cooking oil

175 ml (6 fl oz) white wine
175 g (6 oz) whipping cream
100 g (4 oz) unsalted butter at
   room temperature
juice of 2 lemons
1 tablespoon minced garlic
1 tablespoon chopped parsley

Sauce
4 shallots, finely chopped

Remove the head and shells from the shrimp or prawns (save these for making seafood stock). Cut through the underside a short way and remove the dark vein, leaving the back intact.

Beat the eggs lightly and add salt, pepper, parsley and garlic. Dredge shrimp in the flour and dip into the seasoned egg batter.

Pan fry the shrimp in oil over a medium heat and turn once. Remove from the oil and repeat the process, holding the shrimps in a low oven until they are ready to serve.

Add shallots and white wine to a saucepan and cook over a high heat until reduced by 80 per cent. Add cream and reduce again until the sauce starts to thicken. Whip in the butter and finish with salt, pepper, garlic, parsley and lemon juice. Serve over the shrimp.

SERVES 6.

5 Indo-China

Throughout its history, Vietnam has suffered four foreign occupations, none of them a happy experience for the indigenous Vietnamese. Yet as one minor compensation, the two colonizers who stayed longest, the Chinese and the French, also happened to possess the world's two most famous cuisines.

The Chinese have been in Vietnam, off and on, since 111 BC. Their influence, therefore, has been strongest, to the point where Vietnamese cuisine may today be fairly described as a more tropical variation on Chinese cookery, incorporating many typical South-East Asian spices and flavourings, plus a small number of herbs and salad leaves of its very own.

The influence of the French, who stayed only one century, has been correspondingly less. From the vast Gallic larder, the Vietnamese chose only selected elements: French bread, pâté, pâtisserie, jams and conserves, butter, coffee, beer, wine, condensed milk, yoghurt, ice cream, and vegetables such as artichokes, cabbages, cauliflowers, carrots and asparagus.

A small number of colonial dishes, about twenty in all, were true French-Vietnamese culinary fusions, anticipating by many decades the great polyglottal culinary fashion at the close of the millennium. Yet on the whole, the Vietnamese kept to their style, and the French to theirs. In Laos and Cambodia, also formerly part of French Indo-China, the French influence has hardly mingled with the indigenous dishes at all, even though in Phnom Penh and Vientiane, when the middle classes dine out, they invariably choose a French restaurant (or perhaps a Chinese).

In Vietnam, however, despite a revival in French restaurants taking place on a scale unmatched elsewhere in Asia, the clientele is mainly French and other European expatriates, plus a few Vietnamese who are there mainly for the purpose of showing off. When it comes down to it, the Vietnamese prefer their own cuisine to the French. This can be seen by the decision of French-owned restaurants such as Globo, in Saigon's fashionable District One, to introduce a page of Vietnamese dishes to their menu, purely for the benefit of those Vietnamese who come in with European business associates to wind up a deal over dinner. The ambience is decidedly more bohemian than corporate and, as the French owner wryly noted, Globo is one French restaurant where the Vietnamese don't come to show off.

And yet those same Vietnamese may well have begun their day with coffee, perhaps a croissant or a baguette (thicker and shorter than its French counterpart) with butter, jam or La Vache Qui Rit processed cheese.

La Vache Qui Rit, along with Air France, was the only French company permitted to maintain its offices and distribution networks in Vietnam during the period of state ownership and collectivization, from the communist takeover in 1975 until 1986, the year Doi Moi, or economic liberalization, began. The resilience of the company is reflected in its product: round segmented packets of the cheese sit out in the tropical sun day after day, without refrigeration, as an optional ingredient for those clients of roadside stalls, seen everywhere in Vietnam, which specialize in baguettes split in half lengthways, buttered and filled with a selection of ingredients that might include mayonnaise, cooked chicken, ham, pork, a few shreds of pickled carrot and white radish, some cucumber, spring onion, a few optional slices of red chilli, and French-inspired pâtés.

Whether *cha lua*, the so-called silky sausage, is French-influenced, is a matter for conjecture. Generally left to commercial manufacturers in Vietnam, it consists of finely pounded pork flavoured with sugar, fish sauce and garlic, which is wrapped into fat logs with banana leaves, boiled, then sliced thinly like luncheon sausage when cold.

Vietnamese chicken liver pâté, which they also call 'pate', is however, clearly French-inspired, even if the frugal Vietnamese use rendered chicken fat rather than butter to fry the livers, garlic and onion prior to grinding them to a paste. They also tend to eke out the mixture with white bread, and usually cannot resist adding a little sugar.

More sophisticated charcuterie, such as the making of *saucissons*, was generally not practised during the period of French rule, due to the climate and its attendant problems of humidity, making the long, slow drying and curing process an impossibility. Only today, in the age of controlled atmospheres, are charcuteries like Patrick and Le Cochon d'Or in Saigon's posh District One operating successfully. Their market is the latest wave of French expatriates, brought in on the crest of investment excitement in the early 1990s. Officially, they number around 1,500, mainly working for corporations such as France Telecom, the Total oil and gas company, shipping companies and the advertising world, although unregistered French expatriates might double that figure.

The intense humidity plays havoc with pâtisserie also. Puff pastry is almost non-existent in Vietnam, while any spun sugar work would collapse and melt within the hour. And whenever chef Laurant Billy of Camargue Restaurant in Saigon makes meringues, he must immediately wrap them in paper and store them in an airtight jar. The Franco-Vietnamese baguette similarly turns limp within hours, and for this reason is made with much less salt than usual (frequently with none at all), since salt draws in moisture from the atmosphere. The addition of a tiny amount of sugar to the baguettes by some Vietnamese bakers also reflects the local palate. The same applies to the baguette as baked in Cambodia.

Since bread is the one food product considered absolutely necessary to the well-being of the French, bakeries were established in Saigon soon after its capture in 1859, as part of an on-going war with King Thieu Tri which was only formally settled with the signing of the Treaty of Protectorate in 1883.

When the French administrators were forced to go on up-country expeditions, however, they had to make do with hard-tack biscuits. Since these had to be either steamed or re-baked after two days, and were thoroughly unpleasant even when fresh, many French in outlying areas developed a taste for white rice instead. Unlike the early years of British India, however, there was no large-scale adoption of the indigenous cuisine. True, a few Vietnamese dishes appealed, such as the ubiquitous *pho*, or *pot au feu annamite* as they called it, a relatively bland noodle soup topped with sliced beef, which the French preferred to be added to the broth at the last moment and served medium rare – a practice which the Vietnamese have retained. It has also been suggested that the extensive garnishes of green leaves and herbs which accompany this soup may also be a French influence.

Then there were the formal banquets held by highly placed Vietnamese aristocrats, officials or financiers, which their French counterparts felt obliged to attend. They would first have been coached in the etiquette of throwing bones to the floor in the absence of a bowl provided for the purpose, and warned not to express surprise at the single communal bowl of *nuoc mam*, or fish sauce, placed in the centre of the table, into which guests would be invited to dip their food. Not that they would have availed themselves of the opportunity, since virtually every French writer on Indo-China, from the first Jesuits, complained about fish sauce, some comparing its odour with tiger's urine.

'As a rule, the vanquishing colonials keep to their European habits, particularly for food,' wrote Charles Lemire in *Les Français en Indochine*, published in 1877. He added that the Vietnamese cooks were quickly instilled with the classic cookery of Normandy and Burgundy, as taught by French bachelors who would take it in turns to oversee the kitchen. 'Each one is *chef de popote* for a month in turn, unless one of the comrades, possessed with distinguished knowledge, accepts this delicate function indefinitely.'

It was a life of both privilege and boredom, of being waited upon hand and foot by servants who would bring tea into their bedroom or light the master's cigarette, all without a word.

At dinner, another servant would be at hand to work the *punkah*, that elephantine overhead fan which originated in British India. 'It is thanks to this invention that we were able to resist a general decline throughout the evening and enjoy our food,' wrote Lemire. As the evening wore on, so did drunkenness, encouraging maudlin discussions about the oppressive heat and humidity and the absence of women.

In the early twentieth century, when more women did begin to arrive, families were established, and the need for domestic servants rose accordingly. A 'boy', who might in fact be a middle-aged or even elderly man, would be employed to do the housework and the laundering of clothes. Oddly, the ironing was often an additional task foisted upon the cook (known by his or her Vietnamese title, *bep*). A nanny would also be employed to look after the children. A dressmaker might be on hand, either full time or part time, to mend clothes and fine lingerie. By the 1930s, a chauffeur was common, since privately owned cars were increasing in number.

'It is frequently said that servants have little honesty,' wrote the anonymous author of the *Guide du Français Arrivant en Indochine*, published in 1935:

> One rages because the cook steals several *sous* while shopping, but one conveniently forgets the same 'dance of the basket handle' in

France. The Vietnamese boy would steal nothing if the mistress did not have the unfortunate habit of leaving keys lying about, and her money on the furniture.

Of more concern, according to the *Guide*, were the 'extremely grievous practices' of certain nannies to get babies to stop crying or to send them to sleep. Children, it was claimed, could contract gastro-enteritis as a result of being fed Vietnamese dishes, and learn swear words from the servants. 'Don't leave your young daughters with male servants and your boys with the dressmakers,' the *Guide* urged. And yet, there was a prevalent attitude among the French that somehow their servants were not men; it was common enough for the mistress of the house to have the boy give her a scrub in the bath, and a massage afterwards.

Compared with the British colonialists, master-servant relations were often intimate. Some servants became so devoted to their masters that they consented to blood transfusions to save them, and even confronted certain dangers on their behalf. The master's children would be given toys by the servants on their birthdays and during the Tet (New Year) festival. For all that, relationships were at best paternalistic: 'Be like the father, indulgent but firm,' concluded the *Guide*.

A firm hand, it was claimed, was needed if the servants were not to begin taking liberties, inviting their wives, parents and friends to live in the house. The cook had to be watched, if the 14- or 15-year-olds who were officially employed as assistants were not in fact being made to do all the work. The mistress was urged to rigorously check the cleanliness of cooking utensils, and to ensure that the cook was aware of her tastes, even to the point of supplying recipes to be cooked.

Nevertheless, any amount of staff supervision still left ample time for socializing. In Saigon, where some 30,000 people – three-quarters of the civilian French of Indo-China – had congregated by 1950, social life revolved around the Rue Catinat, a stretch of road barely 300 m long. It began at the port, with the Majestic Hotel, erected in 1950 for the American tourist trade. Here the high society gathered in the sixth floor jazz bar to drink whisky, which had just displaced the colonialist brandy and soda, and ogle at the Americans in their loud-patterned shirts, worn outside their trousers.

Also down by the port was a collection of sleazy bars run by the Corsican underworld, all chrome, neon strips and mirrors, the hissing of the early espresso machines competing with the loud music. Behind closed doors out the back, the owners received alleged sailors and their smuggled gold.

Around the middle of the Rue Catinat, the ambience became more respectable, with a plethora of café terraces where at noon, and at seven o'clock in the evening, the French would crowd around the tables, drinking aperitifs of Cinzano, sherry, or the favourite of the French, cassis. On special occasions, champagne might be laced with cassis to make kir, but more commonly a cheap white burgundy, such as aligoté, or a white bordeaux was used, and the drink given a tropical twist with the addition of a dash of lime juice and a garnish of lime slice or peel.

Talk at these aperitif hours would be about money, the opium trade, the current state of bribery, the hushed up scandals and who was sleeping with whom. Because of this, the street was nicknamed 'Radio Catinat'.

And yet, despite the fact that everybody knew the faces of everybody else, there was a rigid hierarchy, expressed in who acknowledged whom, and where they dined and drank. The lowest stratum of French society, the clerks and the army privates, did not even dine in the Rue Catinat itself, but in Cholon, the Chinatown adjacent to Saigon. Along the Rue des Marins were Chinese-run restaurants where, to the groanings of a juke box in the corner, mournful waiters presented steak and chips, plates of tiny eggs of dubious origin, bathed in green oil, and 'Châteaubriand Maison' – slabs of bluish grey meat cut from the haunches of some donkey-like animal in the local forest. As for the 'Pommes Lyonnaises', these were likely to be fried slices of cassava.

At the café-restaurant de la Paix on the Rue Catinat, all the old Indo-China hands gathered. Coarse, purple-faced, reeking of garlic, these middle managers were nicknamed 'Colonial eggs' because of their fat bellies and spindly legs. Everything was informal, the food still at the level of steaks and pommes frites, but, even so, their wives did wear diamonds.

Further up the scale was the Pagoda tea-room and Monsieur Franchini's Hotel Continental, while only the high financiers could afford the grand and ceremonious dinners at the Bodega restaurant.

In Saigon, as in all the major cities, the absolute pinnacle of social success was to be admitted as a member into the Cercle Sportif, an exclusive sporting club where the top civil servants and chiefs of the banking and import-export houses would congregate in the dining area or around the swimming pool. There were also tennis courts and a massage room. Although there was no official colour bar, no Vietnamese or Chinese was ever granted membership.

Renamed the workers sporting club after the communist takeover, the Saigon buildings still fulfil their original role today, only with a wholly Vietnamese membership playing tennis on smartly restored courts. On a flat area scattered with trees to one side, as many as six pétanque games might be in progress, the players using ancient rusty balls which may have begun service with the French.

Even the military lived and dined well. The American journalist Howard Sochurek recalled to Harry Maurer in *Strange Ground: Americans in Vietnam, 1945–1975*:

> You'd always start with an aperitif at the bar. Then the head of the mess would formally announce the lunch. All the seats were assigned. There were little nameplates for the visitors. All elegantly set up, with crystal. This in the middle of the jungle. Then there would be an officer who would announce *le menu*. He'd stand up at the head of the table and say, 'The menu for August 14 at 1:00 pm . . . Gentlemen, the menu is . . .' Then he'd recite: 'We will begin with soup. Then we will have fish. Then we will have entrecôte. Then we will have a salad. Then we will have a tart. Then we will have coffee.' The menu was always printed up. Meanwhile, on the perimeter the damn mortars are going off. This went on up until the very end. I'll bet you the last meal at Dien Bien Phu, they still sat down and had somebody announce the menu. That was how it was done.

For some five years prior to the French defeat at Dien Bien Phu, the French restaurants and cafés of Saigon had become targets for Viet Minh grenades. Many restaurateurs responded by enclosing their premises with thick iron curtains and placing bouncers on the door. Along the Rue Catinat, however, the terraces of the cafés remained unprotected, as a matter of pride, and life carried on as if nothing were happening. The Pagoda tea-rooms had protective netting, but it was not often in place, and when one of the frequent bombs did go off, everybody would duck to the floor, those who didn't stand up again afterwards being the dead and the wounded. Then the waiters would come running with floor cloths to mop up the blood, the furniture would be hastily rearranged, and fresh customers would be sitting where an hour previously, people would have lain in agony.

Today, the Rue Catinat has been renamed Dong Khoi Street, and many of its trees have been chopped down. Yet still there are vestiges of its former splendour, such as a branch of Brodard Café and Restaurant. Brodard is a café chain dating back to the French era. It was taken over by the government in 1975 and is now in the hands of Saigon Tourism. Amid the pseudo-Art Nouveau surroundings at the Dong Khoi Street branch, a bottle of chablis or even St Emilion can be had for a price, to drink with a standard French menu selection including salad niçoise, chicken marengo, beef bourguignon and sole provençale.

In the colonial era Brodard was perhaps best known as a purveyor and manufacturer of ice cream – the best in Vietnam. As part of the wider industrial notion of cooking, ice cream was introduced by the French as soon as dairy herds could be successfully established on the Mekong Delta and, particularly, in the relatively cool climate up in Dalat. Within just a few years, the French had been able to reverse the traditional Vietnamese abhorrence for dairy products, and in fashionable cafés café au lait and tea with milk and sugar became the norm, despite purist disapproval. Invariably, the milk would be a home-made version of sweetened condensed milk – a necessity where refrigeration was not available.

Butter was put to novel uses, such as melting it into rice along with fish sauce, while a taste for custard tarts, and especially *crème caramel*, set in so early that the Vietnamese appear to have forgotten that the ubiquitous restaurant dish ever had French origins. Known as *banh flan* or simply flan, some brilliant cook had the idea of incorporating coconut cream:

Banh Flan
(coconut crème caramel)

120 g (4 oz) granulated sugar
250 ml (9 fl oz or 1 cup) milk
250 ml (9 fl oz or 1 cup) coconut
   cream, tinned or fresh
4 eggs, beaten

50 g (2 oz) caster sugar
¼ teaspoon vanilla essence
1–1½ tablespoons freshly grated
   coconut (optional)

Pre-heat the oven to 160°C (325°F/Gas 3).

Over a high heat in a small heavy-bottomed saucepan, stir the granulated sugar with 100 ml (3½ fl oz) of water until it boils. Continue to boil until the sugar caramelizes and darkens slightly to golden brown. Immediately remove from the heat and stir in another 2 tablespoons of water, until any lumps of caramelized sugar dissolve. Pour this mixture into the bottoms of four ramekins, and leave to cool.

Meanwhile, heat the milk and coconut cream until the mixture is just on the verge of boiling. Remove from the heat and add eggs, caster sugar and vanilla essence slowly, in about three lots, whisking continuously.

Pour this mixture into the ramekin dishes over the caramelized sugar. Sprinkle a little freshly grated coconut over each ramekin.

Half fill a roasting dish with water, place a cake rack into it and arrange the ramekin dishes on it. Bake for about 40 minutes, until the flans wobble firmly when gently shaken. Remove and allow to cool. With a small metal spatula or bread and butter knife dipped into a jug of hot water, slide around the edges of the ramekin dishes to loosen them, then place a small plate upside down on each ramekin dish, like a lid. Briskly flip over each ramekin dish, then carefully unmould to reveal crème caramels with the classic caramelized toppings.

SERVES 4.

Yoghurt – *yaourt* – has been completely absorbed into Vietnamese eating habits, as signs all over Vietnamese towns testify. In Dalat, yoghurt production is a cottage industry which, due to the scarcity of milk (a dairy farmer scratching a living from just one or two cows is by no means uncommon), makes yoghurt a luxury. Vietnamese yoghurt is generally excellent, being thick and creamy, rather like Greek strained yoghurt. Often it is sold by itself in little pots at expensive restaurants, sometimes topped with a sprinkling of sultanas, unsalted roast peanuts and cashews, and chopped candied peel and glacé cherries.

As with all dairy products, the manufacture of yoghurt and ice cream ended abruptly when the communists nationalized the means of production in 1975. In the lean years which followed, there was not enough rice or flour to go around (forcing the baguette bakeries to shut down) let alone milk, so what little ice cream there was made in Vietnam was concocted largely from soya bean flour and sugar. With Doi Moi, or economic liberalization, however, a new wave of ice cream making is now occurring in Vietnam, only this time the accent is on

Italian *gelato*. Starting with Pisa in 1992, ice cream is being made with UHT milk imported from Australia and New Zealand. This is largely for safety reasons – pasteurization is not all it should be in Vietnam, although most of the ice cream makers hold out hope for a test farm sponsored by Nestlé in Ba Vi, where milk cows are being introduced, and peasants taught how to feed, milk and care for them. A government-run dairy farm in Dalat is rather less efficient. In the early communist era, Cuba supplied Dutch breeds of cattle to Vietnam, while later, in the late 1970s, the French government introduced the still-popular Jersey and Zebeau breeds.

Like ice cream, ice was unknown before the French arrived, and initially regarded with disapproval. In 1884 the Catholic priest Père Benigne wrote in his memoirs, *Vingt Ans en Annam* (Twenty Years in Vietnam):

> Not all the habits of the Cochinese are good to imitate, but many of them should be examined before they are rejected. If the Europeans of the new colony of Saigon had been wise enough to adopt the habit of drinking hot water instead of indulging too freely in the use of ice, they would probably suffer less frequently from dysentery or anaemia, their stomachs would be less lazy and the cemeteries less crowded.

Ice was, however, purely a luxury of urban areas. Up-country it was unknown, even as late as 1950. Visiting the village of Dak-Song that year, the English travel writer Norman Lewis commented of a lunch provided by his French hosts: 'The drinks were, of course, warm. It has always surprised me that the Frenchman in the tropics lacking ice never made an attempt to cool liquids by keeping them, as the Spanish do, in porous vessels.' Lewis was lucky to have encountered wine and beer at all in these outposts; in earlier times, there would have been only tea. On the other hand, he writes of a 'splendid lunch of wild poultry, the flesh of which was very white and sweet.'

Game being abundant in colonial Vietnam, Cambodia and Laos, and the French being the French, there was very little they were not willing to eat. Duck, pheasant, deer and wild boar were established delicacies, peacock and black-winged stilts less so. 'In flavour they were much inferior to duck,' noted Lewis of the latter. Guy Cheminaud, in his 1939 hunting memoir, *Mes Chasses au Laos*, remembered fondly another exotic not found back in his native France:

Regardless of their size, pythons are always edible. The bigger they are, the tastier their flesh. Its meat is pink and tender . . . Of all edible snakes, the python should be considered the best and the most nourishing. It is also the most copious because of its gigantic size. The finest piece is the last metre of the tail.

Vietnamese cooks would braise python with boar's fat and bamboo shoots, whereas the French favoured a simple court-bouillon, or a red wine sauce.

Vietnamese and Laotian wild boar was especially sought after by French colonials, since its pink, tender flesh did not have the pronounced flavour of the wild boars of Europe. Out in the field, legs of wild pork were roasted in old termite hills. This would had been emptied out for the purpose by taking off the cap, clearing out the debris from the inside through a 'door' pierced into the side, then replacing the top and shutting up the door with a sheet of iron. Before using the 'oven' it would be fired up to kill off any remaining termites.

Equally as well regarded was the flesh of a type of deer, *Cervus porcinus*, 'pig deer' known by the Vietnamese as *con huu* and by the Laotians as *neua*. Unlike other types South-East Asian deer, Cheminaud noted, its flesh could be eaten frequently without tiring of it.

A number of species of wild cattle were sought after, notably the banting, the flesh of which was excellent. Exceptions were an animal nearing the end of its life expectancy of about fifteen years, or one that did not belong to a southern sub-species, outwardly identical to the rest, only having an exceptionally strong musty flavoured flesh which was inedible.

There was not much demand for the flesh of wild buffaloes, which, despite being identical to domestic buffaloes, yielded a blackish flesh which had little gamey flavour. Out in the field, Cheminaud tells us, he would have the meat boiled down to make a type of meat extract which tasted, he claimed, like the Liebig brand popular at the time.

Other non-perishable goods found in every French colonial pantry were Menier chocolate and a food based on lentil flour, known as *revalescière*.

The other great French import, considered indispensable, was wine. Diluted with bottled mineral water, it was even recommended for medicinal purposes. In 1888 a 200-litre barrel of 'superior wine', Lemire tells us, could be bought in Haiphong for around 45 to 70 piastres, or 180 to 280 French francs. If it were to be kept in the barrel, alcohol had to be added in order to preserve it, but bottled wine endured far better.

Rice wine had always been a part of Vietnamese life, offered as a gift and much used in rituals and celebrations. Traditionally, it had been made in the villages, but under French rule its production and sale was prohibited, and an alcohol monopoly granted to two French firms. Anxious to increase their profits, the Société Française des Distilleries de L'Indochine pressured the colonial government to force each village to meet an alcohol quota, calculated according to the number of inhabitants. This the French were pleased to do, since the sales tax on salt and alcohol provided the largest source of revenue for their colonial government. Failure to meet the quota was taken as evidence that the villagers were making illegal alcohol.

Consequently, French wine managed to infiltrate even the most deeply traditional Vietnamese households. In *The Sacred Willow: Four Generations in the Life of a Vietnamese Family*, Duong Van Mai Elliott recalls that even her strictly Confucian grandfather sat down to dinner with a half-bottle of French wine served in a special glass reserved only for him.

In the mountainous areas of Vietnam, grapes were planted with the hope of making domestic wine. The vine certainly produced grapes which, according to Père Benigne 'by their size announce the Promised Land', but which, disappointingly, yielded nothing but a sour vinegar. Despite the British firm Allied Domecq's attempts to revive the industry with the Ninh Thuan Winery 350 kms (250 miles) north east of Saigon, the results today are little better. The winery, with a one-million bottle capacity, is supplied from an existing vineyard situated on a hot and steamy coastal plain, where, despite ruthless pruning to contain the tropical vigour and limit the more or less continuous output to three 'vintages' a year, some 50,000 tonnes of rather characterless red Cardinal grapes are produced annually. In the north especially, about two-thirds of wine consumption is red, a colour considered auspicious, fiery and warming (an important consideration when you consider the climate in Hanoi hovers around 12°C in February).

Evidence of a lasting palate for French wine among the Vietnamese is to be seen today in Ho Chi Minh City, where La Cave, a wine shop done out like an old French cellar, caters to the emerging Vietnamese middle class while doing its main trade to the French restaurants of the city.

But if most wine is imported, beer is nearly all brewed locally, due to the exorbitant taxes on the imported product. The French company BGI returned to Vietnam in the 1990s to produce the prestigious Tiger brand, a revival of a colonial label, which today is a close number two to '333' brand. These are the aspirational labels for the Vietnamese, perhaps only drunk once workers have had their fill of cheap, gaseous beer (brewed the day before) at their *bia oi* or afternoon boozing session.

But if beer is the preserve of men, both sexes drink coffee. The coffee-growing industry established by the French in Vietnam expanded greatly in the 1990s, to the extent that Vietnam overtook New Guinea as Asia's largest exporter of beans. While there are some robusta trees, the majority of trees in the main growing area – the foothills below Dalat (see plate 13) – are arabica. One variety unknown to many in the West, and unlikely ever to be exported, is a variety of robusta bean known as *com chua* – fox coffee. Only the reddest berries are favoured by foxes on account of their ripeness. They gorge on them and then the whole bean, minus its fleshy layer, is excreted around the base of the tree. These beans are gathered one by one and sold for exorbitant prices in the markets.

Ironically, many of today's fashionable espresso bars in Saigon import their coffee beans, since the salt and butter commonly added to Vietnamese beans during the roasting process plays havoc with the machines.

One natural affinity between the Vietnamese and French kitchens was a predilection for the products of the pig. The raising of domestic pigs pre-dated the French, of course, but it was they who introduced bacon. Before long, the Vietnamese had incorporated the new product into their own cookery.

Cha Ca Nuong
(fish and bacon brochettes)

Formerly there was a street in Hanoi named Pho Hang Cha Ca, which lends its name to this dish.

500 g (1 lb) firm-fleshed fish
3 tablespoons vegetable oil
2 tablespoons fish sauce
2 tablespoons rice spirit or sherry
1 teaspoon turmeric
1 teaspoon shrimp paste

1 tablespoon grated ginger
2 rashers bacon, de-rinded
2 spring onions, finely chopped
2 tablespoons vegetable oil
2 tablespoons peanuts, chopped

Cut the fish into large chunks (about 2 cm or ¾ in each). Combine vegetable oil, fish sauce, rice spirit, turmeric, shrimp paste and ginger. Pour over the fish and marinate for up to 2 hours (or as little as 20 minutes for a milder flavour).

Cut the rashers of bacon into squares and thread on to bamboo or metal skewers alternately with the chunks of fish.

Combine the spring onions and second measure of oil with the marinade, and use to brush the fish while it is being grilled on both sides, until the flesh is white. Turn once and grill on the other side for another 2–3 minutes, until cooked. Serve sprinkled with peanuts, on a bed of rice, and accompany with vegetables.

SERVES 2–3.

Crab was a familiar luxury to the early French colonial administrators, one of whom is credited with the invention of this dish.

Cua Hap Bia
(crab in beer broth)

6 large hard-shelled crabs
   (any variety)
2 tablespoons oyster sauce
2 teaspoons sesame oil
salt and pepper
8 cloves garlic, finely sliced
2 tablespoons vegetable oil

1 large onion, sliced
1 shallot, finely chopped
1 small red chilli, sliced
250 ml (9 fl oz or 1 cup) beer
2 medium tomatoes, diced
watercress to garnish

Wash the crab in fresh water, remove the carapace, and with a sharp Chinese cleaver or cooks knife, chop away the legs down each side in two clean pieces, taking care to include the meaty part where the legs join the shell.

Marinate the crab for one hour in a mixture of the oyster sauce, sesame oil, salt, pepper, and two of the cloves of garlic.

Heat a little oil in a wok and stir-fry two of the cloves of garlic, shallot and the onion for 4–5 minutes, until browned. Add the crab and chilli, and stir-fry for 3 more minutes. Add the beer, cover, reduce the heat to low, and cook for 12 minutes. Just before serving, add the chopped tomato and stir to mix it through. Deep fry the remaining four cloves of finely sliced garlic in oil, and remove the moment they begin to turn brown. Drain on kitchen paper laid over newspaper. Divide both crab and broth among four bowls, then sprinkle over the sliced deep-fried garlic and garnish with watercress.

In Quérillac's 1931 book, *Cuisine Coloniale: Les Bonnes Recettes de Chlöe Mondésir,* a recipe titled Omelette Saigonnaise calls for an omelette stuffed with sautéed crab and mushrooms, the 'Saigon' element presumably being some spring onions which are chopped into a roux served (rather ponderously by today's standards) over the top.

Crab is also the component of the most famous Franco-Vietnamese culinary fusion of all, crab and asparagus soup. On the menu of almost every Vietnamese restaurant both at home and abroad, the recipe frequently calls for white asparagus, a French import packed in jars or tins. Tinned whole kernel corn, another convenience food introduced by the French, replaces the asparagus in another very similar soup, in which chicken is used instead of crab.

Sup Mang Tay Nau Cua
(crab and asparagus soup)

425 g (15 oz) jar or can white asparagus
1 litre (1¾ pts or 4 cups) chicken broth
2 tablespoons Asian fish sauce
generous pinch each of salt and sugar
1 tablespoon vegetable oil
6 shallots, chopped
2 cloves garlic, chopped
250 g (8 oz) crabmeat, fresh, frozen or canned
freshly ground black pepper
2 tablespoons cornflour
1 egg, lightly beaten
2 tablespoons fresh coriander, chopped
1 spring onion, finely sliced

Cut the asparagus spears into 2–3 cm (1 in) lengths, and reserve the canning liquid. Set aside.

Heat the chicken broth, 1 tablespoon of the fish sauce, and the salt and sugar. Reduce to a simmer.

Heat the oil in a small frying pan and sauté shallots and garlic for several minutes, add the crab meat and the remaining tablespoon of fish sauce, and stir-fry another minute. Grind a sprinkling of black pepper over.

Mix the cornflour with a little cold water, add to the broth, bring to the boil to thicken. Stir the broth gently, then add the egg and stir gently until threads form.

Add the contents of the frying pan along with the asparagus and its canning liquid, then gently heat the soup through. Ladle into six small serving bowls and sprinkle a little fresh coriander and spring onion over each.

SERVES 6.

A great many European vegetables are well entrenched into the Vietnamese diet, having been introduced by seventeenth-century traders, not only from France, but also Portugal, Britain and Holland. To this day, the Vietnamese word for snow pea or mange-tout translates as 'Dutch pea', while a great many European vegetables have French pidgin names which sound remarkably similar to the original, even if the way they are written is quite different. Cabbage or *chou*, for example, is pronounced more or less in the French way but written *su*. Similarly, there are *a-ti-so* (artichoke) and *ca-rot* (carrot). For watercress, another introduction, the Vietnamese took the last syllable from the French name, *cresson*, and prefixed it with 'salad' – hence 'salad-son' or, as it is written, *xa-lach son*.

The cultivation of all these vegetables began in earnest with the establishment, in 1920, of the hill station of Dalat (see plate 16) in the Central Highlands, 1,200 m (4,000 ft) above sea level. Founded by a French physician as an antidote to the enervating effects of the southern tropical climate on the French colonials, it soon became a holiday destination for the wealthy, who built grand villas around the fringes of the town. Whole streets of these remain intact today, the immaculately manicured gardens and perfectly maintained buildings of the privately owned villas standing in direct contrast to the slum-like neglect of those appropriated by the government in 1975, their gardens grubbed to bare earth by free-ranging flocks of ducks and chickens.

Not only was Dalat's climate conducive to the cultivation of Western-style vegetables, but the soil was found to be fertile and free draining.

Due to its resemblance to bamboo shoots, asparagus was dubbed 'Western bamboo'. Bamboo shoots themselves were eaten by the French, who had them brought to the table covered in a white sauce or a hollandaise, or perhaps dressed with vinaigrette. The very young bamboo shoot, asserted Quérillac more optimistically than accurately, attains 'the consistency of an artichoke and has a flavour approaching this vegetable also'. Blanched, then cut into slices and put in a gratin dish, the shoots were covered in a cheese sauce and browned in the oven.

Since the Vietnamese already had the sweet potato, the arrival of the ordinary potato with the French resulted in the name 'French potato', or *khoai tay*. For the Vietnamese, the potato was a luxury food, very much as a whole beef steak still is. Their solution, therefore, was to dice the beef finely, Oriental-style, and then serve it mixed with French fries, in order to stretch the ingredients further:

Thit Bo Va Khoai Tay Chien
(beef and french fries)

vegetable oil for deep frying
2 large potatoes, peeled and cut
   into matchsticks
1 medium onion, thinly sliced
2 cloves garlic, finely chopped
300 g (10 oz) sirloin steak, cut into
   thin slices

1 tablespoon cornflour
1 tablespoon Asian fish sauce
1 teaspoon sugar
1 teaspoon soy sauce

Heat the oil in a wok and deep fry the potato matchsticks, in several batches if necessary (in order to avoid crowding the potatoes in the oil), until browned and cooked. Drain on kitchen paper and set aside.

Pour off most of the oil, saving about 3 tablespoons. Stir-fry the onion and garlic until the onion is transparent, then add the beef and stir-fry for only about a minute, or until the pieces are browned all over.

Mix the cornflour and fish sauce along with about a tablespoon of water to a paste. Stir this through the beef mixture along with the sugar and soy sauce. Just before serving, add the French fries and mix through gently to avoid breaking them up.

A similar recipe known as *bo luc lac* (which uses onions rather than potatoes) involves marinating the meat beforehand in a mixture of garlic, ginger, lemongrass, sugar, salt and pepper.

Bo Luc Lac
(steak and onions Vietnamese-style)

750 g (1½ lb) lean porterhouse steak, cut into 2–3 cm (1 in) pieces
2 stalks lemongrass
¾ teaspoon salt
¾ teaspoon sugar
2 teaspoons ground black pepper
1 thumb-sized knob fresh ginger, grated
2 cloves garlic, crushed
4 tablespoons oil
2 medium onions, each cut into 8 pieces

Chop the lemongrass into rough pieces and then pulverize in a food processor, or chop very finely by hand. Mix with the pieces of steak in a bowl, along with the salt, sugar, black pepper, ginger and garlic. Leave to marinate for at least an hour, preferably 2–3 hours.

Heat 2 tablespoons of the oil in a frying pan over a high heat and sauté the onion, mashing and breaking up the pieces with a wooden spoon, until slightly browned, but still firm. Remove and set aside to drain on absorbent paper.

Shake or wipe the pieces of steak free of their marinade, then sauté each piece on both sides for several minutes in the remaining oil in the pan. Mix with the onions and serve with rice.

SERVES 3–4.

Cambodia has a very similar dish, also called *luc lac* – the name translating as 'dice', a reference to the way the beef is cubed to resemble gambling dice. Like the Vietnamese version, it too is fried with pepper and garlic, only lemon juice is often used instead of lemongrass, and it is often accompanied by a fried egg.

This dish was favoured by both the Vietnamese and Cambodian populace but proved too potent for the palates of French colonial administrators, who preferred the more subtle flavour of the steak marinated whole.

Bip-tech Kieu Phap Thuoc Dia
(French colonial steak)

3 tablespoons black vinegar
  (substitute red wine vinegar)
3 tablespoons bottled Asian sweet
  chilli sauce
2 cloves garlic, crushed
2 large porterhouse steaks, about
  500 g (1 lb) each

4 shallots, sliced finely
olive oil for deep frying
1 tablespoon roast salted peanuts,
  finely chopped

Make a marinade by stirring together the vinegar, chilli sauce and garlic. Brush or spoon the marinade over both sides of the steaks, place in a non-metallic (earthenware or glass) dish, cover with clingfilm and leave for 4 hours or overnight.

Prepare the garnish by deep frying the shallots in olive oil, using a wok to minimize the amount of oil needed. Stir the shallots while frying, and remove as soon as they begin to brown, taking care not to allow them to burn. Remove and spread over two sheets of absorbent kitchen paper laid over newspaper.

Grill the steak for 3 minutes per side for medium-rare, 4 minutes for medium.

Transfer the cooked steaks to a board and slice thinly. Fan the slices over each of four plates, then sprinkle over the chopped peanuts and deep-fried shallots.

SERVES 4.

Beef ragoût has been more or less adopted in its original French form, both in Vietnam and in Cambodia. In Vietnam it has more or less retained its French name – *bo ragout* – and while in Cambodia it is known as *sup sai ko*, it is still a recognizable French stew, with beef and vegetables such as carrot, potato, cabbage, onion and green beans. Significantly, it is cooked without the usual South-East Asian spices and aromatics.

Will the French influence last? In a number of small ways, undoubtedly, but as for the French restaurants, it seems doubtful they will outlive the French corporate presence in Saigon and Hanoi. If the corporate world, which entered Vietnam with such gusto in the early 1990s, now finds itself hampered at every turn by Vietnamese government bureaucracy, then things are doubly hard for the small restaurateur. One French proprietor related how, that very morning, workmen had begun drilling up the pavement outside his restaurant without any prior consultation or warning, while the owner of Globo explained that he would be delighted to pay regular bribes to the police, if only he could be told to whom they could be paid. Anything to avoid repetition of an experience when two policemen had come in and belligerently sat at his bar. Immediately one drew the barmaid's attention to the compact discs on the shelf behind.

'You have too many – there are far too many pirate CDs around these days,' he said, demanding, and receiving, an instant cash 'fine'.

'Take down that picture on the wall,' demanded the other. 'It is obscene.' The poster in question was of a Brazilian dancer, showing a little cleavage and leg. Another on-the-spot 'fine'.

'Take off these,' demanded cop number one, pointing at some wooden knobs protruding from the bar front as part of its design. When asked why, he replied they looked like bullets.

Finally another 'fine' was demanded for the sign outside, which would have to be taken down. Having gone to great lengths to comply with the law which states that any sign in English must be accompanied by the Vietnamese translation in words double the size, the by-now exasperated owner asked what was wrong with a sign which read 'Globo Bar and Grill'.

'Because "grill" sounds like "girls",' came the reply.

With a diminishing expatriate French client base, many of the French restaurants are having to broaden their appeal to Western tourists generally. While tourists may still want to eat French food, the feeling is that it should have less of a northern and more of a Mediterranean slant if it is to be compatible with the Vietnamese climate and relate to modern tastes. Thus a fashionable restaurant like Camargue, in an elegantly renovated Saigon French villa, serves a menu which is strong on salads and pasta, and main courses like roasted seabass with fennel and olive oil, and pan-fried salmon fillet with pistou sauce.

The recently opened BiBi's, whose eponymous, gregarious and somewhat eccentric owner/chef is of mixed French and Vietnamese ancestry, has parquet floors and paintings of Impressionist views of the Mediterranean, a mural of Provençal farmhouses and a Van Gogh seed sower in the setting sun. I dined on a delicious little *amuse-gueule* of dressed cold couscous with red and green pepper, and a mother of all artichokes, fresh from Dalat, served with a thick, deliciously unctuous vinaigrette, with fish meunière and to finish, an exquisite raspberry tart, also made with Dalat produce. Was I in France or Vietnam? Only looking outside and seeing a woman in a conical coolie's hat pass by pushing a cart of bananas brought me back to reality. But again, the clientele here appears to be mainly French, pulling up in their Mercedes Benz and walking through the door barking into their mobile phones.

For the young Vietnamese, every kind of internationalism is being welcomed as a reaction to the long years of isolation from all but Eastern bloc powers. For internationalism, one can largely read Americanization. It's the deepest of ironies, that the children of those who had every conceivable bomb, bullet and defoliant thrown at them by the Americans, today hang out in pool halls, trendy bars and restaurants with names like Montana and Spago, work out in the gym, and wear frat clothing and basketball singlets. The baseball cap is now worn by perhaps seven out of every ten southern Vietnamese men, and now that Baskin Robbins, with its thirty-one ice cream flavours, has arrived in Vietnam, McDonald's and KFC must surely be peering intently at the situation.

On my final day in Saigon, I visited a crass new complex out near the airport called Super Bowl. It's not cheap by Vietnamese standards, yet it is packed with young people drinking Coca-Cola, eating American-style pizza and playing ten-pin bowls. For all their manifest faults, at least the French imperialists brought the refinement of an ancient culture.

6 The Pacific

TAHITI AND FRENCH POLYNESIA

The physical beauty of Tahiti which so awes the tourist is a source of frustration to the cook. For if the island appears to erupt from the sea into gnarled, towering mountains, it is because of an extremely narrow band of flat arable land around the coast. That leaves very little space for market gardening, and even less for the grazing of sheep and cattle. Most of Tahiti's beef and lamb thus has to be imported, mainly from New Zealand, while many of its vegetables come from the temperate Austral group of islands to the south. In Papeete's public market, wilting lettuces and cabbages, limp cucumbers, parched carrots and perspiring plastic bags of tomatoes attest to the lengthy voyage. Along with bunches of thyme and branches of bay leaves, they also indicate a profound French influence on local cuisine, in terms of both ingredients and techniques.

While the easily grown indigenous staples – breadfruit, taro and wild red mountain bananas (see plates 17 and 18) – remain, today they are supplemented with a wealth of tropical fruits introduced from Asia and the Americas: avocado, mango, guava, pistachio, pineapple, tamarind, star apples, 'heart of beef', and the close relative of the grapefruit known as the pamplemousse.

These are the true stars of the Papeete market, along with the fish. It is worth rising early (well before 6 a.m.) just to get to the fish section and marvel at the freshness of everything. There is no odour, and every fish glistens as if sprayed with lacquer. Glowing still with canary yellows, bright reds, oranges and iridescent blues and greens, they seem freshly hauled from a giant tropical aquarium, which, in a sense, they have. Some 300 species teem in the waters of Tahiti and throughout the islands of French Polynesia, a stretch of ocean the size of Europe.

Roughly speaking, Tahitian cooks draw a line between the finely fleshed lagoon fish, which usually receive very simple treatment, and the fuller flavoured ocean fish. Certain species enjoy traditional preparation all of their own. The parrotfish, for example, is imbued with a delicious perfume by baking in an earth oven in a wrapping of leaves from the *'auti* plant (*Cordyline fruticosa*), while the red mullet also has its own leaf wrapping – that of the *nono* tree (*Morinda citrifolia*). It is a short step from leaf wrappings to the French technique of cooking fish *en papillote*, or at least in the aluminium foil which today has replaced the sheet of folded paper.

The French influence on Tahitian cuisine began with Catholic missionaries and the formal annexation of the island in 1842, but has become permanently ingrained as a result of intermarriage. Most Polynesian Tahitians now have some foreign ancestry, if not French (a colonial administrator, perhaps, or a member of the military), then English or Chinese.

It is thus second nature for Tahitian home cooks to poach fish with a French colonial-style court bouillon, by first flavouring the water with thyme, bay leaves and spices. A rock lobster would be annointed with French butter or olive oil before grilling, while clams, crabs and shrimps might be sautéed with garlic and onions before receiving a very Gallic dousing with white wine and chopped parsley.

Given a nice firm piece of shark, a Tahitian cook might stew it with red or white wine as a *matelote*. Mint mayonnaise is a popular accompaniment to lime-marinated dorado fish, while a beer batter is commonly used for the small river fish known as 'ina'a. Until turtles were hunted almost to extinction, they were cooked as French-style ragoûts with pieces of breadfruit and tomatoes, garlic, onion and red wine.

Long before it became wildly fashionable among chefs in Paris and London in the 1990s, cooking fish with vanilla had been practised in Tahiti. Introduced from Manila in 1848, vanilla is grown on several islands (Tahaa, Huahine, Raiatea and Nuku Hiva). Curiously, Tahiti has its own species, despite being an introduced plant. Some say this species was produced by cross-breeding back in the Philippines, though it may be that in nature there is no clear distinction between species and strains. Tahitian growers distinguish between three subspecies, each with its own Tahitian name and distinctive flavour, though all are mixed together for curing and export.

Tahitian vanilla, once rather disparaged, is today recognized as the most highly perfumed in the world. Unfortunately, however, production fell radically after the Second World War, from 3,000 tonnes in 1949 to just two tonnes in 1980. The introduction of synthetic vanilla, and the temptation of alternative regular paid employment by the French armed forces, plus the demanding nature of the crop, all contributed to the decline in its cultivation. Even a 'vanilla plan' inaugurated in 1983 failed to significantly revive the industry, though prospects have brightened considerably since the United States began buying about half the annual crop. Previously, everything went to France.

Turbotin à la Vanille
(vanilla-scented turbot)

1 young turbot or other flatfish, about 1.5 kg (3–3½ lb)	4 egg yolks
3 tablespoons oil	juice of 1 lime
1 vanilla pod	salt and pepper
250 ml (9 fl oz or 1 cup) medium white wine	1 lemon or lime
	2 tomatoes
200 g (7 oz) crème fraîche	1 sprig of flat-leaved parsley

Clean, gut and prepare the turbot, leaving the skin on. Score each side with three deep gashes and brush with oil.

Split the vanilla pod down the middle, scrape out the tiny seeds into a saucepan, then chop the pod finely and add. Pour in the wine, bring to the boil, and boil gently until the amount of liquid has reduced by half.

Grill the turbot, preferably over a charcoal barbecue (it can also be done under an electric grill) for about 8 minutes per side.

In a bowl, beat the crème fraîche, egg yolks and lime juice. Add this to the saucepan containing the wine and vanilla, and over a medium heat, stir continuously until it thickens. Add salt and pepper to taste.

Place the whole fish on a platter and decorate with slices of lemon and tomato, arrange over some leaves of parsley, and serve the sauce separately.

Undoubtedly the most famous Tahitian contribution to the French culinary mainstream has been marinated raw fish with coconut cream, today better known as *poisson cru* than by its Tahitian name, *'i'a ota*. This recipe was given to me during my sojourn at the Hyatt Regency Tahiti, a strikingly designed series of levels set into the forest, which spill like a staircase part way down a hillside towards a sandy beach. It seems an Arcadian idyll but Papeete is visible from its terrace restaurant, which also has spectacular sunset views of the high jagged skyline of neighbouring Moorea Island. The *poisson cru* I ate there was fresh and excellent, and I asked for the recipe.

Poisson Cru
(Tahitian marinated raw fish)

The attitude at the Hyatt was that if your fish is fresh enough then brief marination of only 10 minutes best preserves its delicacy. But some cooks prefer a marination time of 4 or more hours (with sufficient lemon juice to cover the fish) until the flesh turns completely white, and hence more appetizing in appearance.

1 kg (2 lb) fresh tuna, or other meaty, firm-textured fish	salt and pepper
4 limes or lemons	4 tablespoons coconut cream
2 tablespoons finely chopped onion	8 lettuce leaves (iceberg, lollo rosso, endive)
1 tomato, seeded and diced	60 g (generous 2 oz) grated coconut
½ cucumber, peeled and cubed	

Wash and dry the fish, then cut into 5 mm (¼ in) cubes. Marinate the fish with the juice of the lime or lemons for 10 minutes, then remove half of the juice.

Add onion, tomato and cucumber. Sprinkle lightly with salt and pepper. Just before serving, add the coconut cream.

To serve, arrange the fish on the lettuce leaves and sprinkle with grated coconut.

SERVES 4.

Rather more of an acquired taste is the indigenous Tahitian dish known as *fafaru*. Fish is covered in salt water and left in the sun for several days, before straining and reserving the malodorous liquid which results. This is then used as a marinade for raw fish. Timid cooks leave the raw fish in this lusty sulphuric mixture for only ten minutes, others for much longer, but even Tahitians are divided between those who love it and those who loathe it.

Much more popular is the Chinese version of *poisson cru*, to which are added pickled raw vegetables (a common sight in the markets), garlic, ginger, perhaps a little sesame oil, and a sprinkling of roasted peanuts.

After the French, the Chinese have exerted the greatest culinary influence in French Polynesia. Descendants of Hakka peasants from the south Chinese province of Canton, they were first brought out as labourers indentured to the Tahitian Coffee and Plantation Company in 1865 and 1866. A second wave followed between 1907 and 1914,mainly wives and relatives of the first migrants.

Today, the Chinese comprise about a tenth of the population and some have married Tahitians. While a number are high-flying businessmen with interests in shipping, copra, hotels and supermarkets, many more are small-scale tailors and restaurateurs (albeit more anonymously nowadays, after Chinese restaurants in Papeete were singled out for destruction during the riots which followed the announcement of the resumption of French nuclear testing in the Pacific in 1995).

Humbler still is the owner of the *roulotte*, a snack van with a side flap which folds down into a counter. Found all around the waterfront in Papeete, they sell not only Chinese food but also basic European items such as steak and chips, burgers, pizzas, crêpes and croque-monsieur (toasted ham and cheese sandwich). When the latter is served with an egg on top it becomes, not croque-madame as in metropolitan France, but croque-vahine (*vahine* being Tahitian for woman).

About seven per cent of the Chinese are market gardeners, an occupation which is theirs exclusively, hence the regular appearance at village markets of Chinese green-leaved vegetables, yard-long beans, fresh coriander and bean sprouts. Chinese also run general stores in the outlying islands, even in the remote Tuamoto and Marquesas groups. These shops sell everything from tinned goods to petrol, footwear, cement, fishing tackle and toys – as well as sacks of rice and bottles of soy sauce.

Colloquially known as *soyu*, soy sauce is found in practically every domestic store cupboard in French Polynesia, and is used not only in dishes of Chinese origin, such as *chao mein* (chow mein), chop suey and chicken with oyster sauce, but also such unlikely Sino-Franco-Polynesian hybrids as *ma'a tinito*, a stew of pork and kidney beans (in which the soy sauce accompanies bay leaf, thyme and parsley) and in a tasty variation on coleslaw.

Salade de Chou Vert au Soyu
(coleslaw with soy-mustard dressing)

½ green cabbage, finely sliced
½ small red onion, finely chopped
1 tablespoon soy sauce
1 tablespoon mild prepared French-style mustard

1 tablespoon vinegar (wine vinegar or balsamic)
1 tablespoon sugar
salt and pepper
3 tablespoons olive oil

Combine cabbage and onion in a bowl. In a small bowl, mix together soy sauce, mustard and vinegar. Add sugar and stir to dissolve. Lightly season with salt and pepper and then stir in olive oil.

Pour over and serve immediately – the texture of the cabbage does not improve once dressed.

Thanks to the Chinese, rice has become a staple foodstuff for the Polynesians, who today buy it by the 20-kg sack, recognizing its benefits as an easily cooked, readily digested, satisfying accompaniment to meat and fish.

And while the French may have introduced the delights of their breads and pâtisserie to the islands, today the Chinese operate most of the bakeries, producing the bread which today has largely replaced the traditional 'ipo (cassava flour made into a paste and cooked in a leaf wrapping) and popoye (a sour fermented paste made with a base of breadfruit, mixed with coconut cream). French-style Chinese bakeries are also found in the more important outlying islands. Even the French concede these Chinese bakeries turn out excellent baguettes, although the shelf life is even shorter than in France. Rather than drying out and hardening, the baguettes go soft and limp within hours, due to the high humidity. Freshness is thus of utmost importance: the tunnel-shaped receptacles seen outside houses in Tahiti are not for mail, but boxes for the home delivery of bread.

A native ginger already existed in French Polynesia, so the introduction by the Chinese of cultivated root ginger drew an enthusiastic response from the Polynesian populace, who combine it with coconut cream as a flavouring for chicken.

Poulet au Re'a
(chicken with ginger)

1 kg (2 lb) chicken pieces, skinned
  and boned
thumb-sized piece of ginger root,
  grated
2 onions, finely diced
juice of 2 limes or lemons
3 tablespoons olive oil
1 tablespoon soy sauce

¼ teaspoon salt
few grinds black pepper
1 tablespoon flour
200 ml (7 fl oz or ¾ cup) white wine
  or water
250 ml (9 fl oz or 1 cup) coconut
  cream
1 sprig of flat-leaved parsley

Combine chicken, ginger, onion, lime or lemon juice, 1 tablespoon of the olive oil, soy sauce, salt and pepper in a bowl and mix well. Leave to marinate for 30 minutes.

Drain the chicken, reserve the marinade, and pat dry with a paper towel. Heat the remaining 2 tablespoons olive oil in a pot, sauté the chicken pieces until lightly browned. Sprinkle over the flour and mix well. Add the wine (or water), the marinade and the coconut cream and simmer for another 5–10 minutes, until the chicken is properly cooked through.

Decorate with leaves of parsley and serve over plain rice.
SERVES 4.

The chicken was brought to the Marquesas island group with the first great Polynesian migration there around the start of the Christian era. Today, the chicken has partly reverted to its wild state throughout French Polynesia. On the island of Ua Huka, in the Marquesas, a vast arid plateau supports herds of wild cattle and goats, the meat of which is cooked in coconut cream as a local speciality.

The pig, however, is the great livestock animal of French Polynesia, reared in all villages. Europeans added their own breeds to the indigenous pigs, which today still form the centrepiece of the traditional feast, cooked in the earth oven known as the *hima'a*.

As in many other Polynesian cultures, volcanic rocks are heated over a fire, then laid out in a pit made flat to accommodate crates of food. These are covered with earth and baked for about four hours. Unlike their Maori counterparts in New Zealand, Tahitian cooks do not add water to create steam, although the leaves used to wrap fish and meat generate enough moisture for the process to be a combination of baking and steaming. Nowadays, the banana leaves which were once used to cover the food are often replaced with damp sheets and sacking cloth. On some Tahitian *marae* and in the grounds of large tourist hotels, permanent stone-paved pits are in operation, covered over with sheets of corrugated iron, followed by sacking and a thick layer of sand.

The Tahitian earth oven (see plate 19) is associated with large festive gatherings, such as weddings, birthdays, the opening of a new house, or the arrival of an honoured guest. Such a feast, involving from twenty to sixty guests, is known as a *tamaara'a*.

Preparation of a *tamaara'a* is as communal an event as the consumption. Apart from the laying of the earth oven, there are traditional side dishes to be prepared, such as *poisson cru, fafaru,* salted coconut, turbot with native ginger, and breadfruit paste. Traditionally the feast was laid out on coconut leaves spread on the ground and decorated with flowers, although trestle tables are more often used today. However, the custom persists of eating with the fingers (of the right hand only).

The uncovering of the earth oven is accompanied by drumbeats, dancing and the saying of grace (over 90 per cent of the Polynesian population declare some form of religious observance), after which the feasting begins.

There are woven baskets of root vegetables – the sweet potato which has today replaced the native yam, a faintly perfumed form of taro, and of course, the staple carbohydrate, breadfruit, bland in flavour and fibrous in appearance, yet with a beautifully smooth, waxy texture.

Whole fish are removed from their aromatic wrappings, and pots are uncovered to reveal chicken *fafa* (cooked with taro leaves and coconut cream). Pride of place, however, belongs to the whole suckling pig, gutted, splayed out and cooked whole with a kumquat in its mouth.

Drinks may comprise whole green coconuts with a hole cut in the end for a straw to draw out the perfumed (and medically sterile) water within, though just as often there is a French colonial-style planter's punch (rum and fruit juice), bottles of French country wine, and Hinano, the famous brand of lager – light, sweetish yet hoppy – brewed in the same Papeete factory that processes the municipal water supply.

Dessert would be *poe*, a famous Tahitian speciality in which fruits such as bananas or papayas are beaten with cassava starch, sugar and coconut cream, then cooked to a smooth, slightly rubbery mass.

The Polynesians adore sugar, and all the temptation that is today put their way with pâtisserie, sweets and soft drinks has led to health problems of obesity and tooth decay. Ice cream, a particular favourite, dates from the Second World War, when some 6,000 American servicemen were stationed on Bora Bora. From 1942 to 1946 Operation Bobcat transformed the island with the building of a major airport and runway, introducing the islanders to the idea of salads, and to the cool creamy substance they still know as *l'escrime*, their interpretation of the English word 'ice cream'.

A *tamaara'a* would be unthinkable without music and dancing. Near the conclusion of one such feast, put on by a Maeva Beach hotel in Tahiti for the benefit of tourists, a barrage of drumming began, and a dance troupe of breathtakingly beautiful young women began the famously sensuous wiggling of their hips, their hula skirts swishing the floor like over-sized dish mops.

'Ah yes, just like travelogue movies from the 1950s,' I mused, recalling the final scene: the girls lure Whitey on to the dance floor, where he makes a complete dick of himself. 'Well, I'll not be today's fall guy,' I resolved, continuing to scribble my notes. Then I looked up and noted with alarm that the most beguiling of all the dancers was gyrating directly towards me. She stopped in front of my table, draped a waist-length floral *lei* over one wrist, then extended her hand:

'*Veux-tu danser?*'

'*Non, non. Pardonnez-moi, mademoiselle, mais non.*'

She pouted and walked away, making me feel the party-pooper, but I soon felt my obstinacy vindicated by the antics of my replacement, a bald, middle-aged Frenchman whom I had noticed earlier, partaking very freely of the complimentary rum punch. As he lapsed into a series of absurd pelvic thrusts, my spurned dancing partner froze an embarrassed smile and stared into space, while the crowd, Tahitian and tourist alike, hooted and roared, slapping their sides with laughter.

NEW CALEDONIA

With its profusion of flame trees, hibiscus and orchids, its palms and its yacht marinas, New Caledonia's seaside capital of Nouméa just might be somewhere on the French Riviera. The ambience is French, the language is French, and the food is very, very French – oddly so at times. At restaurants, for example, such hearty dishes as *entrecôte au*

Roquefort, coq au vin, pot au feu or *foie gras truffé du Périgord*, appear to have been plucked from the depths of a Gallic winter and transplanted into the sweltering heat of the tropics.

That the French food culture of New Caledonia seems significantly less Pacific in flavour than that of Tahiti may largely be down to demographics: only about 12 per cent of French Polynesians are of full European descent, whereas in New Caledonia the French account for nearly half the population. Furthermore, there has been a lower degree of miscegenation in New Caledonia, where there does not appear to have been the same sexual *frisson* between the early French settlers, or 'Caldoche', and the indigenous Melanesians. For better or for worse, the latter have been labelled 'Kanaks'.

Kanak, in its original Caldoche sense, was a term of racist abuse. One interpretation is *kana-ka* – a land animal, meaning man. In a northern New Caledonian dialect, *kaa-na* means 'to sleep with a woman', an expression learned by the early Caldoches and thought to have been used in derision. Only in the 1970s was Kanak adopted as a badge of pride by the independence movement and turned into a symbol of Melanesian nationalism.

This sexual and cultural apartheid manifests itself in New Caledonia's cuisine. Walking down the aisles of any of the enormous supermarkets in Noumea, it soon becomes obvious that nearly everything has been imported. For those with the money to spend, there is any amount of French wine, perhaps fifty varieties of French cheese, French ice cream, even ready-cooked frozen French vegetable dishes such as ratatouille and celeriac purée. There are also Belgian cream horns, Polish blackcurrants, and frozen pastries and desserts from Denmark. In the charcuterie section is everything dear to the French culinary heart – *saucisson de Paris, saucisson de Lyon, tripes à la mode de Caen, boudin noir*, smoked bacon, *tête de veau farcie* (stuffed calf's head) Burgundian-style parsleyed ham terrine, *foie gras* – the difference here being that some of it is locally produced.

The letters LOC on the labels of fresh meat distinguish the inordinately expensive local beef from the bulk of the meat, which is brought in from elsewhere. Even the vegetables and fresh fruit seem to come mostly from New Zealand. The main challenge, indeed, is to find the indigenous produce – yams, taros and sweet potatoes.

The plethora of imported food and drink can be partly attributed to New Caledonia being considered part of the European Union. This means there are no taxes on imported items, resulting in such anomalies as bargain-priced French wines and cans of Fosters beer, imported from England and brewed there under licence, when the original Australian product is made just across the ditch.

Such luxuries are demanded by highly paid French officials, such as the judiciary and the army, who receive high salaries because they are posted so far from France. They push up the cost of living, so that cheese, for example, is prohibitively expensive for many *kanaks*. In the case of vegetables, importation is partly a necessity due to the extreme scarcity of arable land in New Caledonia. The best farmland typically comprises irregular scattered strips, in some cases no more than a metre wide, at the bottom of otherwise sterile slopes.

And yet, underlying all these factors, one suspects, is an unhealthy degree of colonial culinary cringe: an attitude that if a food product is from France then it must be better, even if comes from the deep-freeze or out of a tin.

To find the true indigenous produce in Noumea, it is necessary to side-step the supermarkets and be at the market on Avenue de la Victoire, down by the Baie de la Moselle at around 6 a.m., when the fishing boats unload their catch. Here are great pink slabs of tuna and of tazar, the tuna-like flesh of a large fish which resembles a shark but isn't. Perroquet (parrotfish), picot (rabbitfish), pouate, bossus, and bec de cane are all to be seen, along with vivaneau, a red fish which grows to the size of a small tuna. The dawa, a bizarre fish with a unicorn-like protuberance in the middle of its forehead, is much sought after by the locals, though the top prize goes to the mahi mahi. Crayfish wave their arms helplessly, mud crabs struggle to break free of their bound claws, and farmed prawns, still alive but in a state of suspended animation, sit in a slurry of salt and crushed ice. Basins of benitiers (large clams) and cigalles (literally 'sea crickets') await a buyer, while dull grey octopus await a beating to tenderize their flesh.

From the adjacent Ile des Pins comes a form of land snail which looks more like a giant shellfish with an elongated spiral shell large enough to cover the palm of your hand. These require over an hour and a half's cooking to make them tender.

From small-scale local farms come headless quails and guinea fowls, as well as domestic rabbits, skinned but with their heads still intact, their eyes staring accusingly at passers-by.

Deer, descended from a pair given as a gift to the colonial government in the nineteenth century, have proliferated in the wild due to the absence of any natural predator. They very quickly established themselves as a pest, devastating plantations of cassavas and yams, making their culling both a necessity and a pleasure for the hunting-mad French.

Perhaps because harmful bacteria bred in the heat of the tropics make the hanging of venison a risky business, the practice of marinating and eating the venison raw has evolved in New Caledonia – a red meat version of Polynesian marinated raw fish. (Do not, however, be tempted to add coconut cream to this recipe – I tried it and believe me, it doesn't work!)

Salade de Caillou
(venison carpaccio New Caledonia-style)

Le Caillou – the rock – is the French name for New Caledonia.

1¼ kg (2¾ lb) venison (shoulder, back steaks or leg)	125 ml (4 fl oz or ½ cup) extra virgin olive oil
1 tablespoon rock salt	2 cloves garlic, crushed
juice of 4 lemons	1 small onion, very finely chopped
juice of 2 limes	10 basil leaves, torn
1½ teaspoons ground black pepper	handful chopped parsley

Cut the venison into paper-thin strips or slices. (This can be better achieved by partially freezing the piece of meat beforehand.) Place in layers in a non-metallic bowl or basin, sprinkle each layer with rock salt and lemon juice, and leave to marinate, covered, for about an hour at room temperature.

Drain off the lemon juice and discard. Now add the lime juice, black pepper, olive oil, garlic, onion and torn basil leaves, and mix well. Leave in the refrigerator for 1–2 hours, then serve sprinkled with chopped parsley. Due to the high level of acidity in this dish, it is usually accompanied with mineral water rather than wine.

SERVES 6.

Tiny though it may be, there is some vestige of culinary tradition in New Caledonia, with a handful of dishes which fit a familiar French colonial pattern. As in the islands of the Indian Ocean, for example, there is the trinity of *rougail, achards* and *brèdes*.

Brèdes (New Caledonia)

In an earthenware casserole, half-cook in butter, onions, garlic, chilli, a small piece of ginger, and salted lard, cut into pieces. Season with salt and pepper. Add *les brèdes* [green leaves such as spinach or Peking cabbage, or wild green leaves – see page 60] and when they are wilted, add water and simmer until it comes to the boil.

Translated from *Cuisine Coloniale: Les bonnes recettes de Chlöe Mondésir*, collected by A. Quérillac, Paris, 1931.

Rougails have also been long established in New Caledonian cooking, albeit with names that are variations on the familiar spelling. A *rougaiede* of coconut for example, is served as a condiment or adjunct to a meal in the same way as a *rougail*. It is made simply by stirring a little oil, salt, pepper and chopped parsley into the freshly grated coconut flesh.

Roujaire de Tomates
(tomato and aubergine rougail, New Caledonia-style)

1 large aubergine	3 shallots, chopped
3 medium tomatoes, blanched and peeled	1 teaspoon ground *quatre-épices**
	salt and pepper
2 tablespoons olive oil	2 tablespoons chopped parsley

Pierce a slit in the side of the aubergine with a knife and cook under the grill, on all sides, until the skin is blackened and the aubergine is shrivelled. Drain off any juices which may have accumulated during cooking (these are likely to be bitter), then scoop out the cooked flesh from the blackened skin (which is now discarded) Chop the cooked aubergine flesh finely. Cut the peeled tomatoes in two, squeeze out and discard the pips as you would those of a lemon, then chop the flesh finely.

Heat the oil in a frying pan, add the shallots, *quatre-épices*, salt and pepper, and fry until the shallots turn transparent. Add the chopped aubergine and tomato and cook for a minute or so longer, then mix through the chopped parsley. Serve as a side dish to the meat or fish of a main meal.

SERVES 3–4.

---

* a mixture of nutmeg, ginger, cinnamon and cloves.

In the following condiment of preserved lemons, the linguistic similarity between *achards* and *hachard* seems too close to be coincidental, even if the recipe itself apparently owes less to the islands of the Indian Ocean than to the famous preserved lemons of North Africa. It may be that the recipe was brought to New Caledonia by *pieds-noirs* from Algeria, about 2,500 of whom settled there during and after the Algerian war of independence in the 1950s and 1960s. Today, their cemetery can be seen outside Noumea.

Hachard de Citrons
(preserved lemons)

30–35 small lemons, not too ripe
a good handful of salt
juice of 12 lemons
1 tablespoon saffron

500 ml (scant 1 pt or 2 cups) oil
2 teaspoons curry powder
8 cloves garlic, crushed
8–10 dried red chillies, left whole

Wash the lemons, cut in half and place in a large non-metallic container. Sprinkle with the salt and add lemon juice, ensuring there is enough juice to completely cover the lemons (add extra lemon juice if necessary). Leave for three or four weeks, stirring every day. A little more salt can be added.

Pour off the salted lemon juice (this can be reserved for the next batch of preserved lemons). Rinse the lemons in fresh water, then bring a pot of boiling water to the boil and steep them in this for half an hour.

Heat the saffron gently in a dry pan until it just begins to turn a darker shade of red, then place in a mortar with a teaspoon of boiling water and crush with a pestle to a fine paste. Gently heat the oil and add the saffron, the curry powder and the garlic. Remove from the heat and pour over the lemons. Pack the lemons and chillies in glass jars and pour over the flavoured oil. The oil should cover the surface – add extra plain unflavoured oil, if necessary, to top it up. Store for a week before using. These lemons will keep for about a year. They can be eaten with meat, or sliced finely into melted butter as an accompaniment to fish.

While the town-based Caldoches eat strictly French food, the cattle ranchers out in the bush tend to eat as their Kanak employees do, a diet of meat and fish with plenty of taro, sweet potato and yam.

These root vegetables formed the basis of vegetable cultivation prior to European contact, when the Kanak population also lived by hunting, fishing and foraging for coconuts and other native fruits. They also ate a great deal of wild sugar cane, which is native to the South Pacific and has been growing in New Caledonia since at least 8,000 BC.

The sapwood of the *bourao*, a member of the hibiscus family, was eaten after a long process which involved making ring cuts on the trunk or branches. These were left for six months, provoking an accumulated store in the sapwood. The now thickened section of trunk or branch was then cut, sliced, boiled and finally threshed to extract the sapwood. These fibres were chewed for lengthy periods, yielding a flavour similar to chestnuts.

As fishermen, the Kanaks acquired finely tuned skills, being able to hear movement of fish under water and thus accurately throw their harpoons at night. The larger fish and creatures such as green turtles and dugongs (sea cows) were essential in making up a shortfall in the meat which could be obtained from forest animals. There were no pigs prior to European contact, and game consisted largely of pigeons, bats and rats. Fat grubs were also extracted from rotting vegetation.

In the mountains of la Chaîne Centrale a certain amount of cannibalism took place. The early French colonists were both fascinated and horrified by the practice, and their accounts are probably not very objective or accurate – especially Quérillac's contention that cannibalism was a simple response to hunger, and that only the fattest and the youngest humans were chosen as victims. Also of dubious veracity is H. E. L. Priday's claim, in *Cannibal Island*, that human eyeballs and the breasts of nubile girls were set aside for the chiefs.

While the Kanaks had domestic earthenware pots for cooking prior to European contact, any large-scale cooking, such as that of humans and later pigs, was done in the *bounia*, a classic Pacific earth oven, very similar to that used in French Polynesia. The meat and vegetables are wrapped in coconut leaves and then cooked over stones, previously heated in a fire. The coconut leaves are covered with a layer of soil to keep the heat in. A New Caledonian expression, 'having his hot stones' – meaning 'he is exposing himself to grave danger' – refers to this old method of cooking human flesh, even though the earth oven was also used for all types of wild animals, shellfish and fish, and later, with the introduction of European livestock by the French in the mid-nineteenth century, for pork, beef and chicken.

Usually the meat is accompanied by root vegetables and flavoured with wild onion stalks and coconut cream, prior to being placed in the centre of overlapping coconut leaves, which are wrapped into a large bundle. The presentation of the cooked food by unwrapping layer after layer of the leaves in front of guests is an important ritual element at a *loi-loi*, or feast.

The preparation of Kanak foods was quickly influenced by French kitchen techniques. Fruit bats, for example, when braised with parsley, thyme and shallots, and with a dash of crème fraîche and a bottle of red burgundy, were transformed into *civet de chauve-souris* (a dish found in several other parts of the Francophone world – in Mauritius and Vietnam, and also in neighbouring Vanuatu, formerly an Anglo-French condominium). Today the fruit bat is a protected species (though still shot and sold illegally at the markets) but until the 1980s fruit bat pâté was on the menu, among the couscous and the chicken with tomato and peppers, at Eau Vive, a celebrated restaurant at a nunnery. The sisters would lay down their kitchen knives and serenade the diners after the main course.

A typical modern kanak dish, which must date from the French introduction of chickens, is to cut root vegetables such as taro, yams or cassava, place them in a large Dutch oven, then cover them in coconut cream and place a chicken on top. The dish is done when the chicken is cooked.

Rice is an important staple in the contemporary kanak diet. Introduced by the French, it was grown experimentally as early as 1852. By 1865 rice was being cultivated for the Noumea market, though demand was greatly reduced by imports from Indo-China. Today, most rice comes from Australia.

The kanaks also eat French bread such as baguettes, and all races contribute to the labour force in French-style bakeries. Kanaks also share the French habit of using doughnut-like bread sticks for dipping into their early morning café au lait. Powdered milk is seen all over New Caledonia, the empty tins forming pot plant holders on the verandahs of kanak houses.

The fruit trees introduced after French annexation in 1852 –mangoes, custard apples, oranges and mandarins – all had their impact on the kanak diet, but possibly the most significant French influence is coffee. Many kanak smallholders on the rugged western side of the island grow excellent arabica coffee, rich and chocolatey, though perhaps not sufficiently potent for some tastes. Some kanak families still prepare their own beans in small, hand-turned cylindrical roasters. All New Caledonian coffee is consumed on the domestic market and indeed must be supplemented with imported beans from neighbouring Papua-New Guinea and Vanuatu. In the 1990s a co-operative of small kanak producers began marketing a purely New Caledonian blend of beans.

Other ethnic groups – mainly Polynesians and Wallis Islanders, but also Indonesians, Javanese, Chinese, Japanese and Vietnamese – comprise 16 per cent of New Caledonia's population and have a noticeable presence. There is a Chinatown in Noumea, whose predominantly Vietnamese inhabitants are incorrectly referred to as *Chinoise*. Imported as labourers to work the nickel and copper mines from 1891 onwards, each Vietnamese labourer received a little book, issued by the employer, setting out the conditions of employment – wages, the conditions of repatriation, etc. Article 16 of the contract stipulated that food would be adapted to the tastes of the employee, sufficient in quantity and of good quality. The following was to be dispensed each day: 250 g (8 oz) bread, 200 g (7 oz) rice, 200 g (7 oz) fresh meat (or 120 g/4 oz if salted), 400 g (14 oz) fresh fish, 300 g (10 oz) fresh vegetables (or failing that, plantation crops of sweet potato, potato, cassava), 20 g (¾ oz) pork lard, 20 g (¾ oz) salt, 40 g (1½ oz) sugar and 5 g tea.

The Vietnamese mostly kept their cuisine to themselves, until the arrival of American soldiers during the Second World War, on 12 March 1942. They had spare money to spend, and this created a demand for hawker foods still seen today in the markets, such as noodle soups flavoured with fresh coriander.

Surprisingly, there is no culinary legacy from a large Japanese immigrant population, also brought out in the nineteenth century to work the nickel mines, and repatriated after the First World War. The *sushi* and *sashimi* seen on grand hotel buffets today speaks more about international food fashion and mass tourism.

The growth of tourism, combined with the rise of Kanak nationalism, has had some interesting outcomes in the world of cuisine. Today there is more confidence about using traditional ingredients on the part of Kanak chefs, and an increasing demand from tourists for local cuisine. In the early 1990s, the Lycée Escoffier in Noumea decided to incorporate into its three-year chef's course a section on New

Caledonian cuisine. To be sure, the making of *pot au feu* or a bouillabaisse are still taught, only nowadays, both dishes are likely to incorporate local root vegetables such as taro, while the bouillabaisse might
include a heretical dash of curry powder and give prominence to local
crabs, as well as native fish from the lagoon.

AKAROA, NEW ZEALAND

Alighting from The French Connection in Akaroa, and having checked
into l'Hotel, tourists can stroll along Rue Lavaud and have a three-
course French meal at a restaurant called C'est La Vie, accompanied by
pinot noir made at the French Farm Winery. Later, they might check
out the pictures at le Galerie, having passed the local service station
offering *l'essence* and *réparations d'automobile*.

But before too long, it begins to dawn upon even the most gullible
visitor that there are not terribly many Gallic accents to be heard in this
tiny former French settlement on remote Bank's Peninsula, not far
from Christchurch.

For the fact is, Akaroa's 'French' ambience is largely a modern con-
struct of the tourism industry, a marketing tool designed to appeal to
the aspirations of an expanded post-war New Zealand and indeed,
Western middle class, determined to acquire the trappings of culture in
its wider sense of architecture, gardens, wine and fine cuisine. Even the
French street names of Akaroa date back only to a local council
decision in 1968.

However, not all is bogus: there are a number of genuine early
French buildings still standing, such as the Langlois-Etéveneux cottage,
which is today part of the Akaroa Museum, and an old French wine
cellar on private land up behind French Farm Winery. Excavated into
the hillside, its entrance is lined with bricks. Around some of the old
French houses are roses and grape vines, said to have been planted by
their original inhabitants, and there are also walnut trees left by the
French, now in full maturity. Moreover, there are prominent families
still living in Akaroa and Christchurch, such as the Brocheries, the Le
Lièvres and the de Malmanches, who can trace their ancestry to the
original settlers.

'French' Akaroa was doomed from its inception: disembarking from
the *Comte de Paris* in August 1840, the first French settlers were
dismayed to find a flag pole flying, not the Tricolore as they had been

led to expect, but the Union Jack. Having validated their settlement of the whole of New Zealand by signing the Treaty of Waitangi with Maori chiefs in February 1840, the British had pre-empted, by just six months, French plans to annexe the South Island. British sovereignty threw into immediate jeopardy the legality of a land purchase agreement signed with Akaroa Maori by the colony's founder, a young whaling captain named Jean-François Langlois. In the event, however, the British tolerated the presence of the French colonists, and they were permitted to remain, their land ownership recognized officially with Crown Grants in the 1850s.

The fifty-seven colonists, apart from twelve Germans and two Parisians, had all been recruited either from Normandy or the Charente, north of Bordeaux. All were working-class peasants, wine growers, agricultural labourers, carpenters, a shoemaker, a locksmith, a miner and a baker – attracted by the promise of a grant of land and free rations for the first year of settlement. Having paid off their debts in France, some were left with no more than the clothes they stood up in. Nor had the Charentais, at least, left behind a particularly rich culinary tradition.

By all accounts, peasant life in the Charente was not particularly salubrious in the first half of the nineteenth century. Agricultural methods were primitive, and despite the reforms the French Revolution had wrought elsewhere, Charentais squires still held sway over their tenants, who commonly lived in tiny one-roomed houses with their families and livestock. Their diet consisted mainly of coarse gruel, either made from buckwheat or the *châtaigne*, an inferior, rather tasteless type of chestnut, ground and cooked to a pap with milk. Alternatively, they might make a meal of bread rubbed with garlic.

Those from Normandy fared a little better, with apples, butter and cream entering their diet. From both the Charente and Normandy, a strong tradition of pancake-making was transplanted to Akaroa, where it still exists.

When Ursula Brocherie, who lives in Rue Lavaud in Akaroa, sets about making pancakes, she has a family recipe to draw upon, handed down the generations from her maternal great-grandmother, Rose de Malmanche, one of the original 1840 settlers who later went on to cook professionally at the hotel at nearby Duvachelle. At least one satisfied guest wrote in praise of Madame de Malmanche's beautiful cooking.

Her recipe is now known simply as 'French pancakes'. The original settlers, Ursula Brocherie explains, continued speaking French and had only broken English, but while the second generation learned to speak French at home with their parents, English took over as the primary language.

French Pancakes

50 g (2 oz) butter
3 eggs
100 g (4 oz or 1 cup) flour

70 g (2½ oz or ⅓ cup) sugar
500 ml (scant 1 pt or 2 cups) milk

Melt the butter, put in the remaining ingredients, and beat well. The mixture, Mrs Brocherie explains, should be quite wet. Pour enough of the mixture to cover a hot greased frying pan and cook like a crêpe, first one side, then the other. Sprinkle the pancakes with a little sugar and roll them up.

The ingredients initially used to cook these pancakes would have been supplied by the sponsors of the colonizing venture, the Nanto-Bordelaise Company. Under agreement with the colonists, they supplied enough free rations for seventeen months after the date of their departure from France, along with five acres of land for each male, and two-and-half acres for younger males, provided they cleared it within five years.

Clearing the land was hard work, as the prevailing fern roots ran deep. There was not even an ox to draw a plough, since they had all died on the voyage out, and only a duck, a hen and a goose had survived.

The first main crop planted was potatoes, which flourished, along with cabbages, lettuces, tobacco and broad beans. Runner beans, peas and corn had been planted too soon, and failed due to cold spells, winds and hailstorms.

There was not the cleared space available at first to plant wheat, but a crop of barley went in. Walnut trees immediately took root, and still grow very well around Akaroa. The French settlers also planted mulberries, pears and apples (from which they made cider in the Normandy way). Across the harbour from Akaroa, a plot of land later known as French Farm was planted for the purpose of supplying French naval ships with vegetables. In 1840 and 1841 these comprised potatoes, cabbages, salad greens and broad beans, and in 1841, a huge crop of beet. Plenty of seed was gathered from these gardens, and handed on to the settlers for their own private gardens.

Everybody kept pigs (which were allowed to wander about the village freely, doing indiscriminate damage) and the familiar colonial ritual of the *boucherie* was observed, with communal butchery and the dividing up of the spoils whenever one person wanted to kill a pig.

While there were wild pigs in the forest, they proved elusive. However, a large part of the early diet was provided by the meat of the native pigeon, or kereru, fat-breasted and succulent (and a favourite food of the Maori).

Around the rocky shores were paua (black abalone), oysters and mussels. Working initially from a ship's boat borrowed from the French warship, *L'Aube*, the settlers caught large hauls of fish with a seine net near the shore. This they almost certainly would have turned into a traditional Charentais chowder, known as *chaudrée*, meaning the portion of fish that could be packed into the large black iron cauldron, or *chaudière* – the basic piece of galley equipment allotted to the captain and crew of a fishing boat.

La Chaudrée
(fish chowder)

1.5 kg (3–3½ lb) fish, such as sole, hoki or eel
2 onions, quartered and studded with 4 cloves
1 large potato, peeled and cut into cubes
4 large cloves garlic, crushed
1 large bouquet garni
100 g (4 oz) butter, cut into pieces
salt and pepper
500 ml (scant 1 pt or 2 cups) dry white wine

Clean, scale and gut the fish. Cut off the heads, fins and tails, then cut the fish into sections, through the bone.

Place in a pot with the onions studded with cloves, the potato cubes, garlic, bouquet garni, and half the butter. Sprinkle with salt and pepper, pour over the wine, then add enough water to bring up the level of liquid until it is just covering the fish. Bring to the boil and simmer very gently for 10 minutes, covered, until the fish is barely cooked.

Remove the fish, bouquet garni, onions and potatoes. Pick out and discard the cloves. Keep the fish mixture covered, in a low oven (where it will finish cooking through) while you finish making the sauce: bring the liquid to the boil and continue to boil, uncovered, for about 20 minutes, until its has reduced down to a tasty sauce. Add the remaining butter, stir until it has melted into the sauce, then pour over the fish.

SERVES 4–6.

The *chaudrée* would have been cooked in a pot, similar in shape to the *chaudière* but smaller, suspended by a hook over an open fire in the cottage. This rather primitive set-up carried its hazards; a young housewife, Margaret Michel, died of burns after her clothes caught on fire while she was roasting coffee beans in a frying pan over an open fire.

The batterie de cuisine of the average household was not elaborate. One household inventory which survives, that of Jules Véron (1819–75) lists, besides the usual black iron pot, half a dozen smaller tin or iron pots and pans, six iron forks and spoons (no knives), six tin goblets, three cups and two dozen plates, mostly earthenware.

Little wheat was grown at first, meaning that for the first two years, the settlers had to go without bread for weeks on end if a supply ship did not turn up from Wellington. By 1844, however, forty-one acres were planted with wheat and another thirty-six with potatoes. At about this time the new vines were yielding their first grapes, which at first were sold almost exclusively to the visiting whaling ships.

Indeed, it was the victualling trade with the whalers that provided Akaroa with its initial prosperity in the 1840s. The ships tended to call in the late summer to lay in supplies for the winter whaling season, which coincided neatly with the main harvest time for the vegetables. In return, the settlers bought or bartered supplies from the whaling ships, such as barrels of black molasses. Tea was also bought from the ships, but it was a luxury and, like their British counterparts, the early French settlers often resorted to a brew from the young leaves at the tips of the manuka tree (*Leptospermum scoparium*). While I have not been able to find any reference, it is possible the French might have learned from Akaroa Maori the infusing of the chopped fresh kawakawa (*Macropiper excelsum*) to make kawakawa tea, which has a marginally appealing medicinal astringency about its aroma.

Ironically, just as the production from the vegetable gardens and the fruit trees (peaches, apricots, cherries, plums, pears and apples) began to come into full swing after 1845, the whaling trade died off, and the settlers were left without markets for their produce.

The disappearance of the whalers also had dire economic consequences for the township of Akaroa, where a number of inhabitants had been making a tidy income selling grog to the sailors. Besides the Hôtel Français, which operated with a publican's licence, Jacques Benoît sold alcohol illegally from his coffee house (until he was caught and fined heavily in 1846).

The French had their own hotel, Jules Véron's Hôtel de Normandie, where they could feel comfortable speaking to each other in French. There was also the cosy little coffee house of the *limonadier*, Adolph François, where in the evening one of the settlers might bring out his fiddle, and music and dancing would follow. Further up the harbour, François Lelièvre ran an inn, later called The Traveller's Rest, from 1851.

In the 1850s, the Canterbury Association settlement of British colonists provided a fresh outlet for Akaroa fruit and produce. By the 1860s Akaroa was shipping 800 consignments of fruit to Christchurch markets each year.

Since many of the settlers came from the wine districts of the Charente, they brought with them a detailed knowledge of viticulture to Akaroa. In 1842, Captain Smith, Surveyor General to the New Zealand Company, wrote in a report: 'The French at once started to prepare their gardens and grow grapes, some of them developing their branch of horticulture to a high degree of efficiency making excellent wine therefrom.'

However, despite subsequent reports of 'very good red wine', the vineyards gradually went into decline. In 1895, the viticulturist Romeo Bragato, writing a government report on the potential for wine making and viticulture in New Zealand, noted that he had been presented with some fine-flavoured grapes of chasselas, la folle and muscat frontignan varieties at Akaroa by M. Le Lièvre, the oldest French settler. They were of such quality that they caused Bragato to think that:

If the settlers in this district would only enter upon the vine industry in a proper spirit and upon an extensive scale, they would be able to produce a good light wine of similar character to that of the Rhine and Moselle . . . The wine industry prospered as long as those by whom it was started remained at the helm, but immediately they began to die off, the vineyards became neglected, and in consequence the vines died out.

Alternatively, he suggests that the vines died because they were attacked by oidium. However, a novel suggestion was put to me by a descendant of the Le Lièvre family, Antoine Le Lièvre of Christchurch.

A factor in the decline of the Akaroa wine industry, he believes, was the inability of the early settlers to obtain sterile conditions in their fermentation tanks. This drove the second generation into using their horticultural skills to grow enormous pumpkins, whose interiors are free of all bacterial contamination. These were then used as fermentation tanks, with a hole cut around the top, the cavity filled with fruit (not necessarily grapes) and sugar, then the top placed back and sealed. The pumpkins would then be hung from the rafters, and when the fruit inside had fermented and turned itself into wine, a hole would be pierced in the bottom of the pumpkin, and out would spurt a Bacchanalian stream. Another member of the Le Lièvre family, Marie Le Lièvre, recalls her late grandfather, Henry, making elderberry wine.

Romeo Bragato confidently predicted that, in time, Akaroa would become known as the 'Vineyard of Christchurch'. As it happens, the main focus of the modern wine industry has been around Waipara and on the Canterbury Plains around Christchurch. However, in 1989 a vineyard was planted on the historic French Farm, amid divided opinion as to the suitability of the site for viticulture. But the owners went ahead and planted 3.4 hectares in chardonnay and pinot noir anyway, and despite a two-year period when the winery ran into difficulties and was leased out as a restaurant, the operation has bounced back and proved the detractors wrong. French Farm today makes wine for three other vineyards around Akaroa, and in the ten years from 1989 to 1999 the district's vineyard area quadrupled.

So what happened to the French at Akaroa? Some returned to France, others simply died childless, while a great many more married British settlers. With this merging into the cultural mainstream, and increasing British migration to an area where the French were a tiny minority, the French language died out, and their food and wine culture with it. While there is some evidence of French cuisine having been established later in the nineteenth century (the Akaroa Museum has a settler's copy of an 1889 Parisian cookery book, *La Bonne Cuisine*, by Emile Dumont, for example), this would have been steadily diluted in the face of an Anglo-Celtic deluge of plain roast mutton and three veg.

Probably the rot, as it were, had set in very early – before even the first year at Akaroa was up. Having run out of supplies, the French were forced to send to Wellington for more. The solid British Empire stodge which arrived back – including 14,000 kg of ship's biscuit, 1,130 kg of salt pork and sacks of pease (pea meal) – must have provided a challenge to even the most creative French cook!

But what if the French *had* managed to get in before the British and claim Akaroa, then use it as a platform for colonizing the whole of New Zealand's South Island – as was their plan back in 1840? Probably only shortly later a Burgundian viticulturist would have done some sniffing around and become very excited by the limestone soils around Waipara, in north Canterbury, along with the seaward row of hills to block cooling sea breezes and cause warmer ripening conditions in summer, followed by months of extended, low heat sunshine hours allowing growers to hang their grapes on the vines well into autumn. Waipara might well have begun producing excellent pinot noir in the nineteenth century instead of the twentieth.

On the other hand, had John Bull, that corpulent, gout-ridden connoisseur of claret and burgundy, not been allowed the novelty of owning his own vineyards out in the Antipodes, the New Zealand wine industry might not enjoy the same independence and spirit of innovation today, since you can bet that under French administration, the vineyards would have been smothered to death with affection at the same time as being subjected to strict paternalistic control from la Metropole.

Who is to say that the Algerian experience (see pages 205–6) would not have been repeated and elaborated, with surreptitious blendings of the colonial product into the *first* growths of Burgundy? Granted, that might have been a small price to pay for a hundred years of British Empire cooking, of over-cooked lamb and bad bread, but that era is history now, and New Zealand is a very different place today. Now there is decent blue cheese and baguettes, and all the coastal lamb is *pre-salé*, just as it always was, only nowadays it is cooked pink in the middle.

Also, we still have the toheroa, that giant triangular surf clam, albeit in much diminished numbers, and the koura. If the South Island had become a French colony, today there would not only be koura farms as have already been established in Otago (since the koura is none other than the French *écrevisse*), but marine biologists would also be engaged in frenetic scientific research to achieve the seemingly impossible quest for successful toheroa aquaculture. Perhaps, also, there might exist a Confrérie des Chevaliers de la Toheroa, of grey-haired gents got up in medieval robes and caps, with silver chains wrought as toheroas hung around their necks, gathering at the remaining Southland beaches where the toheroa is still found, sitting at outdoor tables laid with linen and Limoges tureens, supping Bisque de Toheroa and recalling the old days when they gathered enough to fill the back seats of their Citroëns to the ceiling.

For, make no mistake, the flavour of this shellfish is *très recherché*. This is due in no small part to the fact that the toheroa (which, along with the much smaller tuatua and pipi, form a class of bi-valves unique to New Zealand) sends up long siphon tubes around the low tide mark and feeds on an exclusive diet of plankton. This not only gives the minced flesh its colour (a curiously appealing olive green) but, more importantly, its unique flavour. It is not mere romantic fancy to suggest that toheroa taste like oysters fed on asparagus. James Beard, the famous American gastronome, is supposed to have declared toheroa soup the most delicious soup he had ever tasted, despite it having been prepared with toheroa from a Meredith Bros. export tin.

Mes amis, je vous propose la recette de notre Confrérie manquée:

Bisque de Toheroa

50 fresh toheroa
1 litre (1¾ pts or 4 cups) light
   chicken stock
1 carrot, sliced
1 stick celery
1 onion, chopped

2 bay leaves
250 ml (9 fl oz or 1 cup) off-dry
   wine, such as a New
   Zealand riesling
250 ml (9 fl oz or 1 cup) crème
   fraîche

Mince the toheroa in batches of five at a time in a large and powerful food processor, until the flesh is thoroughly minced to a smooth, consistent paste. (The flesh is very tough, so eating toheroa whole or raw is not an option; finely mincing it, on the other hand, brings out the green colour.)

Take half the toheroa and make a stock with it, by simmering it for 2 hours in the chicken stock with carrot, celery, onion, bay leaves and riesling.

Once stock has cooled completely, strain through a muslim cloth and return to the pan. Add the remaining minced toheroa and slowly bring up the heat, without actually boiling. Keep at this heat for about 5 minutes, until the toheroa is cooked through, then whisk in the crème fraîche, little by little. Heat but do not boil, and serve immediately.

7 Africa

Based on fish, olive oil, spices, fresh herbs and vegetables such as tomatoes, peppers, artichokes and aubergines, and combining French sophistication with rustic influences from around the Mediterranean – from Spain, Italy and North Africa – it is perhaps not surprising that the lost cuisine of the European settlers in French North Africa has a fashionably contemporary ring.

If these white settlers identified themselves, in their own famous expression, as *mediterranéens-et-demi*, then they were most assuredly Mediterranean-and-a-half with regard to their food. It was, indeed, one of the very first eclectic modernist cuisines, deriving from the cosmopolitan mix of races thrown together as a result of French colonial policy.

Collectively, these Europeans were known as *pieds-noirs*, a name said to have been coined by sandal-wearing Arabs, who looked with fascination upon the highly polished boots or 'black feet' of the French military. (Among the *pieds-noirs* themselves, however, the name only gained currency after it was adopted, somewhat pejoratively, by the French press during the Algerian war of independence.)

Cuisine pied-noir is all the more startling for having appeared by accident, for the French never intended to colonize Algeria. Their conquest in 1830 was intended more to teach the ruling corsairs a lesson, and it was only when unofficial groups of Europeans established small farms and market gardens around the towns and began to exert political influence, that the French army realized withdrawal was impossible.

In 1848 Algeria was declared an integral part of France, and colonization continued apace, by the unwanted and unemployed Parisians from the revolution of 1848, followed by hard-working Alsacians, refugees from the provinces forfeited to a triumphant Prussia. There followed immense, successive waves of Spaniards, Italians and Maltese, who by a law of 1889 were all granted French citizenship. By 1917, it was estimated that only one in five of the non-Muslim population was of French ancestry. As Anatole France noted angrily, 'We have despoiled, pursued and hunted down the Arabs in order to populate Algeria with Italians and Spaniards.'

Immense, beautiful and harsh, the savage sun-baked landscape of Algeria accentuated the Latin temperament of the *pieds-noirs.* Typically, they were passionate and fiery, capable both of extreme hatred and affection, macho, patriarchal, with a strong sense of family and respect for the mother. Sensual rather than intellectual, they were also intensely hospitable, placing a high value on eating and drinking, and well able to enjoy their leisure hours, fishing from the rocks or swimming at the beach, gossiping over a pastis at an outdoor café or playing a game of *boules* in their dusty town squares, lined with pollarded plane trees and dominated by the inevitable, graceless *monument aux morts.*

Since the various immigrant groups gravitated towards specific parts of the country, colonial Algerian cookery quickly developed a regional character. In the east, in the port city of Oran, there was largely a Spanish settlement. In fact, with 300,000 *pied-noir* inhabitants to 150,000 Muslims, Oran was the only European-dominated city of Algeria. Albert Camus damned it as a city of ineffable boredom, where the youths had only two pleasures – 'getting their shoes shined and displaying those same shoes on the boulevard'. Its streets were 'doomed to dust, pebble and heat', while its shops combined 'all the bad taste of Europe and the Orient'. But Camus could not deny Oran's Spanish character, and indeed, in the 1950s, René Lespès estimated that 45 per cent of its population was of Spanish descent, as opposed to 18 to 19 per cent which was French.

In such circumstances, the community retained both its Spanish language and its cuisine. Traditional Andalucian-style gazpacho was common, along with a version peculiar to Oran. This was called *gaspacho oranais* but in reality it was a stew of rabbit, chicken, pork and pigeon, stewed with onion, garlic and tomatoes, then thickened near the end of cooking with crumbled home-made pastry *galettes.*

Paella

For all *pieds-noirs*, whether of Spanish ancestry or not, paella was party food, cooked for crowds in special over-sized paella pans with four handles, custom-made in Bab el-Oeud, a sprawling Spanish suburb of

Algiers. Every family claimed to have its 'secret' recipe, but the list of ingredients was always loose. To those listed below, you might add rabbit, lamb or snails.

500 g (1 lb) mussels in the shell, scrubbed
24 uncooked prawns
250 ml (9 fl oz or 1 cup) olive oil
500 g (1 lb) squid, prepared as for Calmars sauce paprika (see page 194)
1 chicken, cut into pieces
400 g (14 oz) pork, cubed
1 tablespoon tomato concentrate
6 cloves garlic, chopped
pinch of saffron threads

500 g (1 lb or 2 cups) short-grain rice (ideally Valencian)
salt and pepper
200 g (7 oz) chorizo, sliced
2 red peppers, prepared as for frita (see page 200)
2 tomatoes, blanched, peeled and chopped
6 preserved artichoke hearts
125 g (4 oz or 1 cup) green peas
50 g (2 oz or 1 cup) chopped parsley

Steam open the mussels and leave them in their juices. In another pot, boil about 500 ml (1 pt or 2 cups) of water, then plunge in the prawns and boil for 3 minutes only. Remove from the stove and leave the prawns in their water.

Heat half the olive oil in a pot, then sauté the squid until it changes colour and is barely cooked through. Remove with a slotted spoon and set aside. Add the chicken and the pork to the oil remaining in the pot and stir-fry until lightly browned. Add tomato concentrate, garlic and saffron threads (previously ground to a paste in a mortar and pestle with a dash of hot water). Cover and simmer gently for 10 minutes.

Into another pot, strain the cooking liquid from both the mussels and the prawns. Add 2 litres (3½ pts or 8 cups) of fresh water, taste, then add salt accordingly. Bring to the boil.

In a large paella pan (failing that, use a large wok) heat the remaining olive oil. Add the rice and stir to coat each grain, then add the water little by little with a soup ladle. Add the meat mixture, stir in, and cook the rice, uncovered, for about 15 minutes on a low but steady simmer. About 3 minutes before the end of cooking, gently stir in the chorizo, grilled and sliced red peppers, tomatoes, artichoke hearts, peas and parsley.

Gently press the mussels (still in their shells), prawns and squid part-way into the top of the rice, cover the pan or wok, turn off the heat and leave for 5 minutes before serving.

SERVES 8.

Thon à la Catalane
(tuna with gherkins and capers in tomato sauce)

Although, as the name suggests, this dish is apparently of Catalonian origin, it was acclimatized to Algeria by the use of fresh coriander, which the *pieds-noirs* called 'Arab parsley'.

1 kg (2 lb) tomatoes
200 ml (7 fl oz or ¾ cup) olive oil
1 kg (2 lb) tuna (1–2 thick slices)
salt and pepper
1 tablespoon tomato concentrate
1 teaspoon mild chilli powder
200 g (7 oz) small gherkins, sliced
   lengthways

200 g (7 oz) pickled onions, thickly
   sliced
2 tablespoons capers
3 tablespoons fresh chopped
   coriander

Place the tomatoes in a bowl of boiling water, leave for 30 seconds, remove and peel. Cut each tomato into two crossways and squeeze out the pips, as you would a lemon. Cut the tomatoes into small pieces.

Heat half the olive oil in a large heatproof casserole dish, add the tomatoes and stir. Place over the tuna, sprinkle it with salt and pepper. Mix the other half of the olive oil with the tomato concentrate and the chilli powder, and sprinkle over the tuna. Scatter the gherkins, pickled onions and capers across the top. Cover the pot and cook on a low heat for 30 minutes. Sprinkle over the chopped coriander and serve cold. This dish will keep for several days in the refrigerator.

In Bab el-Oued, the working-class district of Algiers, the tenements were so impregnated with Spanish blood that their inhabitants were known collectively as the 'Hernandez-and-Perez.' From the street corners came the aromas of grilled liver and kidney on spits, of red sausages cooking on charcoal braziers, of fritters fried in oil, and fish mingled with incense, cumin and amber. From hawkers came the tapping sound of a knife against an iron plate, and the plaintive cry of *'la calentita! la calentita toute chaude!'* This was a deceptively simple Spanish cake of chick-pea flour, mixed with water, olive oil and salt, and baked until set. Perfectly cooked, calentita was light underneath its golden skin, gradually becoming denser towards the base.

At Bab el-Oued market, calentita sellers set up trestle tables, and laid a clean cloth over the calentita to keep it warm. Their cries would have to compete with the seller of carrots, of mackerel 'fresher than you', of figs, ten different varieties of olives, strings of onions and chillies, oranges, tubs of sardines and roses, all in weird juxtaposition. Near Notre-Dame-des-Victoires was a Spanish spice shop, selling special spices for rice dishes, along with dried salt cod and delicious Málaga raisins. Then there were pâtisseries, their windows piled with pyramids of nougat, anis-flavoured rolls and *montecaos* (spicy ball-shaped confectionery) ready to tempt workers on their way home from Bab el-Oued's furniture, shoe and tobacco factories.

In every Algerian town in the early evening, loud conversation, often seeming on the verge of quarrelling, billowed forth from brightly lit, cavernous cafés, along with a dense blue cloud of tobacco smoke. Glasses of anisette would be lined up along the bar, along with little saucers of complimentary olives, anchovies, fried broad beans, little herbed snails, salted almonds, peanuts, preserved lupin seeds, grilled watermelon seeds and chips.

This was the *kémia* hour, when the *pieds-noirs* gathered to discuss the day's events. *Kémia*, a word of uncertain origin which may derive from the Arabic *kmeh* – to smoke, was the *pied-noir* equivalent of the Spanish tapas, the Greek mezze, or the Turkish raki table.

When *kémia* was served in the home, a brass pestle and mortar would be placed in the middle of the table to crack the shells of the nuts and to split the olives in order to remove their stones. The *kémia* themselves might also be more luxurious, such as slices of *boudin*, garlic sausage, *chorizo* or *merguez*. If guests were present, there might also be rather more substantial, involved dishes, such as calf's brain pâté *(méguéna)*, anchovies baked in pastry *(alumettes aux anchois)*, kebabs of kidneys and vegetables, and a *pied-noir* favourite, squid in paprika sauce.

Calmars Sauce Paprika
(squid in paprika sauce)

1.5 kg (3–3½ lb) squid	2 sprigs of fresh thyme
4 tablespoons olive oil	2 sprigs of fresh rosemary
1 large onion, finely chopped	2 bay leaves
6 cloves garlic, chopped	salt and pepper
1 tablespoon tomato concentrate	400 ml (14 fl oz or 1½ cups) white
1 teaspoon mild paprika	wine

Prepare the squid. Under a cold running tap, strip the small discs of cartilage from the tentacles by pulling them through your hands. Take a dishwashing brush, and hold the squid under the cold tap while you scrub off the purplish outer skin. Turn the sac or hood inside out, rip out the contents, including the guts and the long strip of semi-transparent backbone. Cut out the beak and the eyes. Slice the hood into rings and the tentacles into lengths.

Heat the olive oil in a pot, add the chopped onion and fry until translucent. Add the squid and the remaining ingredients and simmer over a medium heat for 45 minutes to an hour, until the squid is completely tender. After 20 minutes, pick out and discard the sprigs of rosemary and thyme before their leaves fall off. This dish can either be served cold, or hot with rice.

Perhaps the greatest contribution from the Italian *pieds-noirs* was pasta.

Spaghetti à l'Algéroise
(spaghetti Algiers-style)

500 g (1 lb) spaghetti	2 cloves garlic, chopped
salt	200 g (7 oz) grated gruyère cheese
200 g (7 oz) smoked bacon, diced	1 tablespoon chopped parsley
olive oil	

Boil the spaghetti in salted water until cooked. Meanwhile, heat a couple of tablespoons of oil in a pan and fry the bacon for several minutes, then lower the heat, cover the pan and allow to complete cooking until the pasta is done. Several minutes before the end of cooking, add the chopped garlic to the bacon.

Drain the spaghetti, toss with a little olive oil, then add the cooked bacon, the gruyère and parsley, and toss together.
SERVES 3–4.

One other minority group deeply influenced the cuisine of the *pieds-noirs* – the Jews of Algeria. Comprising about one-fifth of the non-Muslim population, they arrived in Algeria many centuries before the French. While they had never suffered the same official oppression as Jewish communities elsewhere, they tended to identify with the French after the conquest in 1830. Moreover, the Crémieux Decrees of 1870, conferring automatic French citizenship, attracted significant numbers of prosperous Jews from outside Algeria.

It was through Jewish friends that many indigenous North African dishes reached the kitchens of the French settlers. Not only had the Jews assimilated these dishes when large groups settled in Algeria following expulsion from sixteenth-century Spain, but they claimed a part in having invented them. The first Jews, it was said, had been established in Algeria even before the arrival of the Romans, and managed to convert a number of Berber tribes to Judaism. These Berbers unsuccessfully fought the Arab invaders at the end of the twelfth century, and while the majority converted to Islam, some remained loyal to Judaism. Hence, a number of Algerian Jews are said to be of Berber ancestry, having blonde hair and blue eyes to substantiate their claim.

Algerian Jewish cuisine, therefore, had many similarities to that of the Algerian Arabs. While some dishes were particular to each community, a great many more were common to both. When the French arrived, the Algerian Jews adopted dishes such as fried beefsteak and béchamel sauce, but their own cooking contributed far more significantly to the *pied-noir* cocktail. In the *pied-noir* version of *caldero* for example, the influences of Spain, southern France and the Algerian Jews converged to create a new variation on bouillabaisse, served with rice rather than croûtons, and with the rouille spiced up with a little harissa (see page 211).

Other important examples of Algerian Jewish influence are *boulettes de poisson* and a fish pickle known as *escabèche*.

Sauce Escabèche
(marinade for sardines or mussels)

Probably brought to North Africa by Spanish Jews in the sixteenth century, this dish had been introduced to them in the Iberian Peninsula long ago by Moorish invaders (*escabèche* or *escabech* being derived from an Arab word, *cisbech*, itself a corruption of the Persian *siquisbé*, meaning 'acidulated food').

2 tablespoons olive oil	½ teaspoon mild chilli powder
5 cloves garlic, chopped	125 ml (4 fl oz or ½ cup) white wine
1 teaspoon ground cumin	vinegar
1 teaspoon mild paprika	salt and pepper

Heat the oil and gently fry the garlic, cumin, paprika and chilli powder for about 2 minutes. Pour in the wine vinegar along with 250 ml (9 fl oz or 1 cup) of water, add salt and pepper, and leave for 15 minutes.

The escabèche can then be used to marinate fried sardines or steamed mussels. If using mussels, replace the plain water with the water used to steam them open, together with accumulated juices, and omit the salt. Eat hot or cold. This dish keeps several days in the refrigerator.

Since Algeria borders the Mediterranean, the importance of fish in the *pied-noir* diet is easily understood. Both Oran and Algiers were important fishing ports, the latter with significant communities of both Napolitan and Maltese fishermen. Some of these, berets on their heads and dressed in blue, would hawk their catch in wicker baskets door to door.

At the fish market in Algiers, which used to be referred to simply as La Pêcherie, customers would await the arrival of the trawlers at around 6 o'clock each morning, bringing fresh tuna, red gurnard, whiting, anchovies and sardines. Despite the heat, the fish was rarely put on ice, since it was customarily sold and cooked the same day. In summer, fish was often simply grilled or fried; in winter, more elaborate recipes came into their own.

Boulettes de Poisson
(fish balls with tomato and coriander sauce)

Sauce
3 cloves garlic, chopped
2 tablespoons olive oil
3 medium tomatoes, peeled and
  chopped
3 tablespoons tomato concentrate
1 teaspoon sugar
salt to taste
1 red chilli
250 ml (9 fl oz or 1 cup) white wine

Fish balls
500 g (1 lb) white fish fillets
4 tablespoons dry white breadcrumbs
1 egg, lightly beaten
1 teaspoon mild French mustard
a good pinch of nutmeg
salt and pepper
4 tablespoons chopped fresh
  coriander

Briefly sauté the garlic in the olive oil and before it browns, add the remaining sauce ingredients along with about 250 ml (9 fl oz or 1 cup) of water. Simmer for 20 minutes, covered, while you make the fish balls.

Either finely chop the fish by hand until you have the consistency of minced meat, or chop the fillets roughly and grind in a food processor, using the pulse button. Be careful not to over-process; you want tiny pieces, not a gluey purée. Transfer to a bowl, add breadcrumbs, egg, mustard, nutmeg, salt, pepper and 3 tablespoons of the coriander, and mix well. With wet hands, shape the mixture into balls about the size of golf balls.

Drop the fish balls into the sauce and simmer for about 25 minutes. Turn them once during cooking. Just before serving, stir the remaining table-spoon of fresh coriander into the sauce.

SERVES 4.

Daurade au Four
(baked whole fish with coriander aïoli)

For the fish	*Aïoli*
1 whole gilt-head bream or other fish, about 1.5 kg (3–3½ lb)	1 large clove garlic
3 cloves garlic, chopped	1 egg
2 lemons, sliced thinly	250 ml (9 fl oz or 1 cup) light olive oil
25 g (1 oz) butter	¼ teaspoon salt
125 ml (4 fl oz or ½ cup) white wine	few grinds of black pepper
salt and pepper	juice of 1 lemon
8 small potatoes	2 packed tablespoons chopped fresh coriander
4 peeled tomatoes	
2 large carrots, sliced	
8 button mushrooms, left whole	
olive oil	

Scale and then gut the fish, if this has not already been done for you.

Place the fish on a large sheet of aluminium foil, on top of an oven tray. Scatter the chopped garlic and sliced lemons over the top of the fish and dot with pieces of butter. Bring up the sides of the foil to form a sort of leak-proof container, then pour over the wine. Sprinkle with salt and pepper. Bring the edges of the foil together, fold and crimp to seal the fish in.

Pre-heat the oven to 180°C (350°F/Gas 4). Partly boil the potatoes (allow about 8 minutes). This is to ensure they cook properly and brown nicely dur-ing the allotted time. Drain, then arrange around the fish, along with the tomatoes, carrots and mushrooms, on the spare space around the oven tray. Sprinkle with olive oil and toss lightly to ensure all sides are coated.

Bake for about 30 minutes (cooking time will vary according to the type of fish and its weight) until the fish is just cooked through to the bone.

Meanwhile, make the aïoli (garlic mayonnaise). Drop the whole clove of garlic into a running food processor. When it is pulverized, break in the whole egg through the feeder tube. When the egg is beaten, slowly dribble in the olive oil, beginning with a very fine stream. You can add the second half a little faster, after the mayonnaise has emulsified and begun to thicken. Add salt and pepper, then place a tea strainer over the top of the feeder tube (to catch the lemon pips) and squeeze in the lemon juice. Stop the machine, add the chopped coriander and use the pulse button to work it through the mayonnaise.

When the fish is cooked, carefully transfer it to an oval serving dish with the aid of two fish slices. If you have squeamish guests, you may like to place a slice of stuffed olive over the eye of the fish, as a sort of blindfold.

Arrange the vegetables around the fish and pour any cooking juices over them. Offer the coriander aïoli separately.

SERVES 3–4.

Filets de Sole Algéroise

Take the fillets of a sole, previously skinned, lay them out on a buttered and salted dish. Sprinkle with 200 ml white wine, several drops of lemon juice, season with salt and pepper, cover with buttered paper, and cook in the oven, basting from time to time. At the end of cooking, place on a long dish, arrange a garnish of prawn tails around them. Incorporate the cooking liquid into 200 ml prawn sauce, pour over the sole fillets and serve immediately.

Translated from *La Cuisine Française et Africaine*, Léon Isnard, Paris 1949.

Amateur fishing was a major pastime. On Sundays, groups of friends would meet on the rocks at Cap Caxine, bringing a packed lunch and staying all day. Football and the racecourse were also important diversions but, above all, there was the beach.

On the many beaches which were within easy reach of Algiers by bus, the young of the poor whites would spend entire weekends lounging under sun umbrellas, playing volleyball or splashing about in the sea. The very expression they used – *se taper un bain* – 'indulge in a swim', rather than simply 'go for a swim', indicates the level of sensuality at which they lived. On Sunday afternoons, at the seaside resort of Aïn Taya, they danced to an orchestra at the Tamaris Hotel, or jived beneath the stars to the tunes of Elvis and Paul Anka, thrashed out by the café juke box at Miliana, before stealing off to make love at a leafy secluded point, named in all seriousness by the authorities Point des Blagueurs (Jokers' Point).

Understandably, food was not the central focus of these expeditions to the beach, and might consist merely of a sandwich filled with grilled green pepper or an omelette of courgettes, potatoes and onions, made just before setting out and kept warm in a tea towel. They might also buy their food at the beach from itinerant sellers of snacks such as *oublies*, a variety of wafer-thin waffle curled into a cone.

On summer evenings, families would gather for light informal meals on the terrace of their apartments, where a charcoal brazier or *kanoun* would be used to grill kebabs of squid or beef. This was the season for salads, many of which had a North African flavour.

Frita lies at the core of *pied-noir* cuisine, mentioned by Albert Camus in *The Plague*, his famous novel set in Oran. It appears *frita* was inspired by a Tunisian dish, *tchoutchouka*, and indeed, went under this name in Algiers. In Oran, however, they made a distinction between *frita* and their version of *tchoutchouka*.

Frita
(grilled red pepper and tomato salad)

6 red peppers
4 ripe tomatoes
4 tablespoons olive oil
1 large onion, finely chopped

5 cloves garlic, chopped
1 small red chilli, thickly sliced
salt and pepper

Grill the red peppers (in Algeria this would have been done over the *kanoun*) until the skins blister and blacken all over. Remove and enclose in a plastic or brown paper bag, leave to 'sweat' and loosen the skins. When cool enough to handle, remove from the bag and peel off the skin. Remove and discard the core and seeds, and slice the red peppers thickly. Place the tomatoes in a bowl, cover with boiling water, leave for a minute, then peel. Slice through the middle crossways, then squeeze out the pips as you would a lemon. Chop the tomatoes.

Heat the oil in a pan, add the onion and fry until cooked through and translucent. Add the tomato pieces and simmer gently. Once the water has come out of the tomatoes and then evaporated, add the peppers, garlic and

chilli. Season to taste with salt and pepper, and cook gently, stirring from time to time, for 20 minutes. This can either be served cold, or hot with rice.
SERVES 4.

Tchoutchouka Oranais
(lamb chops with pied-noir ratatouille)

6 lamb chops
125 ml (4 fl oz or ½ cup) olive oil
3 onions, sliced
1 large aubergine, diced
1 kg (2 lb) peppers, diced
1.5 kg (3 lb) tomatoes, diced

4 cloves garlic
1 small red chilli, chopped
salt and pepper
6 eggs
2 large handfuls basil leaves, torn

In a large heavy-bottomed casserole dish, fry the lamb chops for about 4 minutes per side. Remove the chops and set aside. To the oil remaining in the dish, add the onions and the aubergines. Fry for 5 minutes, then add the peppers, tomatoes, garlic and chilli. Season with salt and pepper, cover the dish, lower the heat and cook for 25 minutes.

About 5 minutes before the end of cooking, bury the lamb chops in the ratatouille. Make six dents in the surface, break in the eggs and poach, covered, until the egg whites are set. Divide the mixture between 6 plates, allowing one chop and one egg per person, then sprinkle with basil.
SERVES 6.

Salade de Pommes de Terre
(pied-noir potato salad)

6 medium potatoes
60 ml (2 fl oz or ¼ cup) dry white
    wine
6 tablespoons extra virgin olive oil
¼ teaspoon salt
2 tablespoons white wine vinegar

1 clove garlic, crushed
3 eggs, hard-boiled and chopped
6 cooked herring fillets (optional)
2 tablespoons chopped parsley
few grinds of black pepper

Boil the potatoes in salted water until soft. Drain, and when cool enough to handle, peel and cut into pieces. Sprinkle with the wine while still warm, then dress with the olive oil, salt, vinegar and garlic mixed together.

Mix through the hard-boiled eggs, herring fillets, chopped parsley and black pepper. If serving with meat (e.g. kebabs) omit the herring.
SERVES 6.

Salade Algérienne

½ cucumber
6 medium tomatoes, peeled and chopped
3 green or red peppers, sliced
1 small onion, finely chopped
20 small black olives (ideally the Coquillos variety)

5 fillets of anchovy (optional)
1 tablespoon wine vinegar
½ teaspoon salt
few grinds of black pepper
3 tablespoons extra virgin olive oil
2 eggs, hard-boiled and sliced (optional)

Peel the cucumber, split down the middle, scoop out and discard the seeds. Chop the cucumber into pieces, place in a sieve, sprinkle with salt and leave to drain for 30 minutes.

Mix together cucumber, tomatoes, peppers, onion, olives and fillets of anchovy (if using). In a cup, mix together the vinegar, salt and pepper, add the oil and stir to make a dressing. Pour over the salad, toss, then arrange the slices of hard-boiled egg over the top.

Variation: use the anchovy fillets to make the dressing. In a blender or with a mortar and pestle, pound them with the yolk of a hard-boiled egg and 10 leaves of fresh basil. Slowly work in 3 tablespoons oil and 1 tablespoon wine vinegar.
SERVES 4–6.

With an improvement in maritime communications in the late nineteenth century, it became possible for the *pieds-noirs* to grow fruit and vegetables to supply the French market, particularly Paris in the off-season.

Near the sea, on the coastal strip where receding coastlines left sheltered sandy beaches with loose warm soil and a damp, mild climate, Spanish and Italian settlers cultivated rectangles of gardens bordered with beach grasses, in which they grew potatoes, carrots and peas. On the Mitidja Plains behind Algiers, vast swamplands were drained and planted with vineyards and market gardens, where Spanish orchardists from Mahón applied their knowledge of irrigation.

French peasant settlers, accustomed to northern winters where the fields shut down over winter, were astounded by the unceasing benefaction of the sun: artichokes, green beans and tomatoes came non-stop into the town markets, with cabbages, cauliflowers, courgettes, cucumbers, aubergines and peppers gathering in piles. Figs, pomegranates and oranges, which had been grown in Algeria since antiquity, were joined by the mandarin in 1850. Later came the clementine, which in Algeria referred to a cross between the Seville orange and the mandarin, created by Père Clément in the Department of Oran.

Each season brought its harvest: in the spring there were strawberries, almonds and cherries. The bigaroon variety from Miliana was particularly celebrated, and the inhabitants held a cherry festival in its honour each year. With the onset of summer came an avalanche of fruit – meltingly soft peaches, apricots, greengages, an unusually sweet variety of medlar. 'The juicy plum turns golden under the sun,' gushed Léon Isnard in *La Cuisine Française et Africaine*, 'while the perfumed pear turns yellow and grows heavy on its frail stem . . . In the autumn, there are apples, round and firm like the breast of a young woman.'

Watermelon, which completed many a *pied-noir* dinner in summer, was sold on the streets of Algerian towns and cities, the canny buyer knowing what to look for: watermelons needed to be large but light, while cantaloupe melons were best when heavy and scented. Ideally, melons were refrigerated before eating; failing that, they were immersed in rivers, in the sea, or under running cold water.

For Algerian Jews, their new year's celebration, Rosh Hashanah, in late September or early October conveniently coincided with the arrival of autumn fruits: pomegranates, jujubes, kakis (persimmons), apples, fresh figs and dates. In the middle of the table laid for the Rosh Hashanah celebration there would be a pot of honey, dates and figs, their sweetness symbolizing what everybody hoped the new year would bring.

Rosh Hashanah also saw the first of the new season's olives. The olive, like the vine and the fig, had been cultivated in Algeria since antiquity, having been imported to North Africa from Asia Minor by the Phoenicians. Under Roman rule, the olive was largely responsible for Algeria's prosperity, but with the nomadic invaders who succeeded the Romans, the groves fell into decline and the industry collapsed.

With French colonization, there was a large-scale revival of olive planting, and the indigenous Algerians, noting this success, followed suit. An 1854 census revealed 23,000 hectares under plantation, forming the basis for the modern industry in Algeria, still a significant contributor of olive oil for blending on the international market.

Olives were central to the *pied-noir* diet, not only eaten during the *kémia* hour, but incorporated into their cooking:

Poulet aux Olives Vertes
(chicken with green olives)

1 chicken, about 1.5 kg (3–3½ lb)	250 g (8 oz) green olives,
2 tablespoons olive oil	preferably pitted
1 large onion, finely chopped	5 cloves garlic, chopped
2 tomatoes, peeled and chopped	2 bay leaves
250 g (8 oz) button mushrooms	2 teaspoons chopped fresh thyme
2 medium carrots, sliced	salt and pepper
1 tablespoon flour	chopped parsley to garnish
250 ml (9 fl oz or 1 cup) white wine	

Cut the chicken into 8 pieces. With a modern battery hen, you may want to skin it in order to reduce the fat content. Heat the oil in a large casserole dish and brown the chicken pieces, moving and turning frequently to prevent them sticking. Remove the chicken pieces, and fry the onion in the oil. When the onion is translucent, add the tomatoes, mushrooms and carrots, fry for a further few minutes, then sprinkle with the flour and mix well.

Return the chicken to the pot, add the wine, along with 750 ml (1¼ pts or 3 cups) of water, the olives, garlic, bay leaves, thyme, salt and pepper. Cover and simmer for 30–40 minutes, until the chicken is cooked through. Sprinkle the chicken pieces with parsley before serving.
SERVES 4.

Olive allusions entered *pied-noir* slang: *'Il n'en casse pas une!'* ('He didn't even break one!') refers to the process of splitting green olives with a mortar and pestle, in order to get the flavour of herbs to penetrate them when put into jars to marinate in oil. In other words, with all the speaking and activity going on around an individual, *'Il ne'n casse pas une!'* meant 'The lazy sod said nothing and did nothing either.'

There were also baser connotations: *'faire une olive'* referred to the obscene gesture of 'giving the finger', while *'changer l'eau des olives'* ('changing the olive water' – a reference to the necessity of repeatedly changing the water while pickling olives) was a euphemism for taking a pee.

Besides olive pickling, a great deal of jam making and preserving of quinces, figs, melons and raisins took place during the autumn, in preparation for winter. Dates and figs were also set out in the sun to dry, for use in savoury dishes as well as in desserts and confectionery.

Pruneaux aux Noix
(prunes stuffed with walnuts)

500 g (1 lb) pitted prunes	3 tablespoons raw sugar
250 g (8 oz) shelled walnut pieces	1 teaspoon ground cinnamon
3 tablespoons peanut oil	juice of 2 oranges

Press a piece of walnut into each prune to replace the stone. Pour the oil over the bottom of a heavy-bottomed saucepan, arrange over the stuffed prunes, then sprinkle with sugar, cinnamon and orange juice. Gently simmer, covered, for 20–25 minutes, basting the prunes every so often with the oil and orange juice mixture. These can be served after the meal, but they are also very nice eaten with roast chicken or pork.

Every other agricultural commodity in colonial Algeria paled into insignificance beside the grape. At its peak in 1938, the Algerian wine industry boasted 400,000 hectares (nearly a million acres) under vines, while in the 1950s between one half and two-thirds of the international wine trade was in North African wines, nearly all of it from Algeria. At that time, wine accounted for half of Algeria's exports by value, and for a third of the paid employment in the modern commercialized agricultural sector.

Although vine-growing flourished in Algeria during classical times, like the olive it collapsed with the departure of the Romans. The modern industry began modestly, with the introduction of the vine to the Mitidja by Trappist monks in 1843, followed by another small planting by German wine-growers from Baden. By 1860, there were still only 220 hectares under vines.

The real impetus occurred after France's vines were devastated by the phylloxera pest in 1878. A major influx of French wine-growers from the Midi followed, and indeed, these southerners accounted for the largest group of *pieds-noirs* of French extraction.

Eventually phylloxera hit Algeria too, but despite this and other technical problems, not to mention economic recessions, 188,536 hectares had been planted in 1923–24, yielding 10,243,000 hectolitres, a respectable lake. Yet it was also a ghost lake, in the sense that most of it was surreptitiously blended with French wines in a way which would be illegal today. Being robust, deeply coloured and highly alcoholic, Algerian reds provided the ideal balance for the vast quantity of insipid French *vin ordinaire* made from the aramon grape – until the 1960s, France's most popular variety. It is interesting, if a little embarrassing, to speculate to what extent the body of 'old-fashioned burgundy' was due to the unacknowledged presence of Algerian wine. This never applied to the first growths, to be sure, but certainly many of the lesser burgundies (and bordeaux, for that matter) during the first half of the twentieth century were made with significant input from Algeria. Embarrassing, because the vast bulk of Algerian wine was fruitless and abrasive, its character and acidity largely baked out of existence by a relentless sun.

'It must be confessed that Algerian wines have one and all a rather disagreeable aftertaste, recalling the smell of methylated spirits,' wrote the eminent English authority P. Morton Shand in 1926. 'Also, they are apt to be hot and heady.'

The varieties planted did not help: in terms of hectares, carignan was king, though as regards quality, it was far from noble. Coarse and astringent, entirely lacking in fruit flavour, its one saving grace was to act as a foil for the softer cinsault, an equally uninspiring variety of which 60,000 hectares had been planted by the early 1960s. The sole virtue of Alicante bouschet was its deep red colour, while the wine made from the vast acreage of aramon was no better than its French counterpart.

As for the white grapes, clairette blanc only served to emphasize the drawbacks of the hot Algerian climate, since wine made from this variety is inherently high in alcohol and low in acid. Not that this mattered particularly, since during the colonial period most of Algeria's clairette blanc ended up in French vermouth, heavily disguised by aromatic herbs and wormwood. Algerian ugni blanc was also deeply mediocre, lacking both character and extract, but at least able to provide a certain level of acidity.

The cause of quality was rarely served by the sites chosen for mass production, such as the hot Mitidja Plains inland from Algiers, and in many parts of the Oranais to the east, such as around Ain-Temouchent. Huge fortunes were made by families such as the Borgeauds, of Swiss ancestry, ensconced in the grand mansion of La Trappe at Staouéli, and surrounded by 1,000 hectares of the best land in Algeria, producing four million litres of wine a year.

On the coastal ranges, where the vines were planted up to 1,200 m (4,000 ft) above sea level, the cooler temperatures greatly improved grape quality, leading to a dozen crus being accorded the honour of VDQS recognition by the French in colonial times.

For the *pieds-noirs*, the wine industry was an important source of money and power, while for the non-European population it was a significant source of employment. Yet at the same time, the growing Muslim nationalist movement of the 1950s condemned the wine industry for having enmeshed the Algerian economy, in the classic colonial style, with that of the mother country. Besides which, as teetotallers, these Muslims had no emotional or cultural ties to wine.

The same applied to their attitude to the French in general. Since the indigenous Muslim population could only obtain French citizenship if they abandoned polygamy and renounced Koranic law, it is not surprising that only a handful took up the 'offer'. As for the *pieds-noirs*, their attitude to the indigenous Muslims was largely one of indifference.

It is all too tempting to lump them together with the Afrikaaners of South Africa, or the red-neck whites of the American South, but formal apartheid-style segregation never existed. Certainly the Muslims kept to themselves, living in their own quarter, or casbah, in cities like Algiers, yet they had the same rights of entry to restaurants and public transport as anybody else. Of course there were the outrightly racist *pieds-noirs* who had a string of insulting epithets for the Arabs, accusing them of laziness, dishonesty and uncontrolled lust, but there was a diversity in attitude. Among the professional classes and a large section of the Jewish community, for example, there were many liberals who supported reform. But even these people found it difficult to strike up close friendships with the Muslim Algerians, since the status of women in traditional Muslim society, reclusive and veiled, made social contact between households very difficult. Nevertheless, several significant Algerian Muslim dishes managed to enter the *pied-noir* culinary repertoire.

First, there was *méchoui*, the Algerian method of roasting lamb on a spit, thought to have been introduced to Algeria by the Turks during the period of Ottoman rule. As a convenient method of mass catering, *méchoui* found favour with the French army in Algeria, and was frequently served in the mess, followed by a green salad.

Méchoui

First catch your lamb. Kill, skin and gut it, taking care to leave the kidneys in place. Traditionally, these are given to the guest of honour. Leave the head and feet intact, but singe them all over and wipe clean. Wrap the carcass around a pole. Using thin wire, bind both front and back legs to the pole. This must be done tightly, so the beast will not slip while the spit is turned. (Some spits come with tiny cross bars near each end for this very purpose.)

Melt 1.5 kg (3 lb) unsalted butter and add 200 g (7 oz) salt and 100 g (4 oz) ground white pepper. Rub all over the inside of the gut cavity with some of this mixture, leaving the rest for basting while the beast cooks. Place 250 g (8 oz) peeled garlic cloves into the gut cavity, then sew it up with very thin wire.

While all this is going on, another team of helpers will be preparing the pit and the fires. Dig a trench in the ground, about 1.2 m long and half as wide, and about 30 cm deep (4 x 2 x 1 ft). Build a big fire and burn it down until the embers fill the hole to the top. You will also need another feeder fire constantly on the go nearby, from which the main fire can be refreshed with glowing embers. In all, some 50 kg of embers will be needed. If the embers get too hot and start burning the lamb, damp them down by sprinkling over a little soil.

Erect a Y-shaped stick at each end, to hold the spit. Failing that, the Algerians use tall rocks. The beast should be about 50 cm (18 in) above the embers.

Cook the lamb for approximately 4 hours, turning at least once every 15 minutes, and basting at least once every 30 minutes with the seasoned butter. The indigenous Algerians used a long-handled wooden spoon for this, but under French influence, this evolved into an improvised paint-brush – some clean rags tied to the end of a stick. The basting is essential in order to obtain the desired golden crackling skin. This only stays crisp while the lamb is still hot, so it is essential that the lamb be served straight away. Test the lamb for doneness by inserting a skewer; when no pink juices ooze out, it is ready.

Traditionally, the *méchoui* was laid out on a sheet over some rugs on the ground, but the French tended to place it on a large dish or board in the middle of a table. However, even they adopted the Arab custom of eating the *méchoui* with their fingers, each guest arming themselves with a sharp knife and cutting off the pieces they desired, whether the crackly outside or the juicier inside.

According to Arab custom, the host serves himself first and personally offers the kidneys to his guests. This recipe serves about twelve people.

At a domestic level, *méchoui* was prepared in the fashion of a Tahitian earth oven (see page 170), with a piece of lamb wrapped in leaves and placed in a hole lined with red-hot stones. Nor was the choice of meat necessarily restricted to lamb. A *méchoui* could also be prepared with any of the larger game hunted in colonial Algeria, such as gazelle or mouflon (wild sheep), even a young camel.

There is little evidence that camel featured at all prominently in the diet of the *pieds-noirs*, though French colonial cookbook authors took great delight in featuring numerous recipes, no doubt for their shock value to an audience in *la métropole*:

Pieds de Dromadaire en Vinaigrette
(dromedary feet in vinaigrette)

The feet must be scalded and cleaned with care; then they are cooked at a continuous boil, in well-seasoned water, for 4–5 hours, sometimes longer. Reduce the water, pass it through a fine sieve and allow to congeal into a jelly. Bone the cooked feet and set aside; blend the flesh with the congealed *jus*, along with garlic, spring onion or finely chopped onion, and place in a mould. Eat cold, as an hors d'oeuvre. This pâté is not to be scorned.

Translated from *La Bonne Cuisine aux Colonies*, by R. de Noter, Paris 1931.

Found in the mountains of Algeria, the gazelle was said to taste very much like venison. It was commonly marinated and then casseroled with onions, carrots, tomato and white wine, accompaniments which at the end of cooking would be forced through a sieve and served as a sauce. The mouflon, about the size of an ordinary sheep, was said to taste like chamois.

Lapwing eggs also found their devotees among the French. The lapwing, or black and white plover, has eggs which when hard-boiled, have an albumen which turns opaline; the yolk, which never hardens, is a beautiful shade of orange.

The terfuz or 'truffle' of Algeria was an Arab delicacy eagerly adopted by the *pieds-noirs*. One of the many edible Ascomycetes, its flavour was said to resemble the French mousseron. The terfuz was collected in the sands of the Sahara and, once dried, became an important trading commodity for nomadic Arabs in classical times, sold to the Romans at Carthage (Tunisia) and Libya. A great deal of terfuz was still being consumed in the French era, either raw, or braised like cèpes, cooked in water or milk, and used as a flavouring for other dishes.

Grilled locusts, however, remained largely outside the *pied-noir* culinary orbit, though Charles Moulié, in the *Almanach de Cocagne*, tells of a female friend who tasted it as a challenge:

> She tasted it as if it were poison, while I watched her with amazement.
>
> 'Give me another one,' she said, but this time she chewed the locust with relish.
>
> 'It tastes like salsify.'
>
> Then she swallowed a third one, as if she had lived all her life in the Sahara.
>
> 'You don't like it?' she asked. I looked non-committal.
>
> 'You are wrong,' said my friend, and after a thoughtful silence she concluded: 'What a pity that one has to come to the Sahara in order to taste such a delicacy. What a success they would be in American bars in Paris! Grilled locusts from Ouargla accompanied by English and American drinks and served by Annamites!'

Others claim grilled locusts taste exactly like prawns.

There was no such reservation, on the other hand, towards couscous, those tiny, fluffy, utterly delicious pellets of steamed semolina. Soft, yet firm to the bite, couscous takes on the flavour of any rich stew poured over it. It is North Africa's gift to international cuisine, which the *pieds-noirs* borrowed from the Arabs and made an integral part of their diet. Indeed, the very word 'couscous' is a French corruption of the Arabic *rac keskes*, meaning 'crushed fine'. This is a phonetic derivation from various names used throughout North Africa (*koskos, keuscass, koscosou, kouskous, sekssou, koskosi, kassâa* and *keskès*) all of which refer to the pot in which the couscous is steamed. Pierced with holes on the bottom, it fits on top of another pot containing boiling water or stock.

Traditionally, the couscous pellets were prepared at home. In *La Bonne Cuisine aux Colonies*, de Noter describes them as being 'moulded unceasingly by the expert and . . . dirty hands of indigenous cooks'. It was a laborious process which involved washing and drying, sieving, separating and steaming the couscous grains, before repeating the process again.

For those who are prepared to sacrifice a little authenticity for the sake of convenience, however, the French have invented a pre-cooked product called *couscous rapide*. Encased in bright packets, it has colonized supermarkets of the world for an obvious reason: stir in boiling water, wait for the grains to swell, fork through a little butter, and *voilà*, five-minute couscous!

Lamb and Chicken Couscous

3 tablespoons olive oil
3 small onions, sliced
2 leeks, white part only, sliced
500 g (1 lb) cheap cut of lamb, trimmed of fat and cubed
½ chicken, skinned and cut into 4 pieces
1 large carrot, sliced
2 small turnips or 1 large swede, cut into cubes
50 g (2 oz) tomato concentrate
750 ml (1¼ pts or 3 cups) chicken stock
5 cloves garlic, finely chopped
3 courgettes, sliced

Harissa
2 fresh red chillies, de-seeded and chopped

1 large clove garlic, chopped
1 tablespoon caraway or cumin seed
½ teaspoon coarse salt
1 tablespoon olive oil

Couscous
500 g (1 lb) pre-cooked couscous
500 ml (scant 1 pt or 2 cups) boiling water or chicken stock
2 teaspoons salt
2 tablespoons oil
2 tablespoons butter

Heat the oil in a large pot and add the onions and leeks. Lower the heat, cover the pot, and leave the vegetables to 'sweat' for 5–10 minutes, stirring from time to time. Add the lamb, chicken, carrot, turnips, tomato concentrate, and chicken stock. Bring to the boil, lower the heat, cover and simmer gently for 1 hour. About 10 minutes before the end of cooking, add the garlic and courgettes.

Next, prepare the harissa. Grind together chillies, garlic, caraway or cumin seed, and salt in a blender or with mortar and pestle, then add oil. Ladle off about 3 tablespoons of the cooking broth from the stew, and stir this in.

To prepare the couscous, bring the water or stock to the boil in a large pot (read the instructions on the back of the packet, as ratios of water to couscous vary slightly from brand to brand, and this may need adjusting), add salt and oil, then stir in the couscous. Remove from the heat and leave for

2 minutes, to allow the couscous grains to absorb the moisture and swell up. Return to a low heat and stir in the butter, using a fork to fluff up and separate the grains.

Form a ring of couscous around each plate, spoon stew in the middle, and offer the harissa separately. Or, dish up the couscous, broth and stew in separate bowls, Parisian-style.

SERVES 4.

For large parties, the broth might be served in a soup tureen. 'I have seen this dish thus served,' wrote de Noter, 'at the time of a *difa* [feast] in 1864, in the Kabylie, only the soup tureen had been replaced by a chamber pot . . . it was very funny!'

The *pieds-noirs* even borrowed some of their own customs from the Muslims. There was a traditional outing on Easter Monday, for example, usually to some familiar spot in the woods or the beach, perhaps even a leisurely hunting expedition. The highlight of the day was the ceremonial breaking of the *mouna*, a yeast-risen, hemispherical cake scented with orange blossom water. While apparently of Arabic inspiration, the cake is said to have originated in Oran as, indeed, did the custom of the picnic itself, as a follow-on from the annual procession of Santa Cruz. A popular gathering spot was on top of a hill adjacent to Fort Lamoune, which gave its name to *la mouna*, which followed a traditional Spanish chicken and rice main course.

Despite such cultural borrowings, however, the line between the races was clearly drawn. After the Second World War, attitudes hardened, and in 1954, with the formation of the Front de Libération Nationale – the FLN – came the demand for complete independence. The only alternative for the French, they stated, was whether to leave with a suitcase or in a coffin – *'une valise ou un cercueil'*.

In the end, that was exactly what happened. Having lost the Algerian war of independence in the disastrous summer of 1962, the *pieds-noirs* were forced to leave the land their families had occupied for generations. Boarding ships in one of the largest mass migrations of the twentieth century, more than a million of them descended upon Marseilles with just the two suitcases they were permitted per person.

With the disappearance of the French export market, as well as their expertise, the Algerian wine industry was thrown into a crisis from which it has never recovered; by 1990 only about a quarter of the vines remained. The French left more of a lasting mark on Algerian cuisine, however, particularly in the areas of yeast-risen breads, sweets and hors d'oeuvres, and in a liberal use of tomato purée.

MOROCCO AND TUNISIA

Just as the indigenous cuisines of Morocco, Algeria and Tunisia (collectively known as the Maghreb) bear very close similarities, so too did the cooking of their European communities during French rule. Certain core *pied-noir* dishes, such as *frita*, paella, couscous, *méchoui*, *boulettes de poisson*, *thon à la catalane* and *daurade au four*, were familiar throughout all three societies, which had close links and frequent exchanges of European populations.

Algeria, however, remained pre-eminent. It was, after all, constituted as three *départements* of metropolitan France, whereas Morocco and Tunisia were merely protectorates, still under the nominal rule of the Bey or the Sultan, which made expropriation of land far more difficult. Consequently, while settlers did manage to acquire vast estates in both Morocco and Tunisia, they never developed the same sense of belonging to the land as their counterparts in Algeria. Nor were their numbers ever as great: in Tunisia some 200,000 Europeans had settled by 1939, and in Morocco a little over 250,000, as compared to a million in Algeria. Moreover, there was not the same time span under French control – from 1881 to 1956 in Tunisia, and from 1911 to 1956 in Morocco.

The great *pied-noir* settlement in Morocco was the coastal city of Casablanca, which the French had chosen as the centre of their administration. From a tiny port there arose a glittering white city where luxury apartments and office buildings soared above wide boulevards lined with palm trees. In the exclusive suburb of Anfa handsome villas were built in a pastiche of European and Moorish styles called Mauresque, their gardens overflowing with bougainvillea and frangipani. In complete contrast were nearby *bidonvilles*, slums constructed of wood scraps and oil drums. As elsewhere in French Africa, a class of European *petits blancs* performed such routine jobs as traffic policemen or as cashiers in shops and restaurants.

According to a *pied-noir* saying, every meal begins in the market, or *souk*. Here the vegetable section overflowed with green peppers, aubergines, pale pink heads of garlic, piles of carrots displayed with their leafy tops, all lovingly arranged into pyramids. Along with the baskets of lemon, orange, grapefruits, clementines, apricots, greengages and grapes, this produce testified to the fertility of the coastal regions, in particular the Chaouia area stretching from Rabat to Casablanca and down the southern Atlantic coast, culminating in the vast orange orchards of Agadir.

Since Morocco is bounded by both the Atlantic and the Mediterranean, the fish on sale at the wet and noisy markets was especially varied. Whiting, alose, red mullet, John Dory, turbot, sole, sea bass, grouper, sardines, anchovies, eels, skate, swordfish, tuna, prawns, shrimp, crayfish, squid, baby clams were all vociferously hawked by whole families who would insist theirs was cheaper and fresher than their neighbours', and who, once the bargaining ritual had been completed, would swear they were selling their fish for less than they had paid. Tossing the fish on to their rusty scales, they would know instinctively how many sardines, for example, made the full kilo, always tipping the scales slightly in their favour, and waiting for the call to put another one on, which they always did as if they were throwing in one or two for free.

From the many small urchins hanging about the lanes, a porter would be hired for a pittance to carry the produce home, the fish appearing on the table the same day it had been caught.

Poisson Sauce Chermoula
(fish with chermoula sauce)

1 fish, about 1 kg (2 lb)	1 teaspoon paprika
6 tablespoons extra virgin olive oil	¼ teaspoon chilli powder
juice of 1 lemon	6 tablespoons chopped fresh
1 tablespoon wine vinegar	coriander
3 cloves garlic, crushed	3 tablespoons chopped fresh
salt	flat-leaved parsley
1 teaspoon ground cumin	

The fish can be filleted or left whole. Mix the remaining ingredients together and marinate the fish prior to frying or grilling, or simply pour over the fish once cooked.
SERVES 4.

For some reason, fish dishes are even more popular in Tunisia than in Morocco. The Tunisians, for example, are credited with the invention of fish couscous. Under French rule in Tunisia the *pieds-noirs* also had a simple but effective way with whiting.

Merlan au Cumin
(pan-fried whiting with cumin and harissa)

2 fillets whiting or other fish	½ teaspoon ground cumin
flour	1 teaspoon harissa (see page 211)
2–3 tablespoons extra virgin olive oil	juice of 1 lemon

Dredge the fillets in flour, shake free of excess.

Heat the oil in a large frying pan, stir in the cumin and harissa, then add the fish. Fry on both sides, then remove and arrange on serving plates. To the oil remaining in the pan, stir the lemon juice, then drizzle the flavoured oil over the cooked fish fillets.

SERVES 2.

'Unlike those of Algeria, oxen are large and fat,' wrote the English traveller Lewis Wingfield of Tunisia in his 1868 book, *Under The Palms in Algeria and Tunis*. He goes on:

> Sheep are heavy, and decorated with enormous tails; and camels are wilder and more robust than in the sister country. It is the same with fishes and with vegetables. The Romans, indeed, preferred their kingdom of Carthage to all their other African colonies, and left there as a sign of their partiality the most numerous traces of their dominion.

Langue de Veau Farcie
(stuffed tongue Tunis-style)

This refined *pied-noir* version of a Tunisian classic dish has outlived them and is now part of the Tunisian mainstream.

1 veal tongue, about 1 kg (2 lb)	½ teaspoon black pepper
4 sprigs of fresh flat-leaved parsley, chopped	½ teaspoon mild paprika
1 small onion, finely chopped	4 cloves garlic, chopped
2 tablespoons capers	2 hard-boiled eggs, peeled
½ teaspoon salt	3 tablespoons olive oil
	¼ teaspoon turmeric

1 tablespoon tomato paste
6 slices of lemon
15 black olives

2 medium tomatoes, peeled and
chopped

Place the tongue in a pot, cover with salted water, bring to the boil, lower the heat and simmer, covered, for 45 minutes. Drain, and when cool enough to handle, peel off the skin and discard.

With a thin, long-bladed knife, cut a long section from the centre of the tongue, remove this core of meat and set aside. Using a pestle or similar tool (or your fingers) push into the tongue and gently move around, in order to make the cavity bigger.

Chop the core of tongue meat and mix with the parsley, onion, capers, salt, pepper, paprika and garlic. With the aid of a spoon, stuff this mixture back into the tongue. Finally, press in the two hard-boiled eggs end to end, in order to plug the hole. Curl the tongue into a circle and tie around with string to secure it.

Pour the olive oil into an ovenproof dish. Mix the turmeric and tomato paste with 250 ml (9 fl oz or 1 cup) of water, and pour over. Arrange the lemon slices on top of the tongue, and the olives and tomato around the sides. Bake covered at 180°C (350°F/Gas 4) for 30 minutes. Remove the lid and continue to bake until tender, basting occasionally, for about 20 minutes more. During this time the sauce should reduce to a thick paste, but add more water if it dries out.

When ready to serve, discard the lemon slices, slice the tongue and serve with its sauce while still hot. Alternatively, serve cold with mayonnaise.

SERVES 6.

Brochettes de Boeuf
(spicy beef kebabs)

600 g (1¼ lb) lean steak (fillet of
  porterhouse)
4 tablespoons olive oil
2 cloves garlic, crushed
1 teaspoon ground cumin

1 teaspoon ground coriander seed
¼ teaspoon salt
½ teaspoon ground pepper
1 small onion, finely chopped
1 large onion, quartered

Cut the steak into large cubes. In a bowl, whisk the oil with the garlic, cumin, coriander, salt and pepper. Add the steak and the finely chopped onion, and marinate for 30 minutes.

Pull apart the layers of the onion quarters and alternate these with the meat when threading on to skewers.

Grill under a hot element, or better still, barbeque over hot embers, until just browned on both sides. Serve with plain rice.

Makes about 4 kebabs.

Boulettes de Viande au Sauce Citron
(meatballs with lemon-egg sauce)

500 g (1 lb) beef mince
2 slices white bread, crumbled into
  breadcrumbs
1 small onion, finely chopped
salt and pepper
1 egg

4 tablespoons olive oil
2 egg yolks
3 tablespoons crème fraîche or
  sour cream
4 tablespoons lemon juice

In a bowl, mix together mince, breadcrumbs, onion and egg. Sprinkle liberally with salt and pepper. Form into 12 meatballs.

In a large pot, bring about 250 ml (9 fl oz or 1 cup) of water to the boil with the olive oil. Add the meatballs, cover the pot, lower the heat and gently steam for 20 minutes.

Meanwhile, in a small bowl, beat together the egg yolks, crème fraîche (or sour cream) and lemon juice.

When the meatballs are cooked, remove them and strain off the cooking liquid into a large bowl. Slowly add the egg yolk mixture to the bowl, whisking vigorously with a wire whisk all the while, then return the sauce to the pot. Heat, whisking continuously, until the mixture seems close to the boil, and thickens a little. Immediately remove and pour over the meatballs. Serve with rice.

In Morocco, every *pied-noir* household owned a selection of *tagines*, the earthenware casserole dishes with pointed, 'witch's hat' lids, which lend their name to a whole class of spicy casseroles, often combining dried fruit with meat. These *tagines* have no parallel in classical French cookery, which has an aversion to the sweet-savoury idea underlying them.

While available very cheaply from the *souk*, the *tagines* first had to be seasoned. This was done by simmering vegetables and water in them, then discarding the cooked mixture, and hopefully an earthy taint with it. The procedure also had the effect of impregnating a desired flavour into the clay walls of the *tagine*.

Tagine de Poulet aux Amandes et aux Pruneaux
(tagine of chicken with almonds and prunes)

1 large chicken, about 1.5 kg
　(3–3½ lb)
3 tablespoons olive oil
2 medium onions, finely chopped
generous pinch of saffron threads
70 g (2½ oz) almonds, toasted and
　ground

15 prunes, stoned
125 ml (4 fl oz or ½ cup) white wine
　or water
1 teaspoon powdered ginger
1 red chilli, finely chopped
salt and pepper

Cut the wings from the chicken and skin it. Remove all fat, then cut the breast meat away from the carcass. Cut the breast meat into pieces. Cut the legs in two. Set aside.

Heat the olive oil, fry the onion until it turns translucent, add the chicken and sauté for a further minute or two.

Place the saffron in a mortar with a teaspoon or two of hot water and grind to a smooth orange paste.

Add to the chicken in a *tagine* or other casserole dish (preferably earthenware) along with the remaining ingredients, cover well and simmer for 40–50 minutes until tender.

SERVES 4.

Over winter, the *pieds-noirs* of Morocco cooked *harira*, a hearty soup, rich and well spiced. This they borrowed from the Muslims, for whom it had special significance as the soup used to break the daily fast during the holy month of Ramadan.

Harira

1 medium onion, chopped
1 tablespoon chopped celery
　leaves
½ teaspoon ground cinnamon
1 teaspoon ground turmeric
½ teaspoon ground saffron
½ teaspoon powdered ginger
50 g (2 oz) butter
250 g (8 oz) fatty lamb, cubed
4 chicken wings

2 sets chicken giblets
2 chicken necks
125 g (4½ oz) chickpeas, soaked
　for at least 2 hours
125 g (4½ oz) brown or green
　lentils
4 tomatoes, peeled and chopped
salt and pepper
100 g (4 oz) vermicelli, broken into
　3 sections

2 egg yolks, beaten
juice of 1 lemon
2 tablespoons fresh coriander,
  chopped

2 tablespoons fresh flat-leaved
  parsley, chopped

In a large pot, cook the onion, celery leaves, cinnamon, turmeric, saffron and ginger in the butter for 3–4 minutes, then add lamb and chicken, including the giblets and neck. Cook slowly, stirring often, for 10 minutes.

Pour over 2.5 litres (4½ pts) of water, add the chickpeas, lentils and tomatoes and bring to the boil, skimming regularly. Lower the heat, cover the pot and boil for about 2 hours, until the chickpeas are cooked. About 10 minutes before the end of cooking, season to taste with salt and pepper, then add the vermicelli.

Before serving, beat the egg yolks with the lemon juice. Remove the soup from the heat and slowly pour in this mixture, whisking the soup vigorously as you do so. Add coriander and parsley and serve.

SERVES 6.

Garlic soup, also served over winter, was a *pied-noir* variation on an old Provençal soup, with pasta replacing the traditional bread. It is very quickly made, and *much* nicer than any soup from a tin or packet!

Soupe à l'Ail
(garlic soup)

6 cloves garlic, chopped
1 tablespoon olive oil
salt
100 g (4 oz) (broom-handle-thick
  bunch) vermicelli

50 g (2 oz) butter
2 egg yolks
75 g (3 oz or 1 cup) grated gruyère
  cheese
black pepper

In a saucepan, gently fry the garlic in the oil. As soon as it begins to change colour, pour over 1 litre (1¾ pts or 4 cups) of water and bring to the boil. Add salt to taste, then break in the vermicelli and cook. Meanwhile, melt the butter in a small saucepan and off the heat, stir in the egg yolks. When the vermicelli is cooked, remove the soup from the heat and stir in the egg yolk mixture, preferably with a wire whisk. Stir in the gruyère, season generously with black pepper and serve. There may seem a lot of pasta in relation to soup, but it is needed to offset the richness of everything else; besides, it renders soupe à l'ail sufficiently substantial to serve as a light, easy everyday lunch.

SERVES 3.

Variation: poach an egg for each person and add to each soup bowl before serving.

This soup is interesting for its incorporation of cheese, never a strong feature of the French North African diet, partly for the very practical reason that the climate was not conducive to its storage. A munster or pont l'évêque, for example, would simply have turned into a gaseous, nauseating mess within days of opening a tin, particularly before the era of domestic refrigerators, meaning that what cheese was eaten tended to be sturdier edams and goudas, gruyère and emmenthal, or processed cheeses like La Vache Qui Rit. The heat, moreover, sapped the desire to each such heavy food as cheese, just as it tended to discourage wine drinking. Rather, the constant need to quench one's thirst led to the adoption, by the *pieds-noirs,* of Moroccan mint tea.

Interestingly, Moroccon mint tea is in itself a relatively recent innovation, dating from 1854, during the Crimean wars. British tea traders, denied access to several European markets, off-loaded the surplus in the Maghreb ports of Tangier, Mogador and Constantine. Previously, the peoples of the Maghreb had drunk their infusion of mint leaves with wormwood, but eventually tea came to replace the wormwood (which was eventually banned because of its debilitating effect on the nervous system). In Moroccan cafés today, the tea is often made simply by thrusting a whole branch of fresh mint into a thick tumbler and filling it with sweetened green China tea from a pot.

In Morocco, as in Algeria and Tunisia, the favoured *pied-noir* tipple was anisette, usually in the form of pastis, although generally the sale of alcohol was discouraged, since Morocco was a Muslim country. This was despite the fact that Morocco had a sizeable wine industry. While nothing on the scale of Algeria, some vineyards were established by French settlers in the 1920s, albeit mainly for table grapes, with a major expansion after the Second World War. At independence in 1956, about 55,000 hectares (136,000 acres) were under cultivation, though that figure has declined sharply since.

As in Algeria, carignan and cinsault were major varieties, along with grenache. In terms of quality, the leading region was, and still is, Meknès-Fès, where the vineyards are sited relatively high on the foothills of the Atlas Mountains. The vines benefit both from cooler temperatures and gravelly soils, producing wines of much greater complexity than the soft, heady reds from the coastal plain around Rabat.

Tunisia's wine industry followed the same pattern as its neighbours: it experienced a growth spurt during the French era when ignoble southern grape varieties were used to turn out rough-and ready-red and rosé wines, which today have become difficult to sell internationally. As in Algeria and Morocco, the industry went into a tail-spin after independence. However, Tunisia does produce some sound red wine and, moreover, has an ancient tradition of muscats, both sweet and dry. Indeed, it is thought that the muscat of Alexandria, one of the most ancient cultivated plants known to humanity, may have been introduced when the Phoenicians established the city of Carthage on the coast. Unfortunately, however, as a grape variety the muscat of Alexandria has long been superseded, in quality terms, by the muscat blanc à petits grains. Thus, Tunisian muscat wines, compared to say, a French Beaumes-de-Venise, tend to be rather heavier, lacking in complexity and depth of flavour; but at least they have perfume and fruit, and possess a certain charm when served ice-cold.

FRENCH-SPEAKING AFRICA

Stretching from Mauritania across the arid West African interior of present-day Mali, Burkina Faso, Niger and Chad, and down the palm-fringed coast through modern Senegal, Guinea, Sierra Leone, Ivory Coast, to Togo and Benin, colonial French West Africa comprised nearly one sixth of the entire continent. French Equatorial Africa, which encompassed modern Cameroon, Congo and Central African Republic, was almost as large.

In French West Africa alone, some two hundred different languages were spoken, accompanied, presumably, by two hundred nuances of cuisine, despite an undeniable basic unity in the way a family living in a hut of mud, dung and thatch would congregate in a smoke-filled atmosphere around an iron pot and eat yams and millet porridge with their hands, as their peoples had done for a thousand years.

In the face of this vast African food culture, the French colonials remained profoundly indifferent. With some exceptions, they simply shut it out of their own lives as much as possible, preferring to look upon the landscape only in terms of what might be extracted from it, whether it be slaves, mineral resources or cash crops like sisal, cotton, palm oil or cocoa. Only in a belated rush of conscience near the end of their term of empire did the French in Africa establish research institutes to study what vegetables and other crops might enrich the diet of the inhabitants.

However, while the French were as driven by the profit motive as any other European colonial power, they were not stand-offish. Where the British, for example, remained distant from their subject peoples and practised indirect rule, the French were passionately assimilationist. Less Calvinistic than the British, infinitely more relaxed in their dealings with the Africans, the French thought nothing of taking the African women as mistresses. They also sought to make of the African a Frenchman. As far as they were concerned, they were not in Africa to learn, but to teach the benefits of their civilization, their language – and their wonderful cuisine.

This attitude is encapsulated by a French colonial in Ivory Coast during the early twentieth century, responding to an observation by the traveller Henri Bordeaux that the indigenous peoples seemed to be very thin:

'They don't know how to feed themselves, or even take care of themselves. We are teaching them.'

'But you always know how to feed yourself if you want to.'

'Don't believe it. You not only have to be able to find your food, but cook it as well.'

Thus it is that, today, in major cities of Francophone West Africa such as Dakar, capital of Senegal, and Abidjan, capital of Ivory Coast, among the squares and vast tree-lined boulevards, the concrete and glass high-rise buildings and the solemn remnants of colonial architecture, there are restaurants, pâtisseries and supermarkets which might just as well be in Mediterranean France.

The boutiques sell Hermès scarves, Chanel No. 5, Givenchy soap, heavy linen tablecloths, bone china and silverware. There are pavement cafés serving buttery croissants and excellent coffee, as well as specialist shops, many French-owned and operated, selling French cheeses, charcuterie, pâtés and wines. Even your hairdresser, locksmith or mechanic may be French. At the Dakar markets, perspiring French butchers cut *gigots* from the hind-quarters of sheep and string the shoulders into rolls, surrounded by African counterparts selling halal meat slaughtered according to Muslim rites. Indeed, there are now 30,000 French in Ivory Coast, twice as many as at independence in 1960. The influence, in the cities at least, is overpowering. Little wonder, then, that popular Ivoirian produce such as avocado is frequently set to French culinary music.

Soupe d'Avocat Abidjanaise
(avocado soup Abidjan-style)

2 avocados, peeled and roughly chopped
1 litre (1¾ pts or 4 cups) cold chicken stock
juice of 1 or 2 limes

4 tablespoons plain yoghurt
¼ fresh red chilli, de-seeded and finely minced
salt

Place the avocado in a food processor, purée and then slowly pour in the stock, lime juice and yoghurt. Mix in the chilli and add salt to taste. Refrigerate for 30 minutes to an hour before serving.
SERVES 4–6.

'The French here are just as *gastronome* as they are in France,' the English travel writer Richard West was told by the Poitiers-born chef/patron of the Abidjanaise Restaurant in 1965:

They like to feel at home. At Christmas, for example, when it is very hot outside, we have the traditional meal starting at one o'clock in the morning. Oysters, foie gras, turkey and chestnuts, champagne. Last Christmas we went on until eight o'clock in the morning.

Here in the Ivory Coast one can get a lot of ingredients locally. There is beef from Bamako and Niamey, there are sole and turbots and lobsters in the sea. My speciality is Sole Farcie à l'Abidjanaise, but the recipe is a secret. But a lot of the meat has to be flown in. The chickens come mostly from Denmark and the turkeys from

France. And because of the heat, wine is likely to turn a bit although burgundy keeps better than claret.

At Lomé, capital of Togo, the situation is the same today: what cannot be found in the Grand Marché crams the shelves of the supermarkets, which sell French cheese, foie gras, snails, truffles and all manner of fine French wine. Even in Burkina Faso, one of the world's five poorest countries, the diet of the government élite runs to caviar and Dom Pérignon.

Such urban sophistication has its roots in the period between the two world wars, when the cities of French West Africa began to take on a more settled, domestic appearance. Previously, the atmosphere had been dull and distinctly provincial: in Dakar, for example, the Chamber of Commerce had urged in 1907 that the blowing of ships' whistles be banned at night, just as the beating of tom-toms after 10 p.m. had been outlawed by an ordinance of 1879.

But the 1920s and 1930s saw the arrival of theatres, cinemas, breweries and newspapers, of wide boulevards lined with hairdressers, couturiers, cafés and pâtisseries, and of suburbs, newly electrified and served by tram services and schools, where wealthy Europeans built villas, established families and hired larger retinues of domestic servants. Gardeners, maids and nannies were added to the usual washerwomen and cooks (who were called 'boys' – an obviously English importation which had entered the French colonial vocabulary at the end of the nineteenth century).

This new-found confidence had been inspired by successful eradication of yellow fever and other tropical diseases by branches of the Pasteur Institute. French West Africa, along with Indo-China, had previously been known as the 'white man's graveyard', but now soldiers, businessmen and colonial administrators were willing to bring brides and families out on their colonial tour of service, safe in the knowledge that supplies of filtered water were available, along with greater quantities of tinned food and other imported French provisions.

The economic recession of the 1930s, which led to high unemployment in metropolitan France, further added to the attraction of the colonies, and with the weakening of the metropolitan economy, the bi-annual vacation in France became increasingly less affordable. The local population therefore became more fixed, though nowhere in French

West or Equatorial Africa did the Europeans develop the same sense of identification with the land as the *pieds-noirs* of Algeria. In 1951 the French sociologist Paul Mercier conducted a survey of the French residents of Dakar and concluded that none had any desire to remain permanently in Africa.

With the development of air freight and domestic refrigerators, the French were able to shun the local cuisine more than ever. Since the average Frenchman is prepared to spend vast sums for the sake of eating well, even a French-run hotel in the African interior would frequently offer a range of French cheese, charcuterie and Normandy butter, freshly flown in from *la metropole*. Even fruit and vegetables could be picked in France in the afternoon and delivered in African cities the next day. Richard West quotes the third-ranking restaurant in the provincial Ivory Coast town of Niamey (whose population in 1965 was 40,000) as having a menu which included snails, *terrine du chef*, lobster, steak tartare and several French cheeses. He also recalls, by way of illustration how ill-adapted this cuisine was to the climate, a lunch one sweltering day at a restaurant on the coast near Abidjan:

> It was a tropical scene from a chocolate box. Coconut palms swayed by the side of the lagoon. We ate outdoors under the shelter of woven bamboo to the noise of the long surf and the scent of mangoes. And what were we to eat but hors d'oeuvres followed by pork chops, fat sausages, boiled potatoes and cabbage all the style of Alsace! It was impossible to eat more than a mouthful.

Following the French withdrawal from Vietnam, a rash of Vietnamese restaurants appeared in the French African cities during the 1950s, invariably established by an old Indo-China hand and his Vietnamese wife, and catering to the large number of displaced French colonials who, having been evicted from Vietnam, sought the hot climate of places like Africa and the French West Indies as the next best thing. Having by then erupted into open warfare, Algeria would have been considered out of the question.

At some time during the colonial era, or perhaps even before, Algerian cuisine made its appearance in West Africa, in the form of couscous and *méchoui*. Arlette and Gaston Le Révérend describe the latter, served in the late 1930s at Abomey, a former slave market and the old capital of Benin:

The great treat is to roast a whole sheep over a wood fire in a hole,
dug in the middle of the courtyard. The roast sheep is brought in
on a board and placed in the middle of the table. Everybody tucks
in, without knife or fork, in the manner of old Gaul. I am still too
civilized to obtain pleasure from this dish, above all because it is
spiked with chilli in such an infernal manner, like all the cooking
here. It seems it is indispensable to the health of the indigenous
people, but pouah! how it burns! Mutton thus presented is *le
méchoui.* I hasten to tell you that a sheep here is much smaller than
our fat *Normandie.*

Away the from coast and the cities, the quality of the European diet
took a sharp downward turn. Life in the bush was very much more
spartan and primitive, particularly in the early colonial era, when roads
and communications were bad. 'Drinking water should be supervised
by the European himself and not left to the indigenous boys, who are
too often slovenly and careless,' advised the *Guide de la Colonisation
au Togo* in 1924. In most parts of Togo, the *Guide* advised, well water
was infected, and needed to be boiled or filtered if the unfortunate
colon was not to be struck down with intestinal parasites, diahorrhea or
typhoid fever.

Reading such alarming advice, no wonder the *colons* turned to
alcohol – if boredom and depression had not already driven them to it.
Alcoholism being rife among the French residents of West Africa, the
Guide sternly warned that aperitifs and liqueurs attack the nervous
system far more quickly in Africa than in Europe, manifesting first in
enervation and irritability, later by polyneuritis and outright madness.

'The same goes for food,' the *Guide* continued in the same officious
tone. 'You must, in hot countries, avoid excessive meat intake, especially in the evening. It does not do, under the pretext of economizing,
for example, to have too poor a diet in the colonies.'

In order to have a varied and appetizing diet, a good cook was
necessary. The new arrival in Togo was advised not to choose too
hastily from the many who would come soliciting their services, but to
take on cooks who had already served with Europeans established in
the country. The shops in Togo being limited in their choice, the
intending colonist was advised to take with him a batterie de cuisine,
including aluminium pots and pans, along with a future supply of
clothing.

Singling out the oysters of the Anécho Lagoon as being poisonous, the *Guide* also warned against the many varieties of preserved fruits and vegetables sold in shops, 'for the reason of the intestinal poisoning they provoke'. There was in any case plenty of fresh tropical fruit available – bananas, guavas, papayas, mangoes, pomelos and avocados. The French plantation owner soon realized that he must adapt to such local produce if he was to eat well.

The letters of Henry Hentsch, a *petit blanc* cotton farmer in Paouignan (modern Benin) who died of tropical fever at the tragically young age of twenty-four, reveal many of these adaptations. In 1903 he writes with excitement at having found in the market a superior variety of yam, planted after the dry season. He also grew his own cassava in order to produce tapioca, from which *galettes* could be made as a spartan substitute for bread. Certain wild plants resembled sorrel and spinach. He suppressed his urge for wine, making do with *chapelou*, a beer made with germinated millet, and gave up cooking with lard and butter in favour of palm oil, for which he eventually acquired a taste.

The initiative for meals, Hentsch wrote in response to a question from his concerned grandmother, was generally left to the African cook, an individual who, he claimed, would be just as happy to spend only forty-five minutes in the kitchen each day heating tinned food, and who was often heard to complain, 'I can't make that – it takes too long.'

When his cook was ill or on leave, however, Hentsch admitted his standards dropped even further. Forced to cook for himself, his standbys were often reduced to the level of *cantaloupe d'igname* – a stupendously dull sounding purée of boiled yam, eaten with a 'sauce' of palm oil and chilli.

In addition to what he could grow in his garden, Hentsch lists the various staples commonly found at the local market: 'little bunches of delicious onions, five for a *sou*, papayas, tomatoes and red peppers (which frequently went into a chicken ragoût with rice), dried beans, dried fish or meat, as well as fresh venison, mutton or goat. Fresh pork was difficult to buy, although he was able to obtain English hams on his re-victualling trips to the coast. Game birds were prolific:

> When I need to, I give a cartridge to a man who returns either with a Guinea fowl or a partridge. It's my choice – the Guinea fowl are a bit further away, while partridge is near the entrance to the village.

Marination in citrus juice was routine for game birds of uncertain age, and even for the athletic domestic African chicken. In Senegal, the French borrowed this chicken recipe from the indigenous population:

Poulet Yassa
(chicken Yassa)

1 chicken	salt
juice of 6 limes	1 red chilli, chopped
3 large onions, chopped	oil for frying

Cut the chicken into 8 pieces. Mix together lime juice, onion, salt and chilli, pour over the chicken pieces and allow to marinate at least 2 hours, preferably overnight.

Remove the chicken from the marinade and grill, preferably over charcoal, until nearly cooked. Meanwhile, drain the onion and sauté in some oil. When translucent, add the marinade mixture with a glass of water, and the chicken. Cover the pot and cook gently.

With an African chicken, which is likely to have lived the life of a marathon runner, the chicken is then stewed for another 45 minutes in the sauce until it is tender. Modern supermarket chickens however, will need only 10 minutes or less.

This same technique can be extended to lamb, beef, even fish.
SERVES 4.

As a nation of gourmets known for their propensity towards thrushes, snails and frogs' legs, it is hardly surprising that the French took to African wild foods with alacrity. While a favourite subject of debate among *les colons* as to which was the greatest delicacy, a hierarchy of game preferences eventually emerged, with venison, antelope and crocodile vying for top place. Also highly regarded were lizards, particularly the large multi-coloured varieties, of which the French gourmet knew to eat only the white coloured parts – the dark meat was said to taste of mouse droppings.

In Guinea, as in French Guiana, a French-inspired fricassee of iguana acquired the status of a national dish. Only the back of the animal is used for the fricassee. The meat is cut into pieces, browned in butter, then simmered in water with onions and the classic French triumvirate of parsley, bay leaf and thyme. At certain times of the year, eggs from the females are added a few minutes before serving.

A taste for elephant was learned from the Africans, who favoured the tip of the tongue above all parts of the animal. Zebra was considered a little fatty, while both hippopotamus and giraffe were said to have sweet-tasting flesh. In some cases, hippo was served raw. The guinea pig-like flesh of the agouti appeared on French tables, just as it did in the French West Indies, and before it was shot virtually to extinction, flamingo was also eaten.

In Baoula, formerly part of French Equatorial Africa, monkey with peanut sauce was the national dish. 'According to *le commandant* Baratier, friend of a merchant at Fachoda,' wrote de Noter in *La Bonne Cuisine aux Colonies*, 'this dish is exquisite, but you must have courage to eat it.'

There was also a certain reluctance on the part of the French to partake of the domestic cat, a famous delicacy in Benin, said by the English traveller Peter Biddlecombe to taste like hare. The fact that the cat was introduced to Africa by the Portuguese only relatively late in history, may explain the absence of sentimentality on the part of the Beninese.

In the Sudan, a type of yellowish land-based snail was found on reddish, iron-rich laterite soils, sheltering from the hot tropical sun beneath mimosa shrubs. They were gathered and eaten mainly for nostalgic reasons by homesick *colons*, since the tough flesh only distantly recalled the flavour of a true snail. As in France, the snails were starved for several days, then cooked by classical methods, such as *à la provençale, à la bourguignonne* and *à la bordelaise*.

Those who lived near the marigots (side channels of rivers) in Niger, feasted upon the abundant turtles. As in the English colonies, the French made turtle soup, having first removed the liver. While little known outside Niger, turtle liver was considered a real delicacy, treated in much the same way as duck liver, either sautéed and then sliced, or made into truffled pâtés.

Bisque d'Ecrevisses (freshwater crayfish bisque)

The freshwater crayfish of *Médine* and *Mahéna*, and the crabs of Niger, although of mediocre quality, make good enough *bisques*.

In a casserole, place 2 carrots and a chopped onion with butter. Heat, add thyme, bay leaf and garlic; stir with 20 freshwater crayfish. Sauté for 10 minutes, then stir in half a litre of white wine, a Bordeaux-sized glass of cognac and half a litre of de-fatted bouillon. Let it simmer for half an hour.

Meanwhile, simmer 250 g rice in 1½ litres spicy bouillon.

After cooking, take out the freshwater crayfish, remove the tails from the bodies, and put the tails into a soup tureen. Pound the bodies with a little bouillon, pass through a tammy sieve, and mix with the rice. Adjust the seasoning, reheat and add a good piece of butter before serving.

Translated from *La Bonne Cuisine aux Colonies*, R. de Noter, Paris, 1931.

On the coasts, the French found the African fish generally to be bigger and meatier than in Europe. The capitaine, a type of bream, was especially prized, as were the huge, chunky, flavoursome lobsters – still a prominent menu item in the fine dining restaurants of Francophone Africa.

In French Equatorial Africa, the *colons* discovered several edible varieties of mushroom, found on tilled soil after the first rains. Due to safety concerns, these mushrooms were often boiled and then washed in cold water prior to cooking. Apparently the scent of these mushrooms was such that they could withstand such punishment.

Palm hearts, a food item forbidden in the Sudan due to the scarcity of trees, were nevertheless sold by Africans in many places, often for a minimal price. As in the French West Indies and the French islands of the Indian Ocean, the hearts were julienned and served as a salad, or cooked and served with a béchamel sauce.

In Senegal, the *colons* chopped peanuts and used them for cake decorations, pressing them into the icing to allow them to adhere, though it was the indigenous peoples of West Africa who took to this import from South America with the greatest enthusiasm, grinding peanuts into sauces for chicken, and using them as the basis for soups. There were after all, ample supplies of peanuts, especially in Senegal, for in a decision made on coldly rational business terms, the French gave over the entire colony to peanut production, thus throwing the traditional raising of millet, sorghum and other grains out of kilter. To rectify this domestic food shortfall, therefore, the French decided to import rice into Senegal.

The whole saga, indeed, is a textbook example of colonial dislocation. Since cheap, second-grade broken rice could be imported from the French colonies in Indo-China for less than it cost to grow it in many parts of Africa, it became a major trading commodity landed at the port of Dakar. (The ships would also carry loads of unbroken, premium quality rice, but only a little of this was unloaded for the sake of the local Europeans, the rest destined for Metropolitan France.) Little by little, broken rice became accepted into the indigenous Senegalese diet, to such an extent that it eventually became the preferred option. Indeed, if the rice did not come broken, it would be pounded and made so.

Of the half dozen major tribes of Senegal, the Wolof took to rice with the greatest alacrity, since they needed to, having been successfully instrumental in promoting peanut cultivation at the expense of other equally necessary staple crops. Eventually, a combination of rice with a whole stuffed fish became a famous Wolof – and Senegalese – festive dish: *tieb dien*.

Stemming from the Wolof words *teb* – rice, and *dien* – fish, it has been lately transliterated into French as *thie-bou-dienne*. In the colonial era, however, the dish was simply referred to as *Riz à la sénégalaise*, a name reflecting its status as an adopted native dish on the tables of the *toubab* (white settlers). The preferred fish was red bream or, failing that, the coalfish or saithe. Due to its expense, a Senegalese family would not consider it everyday fare, though they do have many versions, including one particularly tricky variation, peculiar to the city of St Louis at the mouth of the River Senegal, which involves removing the flesh of the fish without disturbing the skin, then chopping the flesh with the stuffing ingredients and cramming everything back into the fish. A distinctly clumsy version involves the stuffing of fish steaks. Here is a relatively accessible, French-oriented method.

Riz à la Sénégalaise

1 whole fish, scaled and gutted, about 1.5 kg (3–3½ lb)
white flour
125 ml (4 fl oz or ½ cup) oil
500 g (1 lb or 2 cups) long-grain rice
½ teaspoon salt or to taste

Stuffing
1 medium leek, white part only, very finely chopped

1 red or green pepper, very finely chopped
2–3 tablespoons chopped parsley
4 cloves garlic, finely chopped

Vegetables
2 onions, chopped
4 tomatoes, chopped
4 medium carrots, chopped
300 g (10 oz or 2 cups) pumpkin, cubed

2 cups chopped cassava root
(optional)
2 sweet potatoes, cubed
1 aubergine, cubed
¼ teaspoon freshly grated nutmeg

¼ teaspoon freshly ground cloves
salt and pepper
2 courgettes, sliced
6 small okra, trimmed and kept whole

Wipe the fish dry, dredge in flour and shake the excess free.

Make a stuffing mixture with the leek, pepper, parsley and garlic. Use this stuffing mixture to fill the gut cavity (which is best slit only as much as is necessary to remove the innards).

Heat the oil in a large flat-bottomed cast iron pot and fry the fish on both sides, allowing 10 minutes per side. Lift the fish with a fish slice several times in the early stages of cooking, to prevent it sticking to the bottom of the pot. Remove the fish, cover and set aside.

In the oil remaining in the pot, sauté the onions until transparent. Stir in the tomatoes, add the carrots, pumpkin, cassava root (if using), sweet potatoes and aubergine. Stir in nutmeg and cloves, and season with salt and pepper. Cover with water, bring to the boil and simmer gently for about 45 minutes, until all the vegetables are becoming soft. Gently stir in the courgettes and okra. Place the whole fish over the vegetables. It should not be covered by liquid (remove and reserve excess liquid for later, if necessary). Gently cook for another 30 minutes.

About 20 minutes before the fish and vegetables are ready, place the rice in a fine sieve and wash under a running cold tap, massaging the rice until the water no longer runs cloudy. Place rinsed rice in a pot, cover with about 750 ml (1¼ pts or 3 cups) boiling water, season with salt. Bring to the boil, lower heat and cook at a low but distinct boil, tightly covered, for 10–12 minutes, or until nearly cooked. (Do not be discouraged if you slightly scorch the rice; the Senegalese have a saying, 'scorched rice behoves the chef' and indeed, any browned and crusty parts which may form on the bottom are considered as *pièces de resistance*.)

Turn off the heat and leave tightly covered for at least another 5 minutes, to allow the rice to absorb the remainder of the steam.

In traditional Senegalese homes, the dish would be presented in a large calabash bowl, whereas in the homes of a wealthy *toubab*, where it often featured as a grand dinner party dish, it would be served on white linen in a deep bone china dish, also surrounded by its garnish. Taking the same idea, there are also versions of *riz à la sénégalaise* with pork, mutton and chicken.

Named after the ancient kingdom of the Wolof people of Senegal and surrounding countries, Jollof rice is famous all over West Africa. Better known in Senegal itself as *benachin*, it was also adopted by the French *toubabs* there. It amounts to a festive African version of paella, and may have been a forerunner of jambalaya (see page 122).

Jollof Rice

500 g (1 lb) chicken or beef, cut
   into pieces
3 tablespoons oil
1 litre (1¾ pts) stock (or water with
   3 stock cubes)
2 medium onions, chopped
200 g (7 oz) mushrooms, quartered
1 chilli, crushed
1 large carrot, sliced
2 peppers, chopped (optional)

6 tomatoes, peeled and chopped
   (or 400 g (14 oz) tin tomatoes)
500 g (1 lb) long-grain or short-
   grain rice
4 cloves garlic, crushed
250 g (8 oz) green beans, cut into
   lengths
4 tablespoons chopped parsley
2 hard-boiled eggs, quartered

In a frying pan, sauté the chicken or beef in the oil until brown on all sides. Remove and transfer to a large pot with the stock. Simmer slowly while you prepare the remaining ingredients.

Fry the onion, mushrooms and chillies in the oil remaining in the pan, then add to the pot along with the carrot, peppers, tomatoes and rice.

Cook, covered, over a low heat until the rice has absorbed the stock and is cooked. You may have to add a further cup or two of water or stock during cooking. Stir from time to time, scraping the bottom of the pot to prevent the mixture sticking. About 6 minutes before the end of cooking, stir in the green beans and the garlic.

To serve, sprinkle with parsley and decorate with quarters of hard-boiled egg.

SERVES 4–6.

But while the French may have popularized peanuts and rice in West African cooking, this was nothing in comparison with the profound changes wrought by the introduction of food plants by the Portuguese.

The peanut brought to Gambia by the Portuguese was just one of many South American plant introductions which changed the African diet forever. Foremost among these was cassava, introduced by the Portuguese to the Niger Delta through Warri and Benin during the mid- to late 1600s, and maize, introduced into the south-west Congo in the same century. These quickly became staple food crops in the rain-forest areas of West and Central Africa, enabling denser population concentrations and, in a cruel irony, only serving to fuel the slave trade further.

Also introduced by the Portuguese from the New World were chillies, peppers, sweet potatoes, tomatoes, bananas, pineapples and papayas. From China, India and Malacca, they brought the orange, the lemon and the lime.

Equally significant, the Portuguese brought to their colonies a fundamentally different attitude from that of France and the other European powers – a willingness to learn all they could from indigenous cultures, despite their determination to remain forever Portuguese.

8 Colonial Crossover: the Empire strikes back

Marseilles is known worldwide as the home of *la vraie bouillabaisse*, and around its neatly manicured port filled with the yachts of the rich, dozens of smart bouillabaisse restaurants fully exploit this fame. Yet not so very far from the port, indeed just a few streets behind the bustling main boulevard of La Canebière, is the impoverished North African quarter, the *kasbah*.

Its narrow, shady streets scarcely rate a mention in the guide books, save to warn tourists not to stay in the Algerian hotels or venture there after dark. And yet, aside from the seedy bars spilling forth on to the pavement with obviously under-employed men for whom white shoes and gold medallions remain fashion statements, the cramped shops selling bargain-priced factory seconds in footwear and clothing, or jumbled masses of cheap tin trunks and key chains hung with medallions of Napoleon III, the quarter provides some of the most fascinating café dining in Marseilles.

Not that the surroundings are necessarily salubrious. Most likely the tables will be covered in gaudily patterned vinyl, and they may even be arranged cafeteria-style in long rows, the better to pack patrons in. On the walls, a painting on black velvet of the Ka'aba sits between a bowl of plastic roses and an ancient bakelite radio, blaring forth execrable wailing music. More than likely, the menu will be chalked up on a blackboard in Arabic as well as French, for the very sound reason that nearly all of their customers are immigrants from the so-called Maghreb – Morocco, Algeria and Tunisia. And more than likely the menu will offer the famous Maghreb soup, *shorba*.

Shorba
(lamb and chickpea soup with fresh coriander)

100 g (4 oz) dried chickpeas	3 cloves garlic, crushed
100 g (4 oz) dried haricot beans	3 tablespoons olive oil
3 lamb chops, trimmed of fat	1 tablespoon paprika
2 onions, chopped	400 g (14 oz) tin tomatoes

1 litre (1¾ pts or 4 cups) stock or
water
75 g (3 oz) vermicelli
1 courgette, finely sliced

salt and pepper
1 small bunch fresh coriander
3 tablespoons chopped parsley

Soak the chickpeas and haricot beans in water for 4 hours or overnight, then boil them with the lamb chops for about 2 hours until completely soft. Remove the lamb chops, chop the meat into pieces and return to the pot, discarding any fat, gristle and bone.

In a frying pan sauté the onion and garlic in the olive oil until the onion turns transparent and begins to brown, then add the beans and meat along with the paprika, tomatoes and stock or water (use more or less, according to how much has been absorbed by the beans in cooking). Boil for a further 30 minutes.

About 10 minutes before the end of cooking, break the vermicelli into three sections and add, along with the courgette. Just before serving add salt and pepper to taste, along with the fresh coriander and parsley.

SERVES 4.

The French are scarcely to be seen in a place like this. They have far too high a regard for their own traditional cuisine to be bothered with that of their former colonial subjects, and besides, many would refuse to set foot in such a restaurant for the very reason that it is Algerian owned. Unfortunately the greatest prejudice is often to be found among the exiled *pieds-noirs.*

Most *pieds-noirs* settled in the south of France, where the sun and the landscape reminded them of the country they had just left. A great many got no further than Marseilles itself, building colonies of white houses with flat roofs, terraces and bougainvillea over the door, to remind them of 'home'.

More sinisterly, some became involved in heroin smuggling and protection rackets, and many joined Marseilles's notoriously corrupt police force, forming the early rump of support for Jean-Marie Le Pen's National Front. The irony is this: these same racist *pieds-noirs* introduced a small but highly significant entry of multi-culturalism into the French culinary mainstream, in the form of couscous, spicy *merguez* sausage, *harissa* and the spice blend known as *ras el hanout* – the cuisine of the people they despised and fought, and continue to harass in France.

During a century of co-existence with the indigenous population, the *pieds-noirs* had adopted a number of Islamic foodstuffs, and once in France set up factories to manufacture their beloved spicy *merguez* sausage and couscous, both of which are now standard items in French supermarkets.

In Paris, couscous is the speciality of many small Algerian and Tunisian restaurants, which opened there in the 1930s or even earlier. Their chefs have been greatly influenced by French food, particularly in the choice of westernized vegetables which go into the stew served with couscous. The side dish of *harissa* also differentiates Algerian and Tunisian couscous from the lighter versions of Morocco.

There is something of a Frenchified ritual at these little restaurants, where you first pile the couscous on to your plate, followed by the vegetables, then the broth, into which you have mixed *harissa* to your taste. Finally you eat the meat or the fish.

Since many of these Maghreb cafés tend to cater to the bottom of the market, the visitor to Paris soon learns to recognize such warning signs as flies or cracked and dirty wall tiles, harbingers of worse horrors in the kitchen and the loos. On the other hand, acting on a recommendation, I visited La Medina on rue de l'Orillon. Here I had the best couscous I have eaten, while seated amid an Orientalist painter's fantasy: etched mirrors, portraits of the famous singer Oum Kaltoum, and glistening blue and yellow tiles imported, I was told, from Algeria, and laid from floor to ceiling in the ordered riot of symmetry that is the triumph of Islamic art.

Like couscous, *merguez* had long been available in Paris – perhaps as early as the nineteenth century – but it only really arrived into French food fashion with the *pieds-noirs*. But while it has been admitted into French charcuterie, it has suffered a certain Europeanization. The spicing has been toned down in response to the French aversion to chilli, and it is also often denatured by the meat used. In Paris it is easy enough to obtain *la vraie merguez* from a number of the Jewish butcheries in rue Richier, or in the Belleville district, but elsewhere, and certainly abroad, it is something of rarity. I have had some fairly weird *merguez* in various parts of the United Kingdom and Australia, for example.

While a modern, somewhat domesticated version, this recipe gives a good idea of what you ought to be tasting in your supermarket *merguez*.

Merguez

1 kg (2 lb) lean beef or lamb
200 g (7 oz) beef or lamb fat
1 head garlic
80 ml (3 fl oz or ⅓ cup) oil
1 tablespoon fennel seeds, ground
2 teaspoons *quatre-épices*
   (cinnamon, peppercorns,
   paprika, dried rosebud)
2 teaspoons *harissa*

1 teaspoon coriander seeds,
   ground
1 tablespoon fine salt
1 teaspoon ground black pepper
3 m (10 ft) sausage casing,
   preferably cleaned and prepared
   sheep's intestines; otherwise,
   whatever your butcher can offer

Cut the meat and fat into pieces and mince separately in a food processor, the meat a little more coarsely than the fat. Put the two minces into a bowl.

Peel the garlic and drop the cloves one by one into a running food processor. Add to the meat/fat mince with the oil, fennel, *quatre-épices*, *harissa*, coriander, salt and pepper. Mix well, preferably by hand, to obtain a homogenous paste. If it seems too compact, add up to half a cup of water and mix well.

Test for holes in the sausage casing by holding it around a tap like a hose, and running water through it. Empty it of water and cut into sections about 60 cm (2 ft) long.

Fill the sausage casing with the aid of a funnel (special sausage-making gadgets are available and make this job easier). To do so, ease the spout of the funnel into the sausage casing, then concertina the casing back down the spout. Take a handful of the mixture and press with your thumb down the neck of the funnel. Do not ram it, and prick the casing with a needle every so often, to release the air pockets which inevitably form. When full, knot both ends of the sausage casing. Alternatively, form into smaller sausages of 10–15 cm (4–6 in), forming knots after having separated them.

It is best to leave the sausages to dry for several hours before grilling them over charcoal or frying in a pan.

Besides serving merguez with couscous, the *pieds-noirs* have a habit of adding it to all types of traditional French ragoûts, in place of meat.

Harissa has today entered the culinary mainstream in France, thinned with olive oil for seasoning olives, and appearing in the dishes of famous chefs, such as Alain Passard's baby roasted pig. It is readily available in tubes and tins in France, but the factory product rarely measures up to the home-made versions, some of which are occasionally to be found for sale in village produce markets throughout the south of France, for example at the Friday market in Beziers. These same markets often sell North African preserved lemons, fresh coriander, North African chilli powder – *piment pour harissa* – and *ras el hanout*, traditionally used to flavour couscous, soups and tagines.

Of those *pieds-noirs* who did move further afield than Marseilles, many stayed in the Midi, becoming farmers or establishing vineyards. Some ventured into the south-west of France and put their Algerian orcharding experience to good use, growing plums for prunes. However, at the end of the 1970s French prunes faced crippling competition from Californian prunes, always much larger and cheaper to produce, and available in seemingly limitless quantities.

As for the Jews of Algeria and Morocco, they had paid dearly for their alliance with the French during colonial rule: despite having inhabited Algeria for centuries, they too were exiled after the Algerian war of independence. While not exactly forced from Morocco after independence, it was clear they were no longer welcome, either. Being urban people, they gravitated to major cities such as Marseilles, Lyons, Bordeaux and Toulouse.

Above all, they settled in Paris, where today they have a strong gastronomic presence along the rue des Rosiers, rue Cadet, rue Richer and the Faubourg-Poissonnière, their restaurants dispersed among food stores and kosher butchers selling *merguez* and a variety of offal so beloved of North African Jewish cooks.

The North African influence continues to manifest itself at Jewish weddings in France. *Henna* nights are held in tents, the bride carried in on a giant tray, decked out in jewels, velvet and gold. A band plays and singers perform nostalgic renditions of songs like 'Fez, Tu Es Mon Amour' and 'Un Soir à Casa', while the food comprises mounds of decorated couscous, *méchoui*, salads and Maghreb confectionery.

At the glorious Izraël, Le Monde des Epices, on rue François-Miron, the shopper can take a gastronomic tour of *la francophonie* – there are sacks of couscous from the Maghreb, vanilla pods from Tahiti, curry powder from south India and rum from Guadeloupe.

The Afro-Caribbean presence is also strong in Paris. By the early 1990s, fifty-three French West Indian were restaurants were operating there, along with a baker's dozen specializing in the cuisine of Réunion, six offering Mauritian food and one each representing the cuisines of the Seychelles, Mayotte, Haiti and French Guiana. Around the 13th arondissement are scattered Vietnamese-owned hotels, Vietnamese *traiteurs* and small restaurants offering classic Vietnamese dishes such as *pho* and caramelized pork.

The influence of these cuisines is slight in comparison with those of the Maghreb, but the clientele of the ethnic restaurants is largely French and, in time, their food will surely become another small tile in the French culinary mosaic.

Bibliography

Achaya, K. T., *Indian Food: A Historical Companion*, Oxford University Press, Delhi, 1994

Arsenault, Bona, *History of the Acadians*, Le Conseil de la Vie Française en Amerique, Quebec, 1966

Alberti, J. B., *L'Indochine d'autrefois et d'aujourd'hui*, Paris, 1934

Asselin, E. Donald, *A French-Canadian Cookbook*, M. G. Hurtig, Edmonton, 1968

Barbet, Charles, *Au Pays des Burnous (Impressions et Croquis d'Algerie)*, Alger, 1898

Barillon, J., *Souvenirs d'Algerie*, Sens 1894

Barnaud, Paul, *Mon voyage à Madagascar*, Cahors, 1921

Bayley, Monica, *Pacific Islands Cook Book*, Determined Productions, San Francisco, 1977

Barthel, J., *Regards sur l'Indochine: l'enquette d'une delegation ouvrière*, Paris, c. 1935

Beauclair, Germain, *Des Mirages au Tam-Tam*, B. Arthaud, Editor, Grenoble, 1937

Beaulieu, Mirelle, *Les meilleures recettes du Québec*, Ottawa, 1974

Beaver Club of Lafayette, *Cajun Men Cook: Recipes, Stories & Food Experiences from Louisiana Cajun Country*, Lafayette, 1994

Bénard, Jules, *Saveurs et Traditions Créoles*, Vols 1 and 2, Editions Noor Akhoun, Saint-Denis, c.1995

Benkirane, Fettouma, *Moroccan Cooking: the best recipes*, [trans. Shirley Kay] Sochepress, Casablanca, 1983

Benoit, Jehane, *The Canadiana Cookbook*, Pagurian Press, Toronto, 1970.

Berglund, Berndt and Bolsby, Clare E., *The Edible Wild; a complete cookbook and guide to Edible Wild Plants in Canada*, Pagurian Press, Toronto, 1971

Betts, Raymond, *Tricouleur: The French Overseas Empire*, Gordon & Cremonesi, London, 1978

Biddlecombe, Peter, *French Lessons in Africa*, Abacus, London, 1993

Bienvenu, Marcelle, *Who's Your Mama, Are You Catholic, And Can You Make A Roux? A Family Album Cajun/Creole Cookbook*, Times of Acadiana Press, Lafayette, 1991

Bikai, Marie Henri, *Cuisine Ethnique: Les Recettes Venues d'Ailleurs*, Montreal, 1994

Boisvenue, Lorraine, *Le Guide de la Cuisine Traditionelle Québécoise*, Stanké, Louiseville, 1979

Bouchard, Cecile Roland, Le Pinereau, *L'Art culinaire au Saguenay – lac Saint-Jean, collections recettes typiques,* Leméac, Ottawa, 1971

Bourgoie, Jean-Jacques, *Souvenirs Créoles et Pittoresque Antillais,* Les Adelys, 1958

Bourgeois, Marie-Eugénie, *Les bons plats de chez nous: recettes de Cuisine Antillaise,* l'Office Départmental du Tourisme de la Guadeloupe, 1966

Bourne, M. J., Lennox, G. W., Seddon, S. A., *Fruits and Vegetables of the Caribbean,* McMillan Press, London, 1988

Boyer-Peyreleau, Le Colonel [Eugène-Édouard], *Les Antilles Francaises,* Paris, 1823

Brown, Dale, *American Cooking: The Northwest,* Time–Life Books, New York, 1970

Brunet, Raymond, *Le Role Gastronomique du Rhum,* Montpellier, 1953

Buick, T. Lindsay, *The French At Akaroa,* Wellington, 1928

Carrier, Robert, *Taste of Morocco,* Century Hutchinson, London, 1987

Canada, Department of Agriculture, *Food – à la Canadienne,* The Queens Printer, Ottawa, 1967

Canadian Government Office of Tourism, *Canadian Menu Manual,* Foodservice and Hospitality Magazine, Toronto

Catat, Louis, *Voyage à Madagascar,* Paris, 1895

Chase, Leah, *The Dooky Chase Cookbook,* Pelican, Gretna, 1990

Clark, Morton G., *French-American Cooking from New Orleans to Quebec,* Funk & Wagnalls, New York, 1967

Collingridge, W. B, *Colonial Cooking: a simplified and abbreviated treatise on food and their cooking as they are prepared in tropical countries, especially Mauritius,* Port-Louis-Ile-Maurice, 1954

Cormier-Boudreau and Gallant, Melvin, *A Taste of Acadie,* Goose Lane, New Brunswick, 1991

Crouse, Elizabeth, *Algiers,* London, 1907

Cuisine Créole, Petits Pratiques Hachette, Paris, 1995

Curpenen, Ludmilla, *La cuisine de l'Ile Maurice,* Publisud, Paris, 1994

Cusick, Heidi Haughy, *Soul and Spice: African Cooking in the Americas,* Chronicle Books, San Francisco, 1995

Dard, Patrice, *Savoir Préparer La Cuisine Creole,* Créalivres, Paris, 1991

David, Elizabeth, *French Provincial Cooking,* Michael Joseph, London, 1960

Davis, Edwin Adams, *Louisiana: A Narrative History,* Clatter's Book Store, Baton Rouge, 2nd Ed., 1956

Debien, Gabriel, *Les Femmes des Premiers Colons aux Antilles 1635-1680,* Le Havre, 1952

Debien, Gabriel, *La Societé Coloniale aux XVII et XVIII Siècles,* Paris, 1952

Debien, Gabriel, *Les Engagés Pour Les Antilles (1634–1715)*, Paris, 1952

Decraene, Jean-Francois, *Le Tour De France Par Un Gourmand*, Horvath, Lyon, 1995

de Galland, M., *Petits Métiers Algeriens*, Paris, 1892

de Haroutunian, Arto, *North African Cookery*, London, 1985

de Jahan, Marie-Reine, *Les Rituels du Rhum et la Cuisine Créole*, Paris, 1992

DeMers, John, *French Quarter Royalty: The Tumultuous Life and Times of the Omni Royal Orleans Hotel*, New Orleans, 1993

DeMers, John, et al, *The Food of New Orleans*, Periplus Editions, Boston and Singapore, 1998

Denuzière, Jacqueline, et Brandt, Charles Henri, *Cuisine de Louisiane*, Paris, 1989

Dinh, Catherine, *Guide Trois Rivières de la Vie Antillais à Paris*, Paris, 1992

Dissler, Roland, *Terres de Soleil*, Strasbourg, 1946

Do Van, Paulette, *Vietnamese Cooking*, Apple Press, London, 1993

Doling, Annabel, *Vietnam On A Plate*, Roundhouse, Hong Kong, 1996

Doyen, Gérard (Ed.), *Savoir Cuisiner Creole: Entrées*, Orphie, Saint-Denis, 1990

Doyen, Gérard, *Savoir Cuisiner Creole: Rougails, Viandes et Poissons*, Orphie, Saint-Denis, 1990

Dubourg, Marie, *La Réunion: les poissons de nôtre ile*, St-Pierre-de-la-Réunion

Dubourg, Marie, *Recettes Réunionnaises*, St-Pierre-de-la-Réunion, 1986

Ebroin, Ary, *Delices de la Cuisine Creole*, red. par Ary Ebroin, Philippe Sarip, Brussels, 1984

Ebroin, Ary, *La Cuisine Créole*, Émile Desormeaux, 1995

Elliott, Duong Van Mai, *The Sacred Willow: Four Generations in the Life of a Vietnamese Family*, Oxford, New York, 1999

Eudel, Paul, *Hivenage en Algérie*, Evreux, 1909

Eudèse, Da, *La Cuisine Créole de Da Eudèse*, Paris, c.1990

Eustis, Celestine, *Cooking in Old Creole Days*, New Orleans, 1904

Feibleman, Peter S., *American Cooking: Creole and Acadian*, Time–Life Books, New York, 1971

Félix, Guy, *Genuine Cuisine of Mauritius*, Editions de L'Océan Indien, Stanley, 1988

Fermor, Patrick Leigh, *The Traveller's Tree: A Journey through the Caribbean Islands*, John Murray, London, 1950

Field, Michael and Frances, *A Quintet of Cuisines*, Time–Life International, 1970

Floyd, Keith, *Floyd on Africa*, Michael Joseph, London, 1996

Foster, Nelson, and Cordell, Linda S., Eds. *Chillies to Chocolate: Food The Americas Gave the World*, The University of Arizona Press, Tucson & London, 1992

Fussell, Betty, *I Hear America Cooking*, Viking, New York, 1986

Gagné, Madame Charles, *Recettes typiques de la côte-du-sud*, Ottawa, 1970

Gay, Gerald, and Huc, Gerald, *Les Meilleurs Recettes de la Cuisine Rèunionnaise*, Times Editions/Flammarion, 1987

Giraud, Marcel, *A History of French Louisiana*, Louisiana State University Press, Baton Rouge, 1974

Gireud, J, *Souvenirs et impressions*, Madagascar, 1897

Gide, André, *Travels in the Congo*, (Trans. Dorothy Bussy), New York , 1929

Girard, Sylvie, *Cuisines Régionales de France: Antilles*, Editions du Fanal, Paris, 1996

Gotlieb, Sondra, *The Gourmet's Canada*, New Press, Toronto, 1972

Graham, Kevin, *Creole Flavors*, Artisan, New York, 1996

Grandmains, D. de, *Cent recettes de cuisine créole*, Editions Berger, Fort-de-France, nd

Guide de la Colonisation au Cameroun, A. Thoyon-Thèze, Paris

Guide de la Colonisation au Togo, A. Thoyon-Thèze, Paris, 1924

Guide des Colonies Francaises, Societé d'Editions Géographiques et Maritimes, Paris, 1931

Guide d'Immigrant à Madagascar, 3 vols, 1895

Guide du Francais arrivent à Indochine, Hanoi, 1935

Guide G. B. Indochinois, Publications G. B., Hanoi, 1926

Guide G. B. Tonkinois, Publications G. B., Hanoi, 1923

Guide General au Voyager en Algerie, Alger, 1871

Guide General Maroc, Editions Maroc-Presse, Casablanca, 1942

Guide Michelin Algerie-Maroc, 1955–56

Guide Touristic Maroc, avec son supplement 'Hotel et restaurants', Paris, 1939

Guillory, Queen Ida, *Cookin' with Queen Ida*, Prima, Rocklin, 1990

Guinaudeau, Z., *Traditional Moroccan Cooking: Recipes from Fez*, (trans. J.E. Harris), Serif, London, 1994

Harris, Dunstan, *Island Barbecue*, Chronicle Books, San Francisco, 1995

Harris, Jessica B., *Iron Pots and Wooden Spoons: Africa's Gifts to New World Cooking*, Atheneum, New York, 1989

Hearn, Lafcadio, *La Cuisine Creole*, Will H. Coleman, New Orleans, 1885

Hearn, Lafcadio, *Gombo Zhèbes*, Will H. Coleman, New Orleans, 1885

Hearn, Lafcadio, *Two Years in the French West Indies*, Harper and Row, New York

Herrin, M. H., *The Creole Aristocracy*, Exposition Press, New York, 1952

Hentsch, Henry, *Deux Annes à Dahomey*, Paris, 1905

Honeychuch, Penelope N., *Caribbean Wild Plants and Their Uses*, Macmillan Education Ltd, London, 1980

Horne, Alistair, *A Savage War of Peace: Algeria 1954–1962*, London, 1977

Horth, Régine, *La Guyane gastronomique et traditionnelle*, Editions Caribéennes, Paris 1988

Huc, Claude, *Les Meilleurs Recettes de la Cuisine Réunionnaise*, Paris, 1988

Institut de tourisme et d'hôtellerie du Québec, *Cuisine du Québec*, Les Editions TransMo Inc, Montreal, 1985

Isnard, H., *Algeria* [trans. O. C. Warden], Nicholas Kaye, London, 1955

Isnard, Léon, *La Cuisine Française et Africaine*, Paris, 1949

Isnard, Léon, *La Gastronomie Africaine*, Paris, 1930

Jaffin, Leone, *150 Recettes et mille souvenirs d'une juive d'Algerie*, Paris, 1987

Janzan, Kathy, *The ABC of Creative Caribbean Cookery*, Macmillan Press, London, 1994

Jones, A. and Sefton, N., *Marine Life of the Caribbean*, Macmillan Education Ltd, London, 1979

Jones, Evan, *American Food: The Gastronomic Story*, New York, 1975

Jones, Paul, and Andrews, Barry, *A Taste of Mauritius*, Macmillan, London, 1982

Junior League of Baton Rouge, Inc, The, *River Road Recipes*, Baton Rouge, 1959

Karsenty, Irène et Lucienne, *Cuisine Pied-Noir*, Editions Denoël, Paris, 1974

Kauffman, William I., and Cooper, Sister Mary Ursula, *The Art of Creole Cookery*, Doubleday, New York, 1962

Kelly, Denis, *Cajun & Creole* [The Pleasure of Cooking Mini-Series], The Book Company, Weldon, Sydney, 1992

King, Grace, *Creole Families of New Orleans*, Macmillan Co, New York, 1921

Kouki, Mohamed, *Cuisine et Pâtisserie Tunisiennes*, Le Patrimonie Tunisien, 1987

La cuisine aux pays du soleil, Les classiques Africains, Versailles, 1976

La Cuisine Creole Tradtionnelle, Emile Désormeaux, Fort-de-France, 1977

La cuisine Guadeloupéenne, Orphie, Saint-Clotilde, 1993

La cuisine Malgache, Orphie, Saint-Clotilde, 1992

La cuisine Mauricienne, Orphie, Saint-Clotilde, 1992

La Cuisine Réunionnaise: recettes d'hier et d'aujourd'hui, St-Denis-de-la-Réunion, 1982

Langlois, [Lieutenant], *Souvenirs de Madagascar*, Paris, 1900

Le Grand Livre de la Cuisine Guyanaise, Orphie, 1992

Le Blanc, Beverley, *The Complete Caribbean Cookbook*, The Apple Press, London, 1996

Leblond, Marius, *Les Iles Soeurs: La Réunion, Maurice*, Paris, 1946

Leclerc, Claire L., *120 recettes aux champignons du Québec*, Editions Garneau, Quebec, 1971

Le Huenen, Augusta, and Poirer, Michel, *Recettes des Iles Saint-Pierre et Miquelon*, Moncton, 1988

Lenoir, Philippe, and de Ravel, Raymond, *L'Ile Maurice à Table*, Editions de l'Ocean Indien, Rose-Hill, 1986

Le Révérend, Arlette and Gaston, *Deux Saisons au Dahomey*, 1940

Leslie, Austin, *Chez Helene, House of Good Food Cookbook*, De Simonin Publications, New Orleans, 1984

Lewis, Norman, *A Dragon Apparent*, Jonathan Cape, London, 1951

Locamus, P., *Madagascar et l'alimentation Europeanne, céréales et viandes*, Paris, 1896

Lowndes, Steve, *Akaroa: A Short History*, Akaroa, 1996

Madame Bégué's Recipes of Old New Orleans Creole Cookery, Harmanson, New Orleans, 2nd Edition, 1937

Marécat, Claire, *Le Poisson dans la Cuisine Québécoise*, Les Editions La Presse, Montreal, 1972

Marks, Copeland, *The Great Book of Couscous*, Donald I. Fine Inc, New York, 1994

Masachs, Paulette, *La Cuisine Calédonienne*, Editions du Cagon (Hachette Nouvelle Calédonie), 1989

Mathilde, Da, *325 recettes de cuisine créole*, Jacques Grancher, Paris, 1975

Matthews, T. T., *Thirty Years in Madagascar*, London, 1904

Michanol, Cibrelis Reine, et Jenue, Jean-Louis, *Le livre de Cérès, ou dictionnaire de cuisine créole*, A àH. Presse centrale Antillaise, Pointe-à-Pitre, 1943

Minh Kim, *200 Recettes de Cuisine Vietnamienne*, Paris, 1988

Mitcham, Howard, *Creole Gumbo and All That Jazz*, 1982

Mitchell, Patricia B., *French Cooking in Early America*, Sims-Mitchell House Bed & Breakfast, Chatham VA, 1991

Morley, Lauren Ann, *Cooking with Caribbean Rum*, Macmillan Education Ltd, London, 1991

Morphy, Countess, *Recipes Of All Nations*, Herbert Joseph, London, 1935

Naipaul, V. S., *The Middle Passage*, André Deutsch, London, 1962

Nathan, Joan, *An American Folklife Cookbook*, Schocken Books, New York, 1984

Navarro, Evelyne et Ambroise, *Manuel de Cuisine Pied-Noir*, Jean Curutchet, les Editions Harriet, Bayonne, 1992

Noter, R de, *La Bonne Cuisine aux colonies: Asie, Afrique, Amerique*, Paris, 1931

Negre, André, *Antilles et Guyane à travers leur cuisine*, Editions Caribéennes, Paris, 1985

Nguyen Thu Tam, *Mon An Viet Nam/Vietnamese Dishes*, Nha Xuat Ban Mui Ca Mau, Ho Chi Minh City, 1997

Obeida, Khadidja, *253 Recettes de cuisine Algerienne*, Paris, 1983
Ortiz, Elisabeth Lambert, *Caribbean Cookery*, André Deutsch, London, 1975

Parents Club of Ursuline Academy Inc., *Recipes and Reminiscences of New Orleans*, New Orleans, 1971
Parents Club of Ursuline Academy Inc., *Recipes and Reminiscences of New Orleans Volume II: Our Cultural Heritage*, New Orleans, 1981
Parkinson, Rosemary, *Culinaria: The Caribbean, A Culinary Discovery*, Köneman, Cologne, 1999
Penicaut, André, *Fleur de Lys and Calumet. Being the Penicaut Narrative of French Adventure in Louisiana*, Translated from the French manuscripts, Louisiana State University Press, Baton Rouge, 1953
Peterson, T. Sarah, *Acquired Taste: The French Origins of Modern Cooking*, Cornell University Press, Ithaca
Pinchedez, Catherine, *La Cuisine Polynésienne*, Publisud, Paris, 1991
Piolet, J. B., *Madagascar, sa description, ses habitants*, Paris, 1895
Petite cuisine bourgeoise en annamite, Saigon, 1914

Quérillac A. *Cuisine Coloniale. Les Bonnes Recettes de Chlöe Mondésir.* Société d'Editions Geographiques, Maritimes et Coloniales, Paris, 1931

Rawlings, Marjorie Kinnan, *The Marjorie Kinnan Rawlings Cookbook: Cross Creek Cookery*, Hammond, Hammond & Co, London, 1960
Reboux, Paul, *L'Algerie et ses vins*, Alger, 1945
Reboux, Paul, *Le Paradis des Antilles*, Paris, 1931
Recettes Haitiennes et exotiques, Ottawa, 1973
Repiquet, Jules, *L'Ile de la Réunion, Centre de Rayonnement de l'Influence Française dans l'Ocean Indien et le Pacifique*, Paris, 1934
Ribère, Roselyne, *La bonne cuisine des Antilles*, Solar, Paris, 1992
Rushton, William Faulkner, *The Cajuns From Acadia to Louisiana*, Farrar, Strauss, Giroux, New York, 1979

Saint-Paul, G., *Souvenirs de Tunisie et Algérie*, Paris, 1904
Sagna, Anna, *Recettes Culinaires Sénégalises*, Dakar, 1972
Segal, Ronald, *The Black Diaspora*, Faber & Faber, London, 1995
Slater, Mary, *Cooking The Caribbean Way*, Hamlyn, London, 1965
Sookia, Devinia, *Caribbean Cooking*, New Burlington Books, London, 1994
So Tay Noi Tro, *A Guide To Typical Vietnamese Cookery*, Nha Xuat Ban Thanh Pho Ho, Ho Chi Minh City, 1995
Soniat, Leon E., *La Bouche Creole*, Pelican, Gretna, 1995
Sonthonaux, *Deux Mois aux Antilles Francaises*, Lyon, 1898
"Suzette", *West Indian Recipes*, Grand Sud, Antilles, 1993

Swartvagher, Michel, *La Cuisine Tahitienne*, Times Editions, Singapore, 1975

Stott. M. D., *The Real Algeria*, London, 1914

Trieu Thi Choi, Isaak, Marcel and Jackson-Doling, Annabel, *The Food of Vietnam*, Periplus Editions, Singapore, 1997

Tan, Terry, *A Little Vietnamese Cookbook*, Chronicle Books, San Francisco, 1995

The Picayune's Creole cook book, Picayune, New Orleans, 1900

Thimodent, Robert, *Tradition Culinaire Créole*, D. F. Editions, Guadeloupe, 1995

Tinker, Edward Larocque, *Lafcadio Hearn's American Days*, Dodd, Mead and Co, 1924

Thomarel, Andrée, *Parfums et Saveurs des Antilles*, Paris, 1934.

Took, Ian F., *Fishes of the Caribbean*, Macmillan Education Ltd, London, 1979

Toussaint-Samat, Maguelonne, *A History of Food* [trans. Anthea Bell], Blackwell, 1992

Tremewan, Peter, *French Akaroa*, University of Canterbury Press, Christchurch, 1994

Trois Siècles de Vie Francais, Nos Antilles, Orleans, 1935

Tuiller, Lucienne, *Terres d'Amour*, Paris, 1955

Valentin, Marie, *La Cuisine Réunionnaise*, Réunion, 1982

Valldejuli, Carmen Aboy, *The Art of Caribbean Cookery*, Garden City, New York, 1957

Vanmai, Jean, *Centenaire de la Présence Vietnamienne en Nouvelle-Caledonie*

Villers, Anne, and Delarozière, M. F., *Cuisines d'Afrique*, Edisud, Aix-en-Provence, 1995

Vincent, Rose (Ed.), *The French in India*, Bombay, 1990

Viola, Herman J., and Margolis, Carolyn, Eds., *Seeds of Change*, Smithsonian Institution Press, Washington, 1991

Vischer, Isabelle, *Now To The Banquet*, Gollancz, London, 1953

West, Richard, *The White Tribes of Africa*, Jonathan Cape, London, 1965

Wheaton, Barbara Ketcham, *Savouring The Past: The French Kitchen & Table from 1300 to 1789*, Chatto & Windus, The Hogarth Press, London, 1983

Wingfield, the Hon. Lewis, *Under The Palms in Algeria and Tunis*, London, 1868

Van der Post, Laurens, *First Catch Your Eland*

Wolfe, Linda, *The Cooking of the Caribbean Islands*, Time–Life International, 1970

Wolfert, P, *Good Food from Morocco*, Rev. Ed. 1989

Zeitoun, Edmond, *250 Recettes de Cuisine Tunisienne*, Jacques Grancher, Paris, 1977

Index